I Think GOD Wants Me To Be a MISSIONARY

ISSUES TO DEAL WITH LONG BEFORE YOU SAY GOOD-BYE

Also by Neal Pirolo:

SERVING AS SENDERS
THE REENTRY TEAM

By Neal & Yvonne Pirolo:
PREPARE FOR BATTLE

I THINK GOD WANTS ME TO BE A MISSIONARY

ISSUES TO DEAL WITH
LONG BEFORE YOU
SAY GOOD-BYE

NEAL PIROLO

Emmaus Road International
7150 Tanner Court, San Diego, CA 92111
Emmaus_Road @eri.org • www.eri.org
858 292-7020

Scripture quotations are paraphrases by the author. All references should be studied in their context.

Though all that is written into the characters, both students and pastors, is drawn from personal experiences of the author with real people, all names and locations have been changed so as to not betray any confidence. All names are fictitious, and are not to reflect on the life or character of any living person.

Published by Emmaus Road International
7150 Tanner Court, San Diego, California 92111 USA
www.eri.org
858 292-7020
Emmaus_road@eri.org

Printed in the United States of America
ISBN 1-880185-50-4

DEDICATION

To
the Lord of the Harvest
Who is still calling workers
to His Fields of Ministry Service

ACKNOWLEDGEMENTS

It is in Christ that we live and move and have our being. Thus, first and foremost, we acknowledge the working of the Spirit of Christ in this effort. From the initial inspiration of using a story format to the gruelling hours of rewriting and editing, the sense of His presence and guidance moved us forward.

Unending appreciation is given to my wife, Yvonne, who continued to stand by me with encouragement and critique, always keeping a balance between the two.

Regularly, we called upon our Prayer Support Team. Though only eternity will tell the full extent of their involvement, we gratefully acknowledge their intercession on our behalf.

The thoughts presented through the words of the students and their pastors came from the hundreds of missions-minded people who seriously counted the cost of cross-cultural ministry. Our appreciation is extended to them for the privilege given to us to relate with them through many years of ministry.

We acknowledge Kimberly Snow, who took a very rough second or third draft and helped enhance the dialogue and develop the characters' personalities.

Through the rewriting process, many—youth and adult—read and reread the manuscript, making good suggestions. Our thanks to each one.

Always accolades to my brother, Paul, who is so skilled in English grammar, yet patiently sorted through my incomplete sentences and rambling tenses.

And finally, *"unto Him who by His power within us is able to do infinitely more than we even dare to ask or imagine; to Him be glory throughout all ages."* (Ephesians 3:20-21)

CONTENTS

AN INVITATION

I would like to retell a story told by a friend of mine. He told it often. Not because it was a success story. It wasn't. But because it was so unbelievable! Unexpected! He told it as if he was still trying to convince himself that it had really happened.

For a number of years he made the final decision for missionaries going to the field through a particular mission agency. Thousands of dollars had already been spent in training each family—training in the Word, training in the culture, training in family and peer relationships. Physical exams. Psychological evaluations. Spiritual readiness. Financial support. Prayer support. Their references were impeccable. All was in order.

He interviewed the whole family individually and as a group. They had the moral support of their church and extended family and friends. They were ready to go, he was sure. By his word, they now had the full support of their agency.

Bags were packed; passports were current; visas were in hand. Tickets were purchased. All loose ends at home were nicely tied up by their logistic support team. The final gala, good-bye parties were held. Bon Voyage!

They were in the air! Headed for a new adventure for Christ in a region they had prayed about. They had studied its history and current events. They had listened to tapes to prepare their ears for a new language.

They landed in the capitol city of their host country. As they gathered their bags, they looked around. All was strange. Yes, there was the driver who would take them to the guest house. He had held up a sign with their names on it—spelled incorrectly, but what a welcome sight, anyway. He was helping them with their bags, but his English at best was difficult to understand. It was hot and humid. It had been a long journey. They were sleep deprived and bloated on the free soda and salty pretzels and their deodorant was no longer protecting them. The smells of their bodies merged with the smells of a foreign land, producing an unsavory aroma. The noise of an unknown language mounted around them, piercing their ears. The family members looked at each other for some reassurance. There was none. Each in his own little world was thinking, *"What in the world have we done?"*

The bags had been gathered. The driver was ready to take them out to the van. But, just a moment, please. The family huddled. There was a buzz of discussion. Then there was agreement. They would return home! They did not even leave the airport lounge. They went to the ticket counter, booked a flight and waited. They returned home!

What happened? What went wrong? Had they not considered the seriousness of this mission? Had their church leadership not taken the time to prayerfully consider their recommendations? Had their prayer support team not been aware of the spiritual warfare they would likely face? What happened? What went wrong?

These and many others are the questions asked by missionaries, their friends and those agencies which send them. Admittedly, all missions are not so quickly truncated. But far too many believers find out too late that they should not have gone to the mission field in the first place.

In fact, 453 mission agencies from 14 sending countries became concerned about the high attrition rate of their missionaries—quitting before their agreed upon term of commitment. They did a study—an extensive study. Over a period of three years, they interviewed 30,600 missionaries who quit. They had them complete questionnaires. They interviewed them again. It took many people several years to review and collate and digest and write out the findings.[1]

The results are astounding. In any study of this magnitude, it is impossible to refine all the statistics into neat, little categories. However, in general terms, the researchers came up with four very broad statistics:

1) Twenty-nine percent of them quit for "understandable" reasons. A spouse died on the field. The surviving spouse did not feel he could remain there. He went home. He quit. This and a number of other reasons were put in this category.

However, there were three other categories which they considered "preventable" reasons. In other words, if one or more of these three things had been better attended to, it is *probable* that the remaining seventy-one percent (21,726) would not have left the field.

2) They did not have an adequate support team. (The study calls it "member care.") Whether provided by the agency, the church or friends who share the burden of this particular mission, there was a lack serious enough for the missionaries to return home.

3) They did not have adequate pre-field training. There is a big difference between pre-field orientation (which most agencies provide) and pre-field training, which, from the statistics, churches and agencies evi-

---

1 The full report is found in the book, *Too Valuable to Lose*, William Carey Library, 1997. The summary excerpted here is from a book review written by David Mays of ACMC.

dently do not provide. Some, it has been reported, provide too much! But obviously not of the kind that truly prepared their missionaries for living and ministering in a second culture. Much more could be said on this topic, but it is not the subject of this book.

4) They should not have gone in the first place. ——!
——? Yes, it is OK to take a long pause! It seems almost unbelievable that one of the three main reasons missionaries quit is because they should not have gone in the first place. This points to the whole process of candidate selection. But it begins before then. It begins in the prayer room of your church. Or even before then. In the prayer closet of your home. In the circle of your friends who can help you process the thousands of thoughts that bombard your mind at a time like this.

In this writing, we are going to give you an opportunity to deal with a number of issues that you should clearly think through in the very early stages of missionary preparation. But not only you. By now you should have a group of people—friends and relatives—who are dialoguing with you and with the Lord on these tough issues. You should be beginning the development of your support team.

Our goal for this book is two-fold:

1) If, in prayerfully considering the ramifications of the issues discussed here, you come to the conclusion that, "Yes, I was just caught up in the emotion of 'It might be fun.' or 'Some of my friends are going. Why don't I try it? I might like it,'" the book will have served its purpose of preventing you from going. For, those who go who should have stayed, have grave issues of failure to deal with when they do come home. As well as the negative attitude toward missions that they spread through the church. Worse, many remain on the field

not only not accomplishing anything, but draining the energies of others who are trying to buoy them up.

2) On the other hand, our greater desire is to see you prepared to enter this commitment with your eyes wide open. As you and your growing team of support discuss your readiness in the issues raised in this book, you will have the tools in your hands to deal with them when they do arise. Nothing in this book is going to be able to avert the occurrence of some issues. But a careful study of these pages will prepare you to meet them head on—to work through them or rise above them.

Missionaries are too valuable to lose. You don't want to get "lost" even before you make it to the field. My prayer is that your study of this book will either keep you from going to the field or, more preferably, be an early step in preparing you to go to the field.

I cannot over emphasize the vital need for you to be developing your support team at these early stages. I am talking more about your prayer and moral—encouragement—support than your financial and reentry support. You can read and hear more about this team development in the book, *Serving As Senders*, and the audio tapes, 'Building Your Support Team.'[2]

The setting of this story is Middletown, USA. It is not Uptown—so sophisticated, so proper, so perfect. Nor is it Downtown, where all is drab and old and run-down. It is Middletown. Middletown, USA. It is where we can make mistakes and not be despised. Yet, where, when we do make mistakes, we don't hide behind the façade of mirror-glassed buildings of uptown, nor behind the broken windows of despair, downtown.

Let's meet four young people who believe that God wants them to be a missionary:

2 *Serving as Senders* and 'Building Your Support Team' are available from ERI: www.eri.org

KEVIN METZGER

Kevin's parents had divorced when he was in the eighth grade. He knew things were not right between them, even though they kept it pretty much behind their closed door. But Dad was seldom home. His flight schedule seemed to include many overnights in other cities. Kevin tumbled into a troublesome four years in high school. His mom remarried early in his senior year. But the man did not (maybe could not) become a good father to Kevin. He remained his mother's husband.

Kevin is now in his final months at a Christian college in the big city, about a half hour's drive from Middletown. Though he could have commuted—his mom wanted him to, Kevin chose to live on campus. He was sure her husband preferred that. But he has come home on the week-ends—some of them, anyway. He wanted to remain connected to his church, though it usually only meant Sunday morning. Once in a while he got in on a Saturday activity; for special speakers, he even stayed for Sunday evening.

Grades came very easy for Kevin, so he was able to fully enjoy several of the extra-curricular activities on campus. He loves soccer. He tried out for the team—twice, but he had not made the cut—either time. The activity he enjoyed the most was tutoring three international students. Taiwo's English was marginal. He needed the most help. And it was obvious that he appreciated Kevin's help. At the end of every session, Taiwo would assure Kevin that his parents would invite Kevin to his home when he returned to Nigeria. He had learned that Taiwo's name meant the "firstborn of twins." Kevin's prayer is that when Taiwo returns to Nigeria, he will be a godly witness to his brother who has chosen the path of Islam.

Kevin had brought the three men home with him one weekend. It was a bit awkward. Though the church is solid in its teaching on world evangelization, it had not yet sent anyone, nor had they captured the opportunity to minister to internationals who live in Middletown. Maybe one or two families of foreign heritage came to the church on a regular basis. So, you can imagine, when Kevin walked in with three huge men, with skin as black as midnight, it caused quite a stir, and some serious embarrassment. Kevin realized—too late—that he probably should have given the church advanced notice!

But, over the next months, a lot is going to change in this Middletown church—and particularly in the life of Kevin Metzger.

HELEN WALKER

Helen is a fine young lady, maturing with poise and a deep love for her Lord. She has been home schooled since kindergarten. Her parents had made that choice even before she was born. Neither she nor they have ever regretted it, though at times it was trying—on both her and them. Helen has learned the disciplines of diligence, commitment and critical thinking, and has developed a positive outlook on life. Her worldview was greatly enhanced by having experienced one semester of her junior year on the sailing yacht, Endeavor. The ship called at many ports in the Mediterranean Sea. Her studies focused on the ancient and modern cultures, governments and languages of several nations.

Her love for music birthed a desire to play the piano and then the organ. She often plays the organ prelude at her church, but her greatest joy is to fill their home with melodies of her own creation.

As her graduation from high school approaches, she is practicing a particularly difficult composition she has been asked to perform. But even as she tries to concentrate on that final arpeggio, other thoughts are forcing their way into her mind. Thoughts about what she believes God wants her to do before launching into her next four years of formal education.

JASON THOMAS
Jason is a carefree, happy-go-lucky young man about to graduate from high school. His thought: Never too soon! Actually, let's be honest, deep inside there is a very serious heart for God. Sometimes, though, words just come out of his mouth before he engages his brain, if you know what I mean. Don't get me wrong. A little maturing will take care of that issue. We'll see a fine young man emerging.

School? Yes, as I said—a necessity. But, motocross! Jason dreams—day and night—about motocross. He draws pictures of them on, in and around every class notebook. His favorite one shows the rider high off the seat, bike in mid-air, just having come off a triple jump. Pictures of fancy bikes, mud-crusted bikes, dirty bikes, bikes with and without riders line the walls and doors and windows of his bedroom. He started a parade of bikes down the hallway, but Dad said, "Turn those bikes around and get them back into your room!" Did Jason own one? No. He rode a beat-up ten-speed. But he talked and dreamed motocross.

That is, until...one day!

KYLE PHILIPS
Kyle is just graduating from a local secular college with a major in English. He is a good student. But he has to

work hard for his grades. He has held down a 20-hour a week job to help pay expenses. He's lived at home. That's helped a lot. With expenses, that is. As a college senior it has been a bit trying to still be under his parents' roof. But they have talked things out, for the most part. They have watched their only child grow into a fine young man. And have given him the space to mature.

Because it tied in so well with his English major, Kyle had been able to squeeze out the time to work on the campus newspaper. Several times he had been able to write solid Christian witness into his articles. Less overtly, but possibly of greater value, he believed that his Christian lifestyle had had an impact on the other staff members.

A relationship has been developing with Melanie, a young lady from his church. Just when they realized it was more than just friends, neither of them can remember. But for some time there has been an unspoken agreement that wedding bells are in their future.

But one Sunday evening...

Middletown is where we can discover truth and live in it. And that is what we want to do as we enter the lives of these four young people as they discuss their issues with their pastors and friends. Let's listen in.

Neal Pirolo
San Diego, CA 92111

1

WHO'S GOOD ENOUGH TO GO?

The sky above the city looked dark like it had been rubbed with a dirty eraser. The rumble of thunder rattled the windows of Kevin Metzger's old Toyota. He wheeled his "buddy" into the parking lot. With the engine still running, he sat for a few minutes, watching the first raindrops splatter against the windshield. He wanted to catch the final sports scores, hoping his college team had won. Unfortunately, they hadn't. He shook his head at what a painful defeat it must have been: eight runs to nothing! He turned off the radio and the ignition. "They wouldn't be going to the playoffs this year," he mumbled, his college pride hurt.

As with a habit developed over the years, he gave the extra push of his shoulder to help open the door. The stuck hinge gave way and the door swung open with a groan. One day he'd get that fixed. One day he'd do a lot of things. Now that his four years of college were almost over, he hoped that one day he'd stop having to say "one day."

Kevin eased his large frame from the car and stood a full six feet. The door slammed shut with the back kick of his foot, followed by the familiar clunk of a latch out of alignment. "One day...," he started to say. He walked three steps, then looked back. He frowned, doubting that anyone would even look at his car much less think of stealing it. He walked back and locked the door. At least, then if someone did take it, his insurance would cover the loss. What loss. The auto recyclers would probably charge him to take it off his hands.

No matter. He had another far more serious issue on his mind as he hurried through the rain, crossing the parking lot with a few giant steps. He stood for a brief moment before the single entrance to his home church. The church had been built on a relatively quiet corner once dedicated for "religious purposes" on the city planning map. Since then, the "cultural diversity" philosophy now designates such land for "community centers." The senior pastor has ministered there since Kevin was three years old. Climbing the steps to the front double doors was so familiar an action to Kevin, it felt like he was coming home.

It was a good church. Solid Bible teaching yielded steady growth numerically, but even more importantly, spiritually. There was a good youth ministry—even though the high school and college were still grouped together. Pastor Jim was at the helm of the youth work. He was a kind man, lean and nearly bald, with gray sideburns, although he was not old. Most thought him handsome, in a rugged, serious way. But when he smiled, his entire countenance softened, as if the very bones of his face altered, rounding out, setting all who know him at ease. He had helped Kevin through some troublesome teen years, and now he would be the first to hear what had been consuming Kevin's thoughts for the past several months. It had to be said out loud, Kevin knew, so that he could get back and concentrate on his final months at college.

The secretary led Kevin through the door into the youth pastor's office. Pastor Jim got up from his worn leather chair and came around the desk to greet him, hand extended.

Kevin gave it a firm shake, feeling the pastor's hand return his strong grip. "Thanks for meeting me on such short notice," Kevin said. He found it comforting to be back in this familiar office with Pastor Jim. His deep-set, blue eyes had not dimmed through the years. *If anything, they were more radiant,* Kevin thought.

"Never a problem, Kevin. You know you can come to me anytime. My door's always open." The pastor gently scrutinized Kevin, He had grown into a rather handsome young man, tall, but not awkward. He had sandy-blonde hair and an athletic square-jawed face. *Strong hands,* Pastor Jim thought, as his own hand still felt the effects of their handshake. Kevin was wearing a plaid shirt; his jeans were neat and clean. *But those large tennis shoes...at least size 14,* Pastor Jim thought. When he looked again in Kevin's eyes, the warm smile for which he was so famous lifted his cheeks. "It's great to see you. I hear school's going well. But from the sound of your voice when you called this morning, I was a little worried. You sounded tense. What's on your mind?"

Kevin hesitated, looking out the window that overlooked the courtyard. "Well...," he began. Then, half to himself, "Oh, man, am I really going to say this?"

The pastor watched as Kevin's fingers tapped ner-

vously at his thighs, his thumbs stuck in his pockets.
"How long have I known you?" Pastor Jim asked.

Kevin raised his face and shrugged.

"Years," the pastor answered his own question. "Since you were a young boy. You know you can trust me." There was assurance in his voice.

Kevin hesitated still, fidgeting awkwardly.

After a patient moment, Pastor Jim encouraged, "Kevin, you didn't drive all the way home to back out now." His voice was calm, steady, and all at once Kevin's shoulders softened and he exhaled a breath he had not realized he had been holding. But despite the ease the pastor gave his mind, there was still a knot in his stomach. "Pastor Jim, I think...." And Kevin hesitated again, butterflies replacing the knot in the pit of his stomach.

"Yes?" Pastor Jim's eyebrows were raised to emphasize his question and anticipated answer.

"OK, here goes," Kevin said to encourage himself. "We held our Annual Missions Conference at the college a few months back."

The pastor nodded. "Yes, your college has a reputation for putting a great focus on cross-cultural ministry. Go on," Pastor Jim encouraged, guessing what Kevin had come to say.

"Well, I went to the conference the year before. And the year before that, and the year before that. But after this last one, something happened."

"Happened?" came Pastor Jim's question, meant to move Kevin forward—to just say it!

"This one really had an effect on me. I just can't seem to get it out of my mind." His large frame melted into the chair facing the desk.

The pastor walked around the desk and took his

own seat, then leaned forward on his elbows and locked his fingers together. "Kevin, I think I know what you're trying to tell me. But it's best you tell me with your own words."

Kevin shifted in his chair. "You're going to think this is crazy. But, well...."

He ran his fingers through his hair, giving the pastor a furtive glance. "Okay, I'll just say it. *I think God wants me to be a missionary!* There! I said it!" Kevin smiled a grin of relief as he wiped his sweaty brow with the back of his hand.

The room was filled with a weighted silence. Only the wall clock could be heard ticking away the seconds that to Kevin seemed like hours.

The pastor raised his brows and the warm smile returned to his face. It was not a smile of amusement, not a mocking grin, but a genuine smile of pleasure. "That's not crazy at all, Kevin. Not crazy at all." Pastor Jim repeated himself, buying some time to think how he should respond. Then, "That's exciting! With our pastor teaching us from the Word, emphasizing that the field is the world, we would expect that God would call someone from our congregation to minister cross-culturally. I say, 'Praise the Lord!'"

Pastor Jim's enthusiasm was meant to give Kevin some encouragement. Kevin's eyes widened as he listened to that response. His body tensed. He shook his head and blurted out, "Well, maybe that sounds alright to you, but you don't understand. I didn't expect it to be me!" He did not mean to raise his voice, but that awful feeling was rising up in his chest again.

"Why not, Kevin? You're young. Full of energy. About to graduate...."

"You don't understand," Kevin interrupted, his

hands gesturing his frustration. "I've been thinking about this for weeks. I realize now that it's a desire that's been growing deep in my spirit—for years. But there is a real problem. I can't get around it. It swallows me up every time I try to think about it. I pray, but that doesn't seem to be helping."

Pastor Jim inched his chair closer and leaned forward, more intent to hear what Kevin had to say. Maybe there was a problem. He was remembering Kevin's teen years. Maybe he had fallen back into some of those ungodly choices.

Kevin hesitated and leaned forward, himself. He cautiously looked this way and that, and whispered, "What are you waiting for? A confession of some terrible secret sin?"

The pastor leaned back and laughed aloud and Kevin chuckled with him. The tension that had built was broken. Kevin was more comfortable now. It seemed right to be talking with Pastor Jim. He remembered the hours he spent in this office, at McDonalds and at the beach with Pastor Jim during his high school years. *How patient he was with me as I tried to make sense out of my mother's divorce. And her subsequent doting on me. I was becoming a man and didn't feel comfortable with such strong affection coming from my mother. And my dad! Where was he? He had just disappeared from my life. And then another man comes into her life who didn't seem to take much interest in me. I am not pleased with the stuff I got into, trying to cover my hurt. But, what a man Pastor Jim had proved to be. I really appreciate the help he gave me when I so needed it. He was patient with me. Yet firm. Like a father. Yes, I guess he was like a father to me during those years.*

Pastor Jim assumed Kevin was reflecting on those

difficult years. So he just let him ponder his thoughts. *Maybe this is what he is having such a difficult time telling me,* Pastor Jim wondered.

Kevin continued, "It's really rather stupid. If I would keep focused on the Lord, this would not be an issue."

"Well, Kevin, as silly as it may sound—spill it! Let's get this issue out in the open so we can examine it." The mood of the room was more congenial now.

Kevin nodded agreement. He leaned back in his chair, finding a more comfortable position. "You know, you're the first person I've told. Whenever I am about to share this with someone, I just clam up. I mean, if it's true, if God really wants me to be a missionary...." He looked down in his lap. "Well, this same thought comes and smothers all excitement and anticipation that it might be true."

"Kevin! Are you going to tell me? Or not?" Pastor Jim blurted in mock exasperation, his arms waving wildly for emphasis. "What is it you're afraid of, Kevin?" he asked in a more sensitive voice.

Kevin raised his eyes to meet the pastor's. "Okay, it's as simple as this: I just don't think I'm good enough to go." As he said it, his eyes welled up with tears that he strained to keep from spilling.

There was a long silence. Finally the pastor exhaled, a slight whistle of air escaping his lips as he tried to put such a statement in perspective with Kevin's life. He shook his head, but Kevin didn't catch disappointment in the pastor's gesture; it was more a shake of surprise. "You have been given so much by the Lord, Kevin. You've been a leader among the youth. You've been a camp counselor each summer. Your grades have been good." Each accomplishment was spoken slowly and thoughtfully, intended to give Kevin encouragement.

The pastor realized that the trauma of his mother's divorce, the lack of a father in her new husband and his years of waywardness in high school could still be giving him these feelings of inadequacy. But he did not think it was right to bring all of that up for discussion now. He continued, hoping for a solution—groping for words. "As I said, Kevin, your grades in school have been outstanding. You're physically fit. You have a supportive mother. You...."

Kevin hung his head, shaking it as the pastor spoke. "Stop! None of that erases my feelings of inadequacy. Pastor Jim, the challenge of cross-cultural ministry really excites me, but then I'm overcome with these feelings of being..." He hesitated, looking for the right word. "...unworthy. I'm not stupid. I know those feelings are destructive to everything I believe in, but I just don't know how to...."

The pastor got up and came around the desk to Kevin's side. He looked at Kevin as a father might look on his own son, with love and care. "Kevin, let's pray. Maybe the Lord can give us direction to help you overcome these feelings." Together they bowed their heads. "Dear Lord," the pastor began, "You are our all-sufficient One. You see the sincerity in Kevin's heart. Please give us some direction in this matter."

Kevin's prayer followed. "I agree with Pastor Jim, dear Lord. You are our Master. I want to do Your will. And I believe it is You calling me. But I need your wisdom and encouragement to get past this issue. We love You, Lord."

When Pastor Jim spoke again, his voice was bright and lively. "I have an idea, Kevin. Why don't we look at some of the men God used in times past? I mean way past, like Bible times. You look up some of them. And I will too. Let's get together again next week and see what we've discovered."

Kevin groaned. "I knew there wouldn't be an easy answer to this," he said, rolling his eyes. "Pastor Jim, I don't mean to sound ungrateful, but finals and term papers are coming up. I have to start focusing on school."

The pastor didn't answer. He waited for Kevin to decide his next move.

Kevin stood up. "But I guess I'm not going to be able to concentrate on my finals if I don't find some resolution here. Why me? Why do I feel this way? It's like I'm filled with excitement and anticipation at the thought of being a missionary, but then my whole being gets stomped on."

The pastor chuckled. "There are a lot of possible reasons," he said. Then his face suddenly grew serious. "Not the least being the enemy's desire to shut you down before you even get started. He is devious in bringing back to the surface issues that have long ago been dealt with."

Kevin shot a knowing look at Pastor Jim. The kindness that came back from his eyes assured Kevin that God had forgiven him for those past failures. And it just struck him that the trauma of those years could be the root of these feelings.

Pastor Jim smiled, and continued, "Let's go ahead with this study. There will still be time, with a clearer mind, for you to tackle your finals."

Kevin nodded. "Okay, I'll do it. I do need to get past this issue."

"See you in church tomorrow?" the pastor asked, putting a hand on Kevin's shoulder.

"I'll be there. Thanks for your help, Pastor."

NEXT SATURDAY MORNING

This time there was no hesitation in Kevin's gait. He took the stairs to the church three at a time and swiftly moved past the secretary and down the hall to Pastor Jim's office. Twice he dropped papers from his over-stuffed folder and had to run back and retrieve them, sliding on the newly waxed floor.

"Pastor Jim!" he called, before even reaching the door. Kevin was chuckling to himself, his face flushed with joy and amusement. "I can't believe what Hezekiah said when he was told that his kingdom would be destroyed and the people taken as slaves," Kevin shouted, as he noisily entered the office. The pastor put up his hand and Kevin stopped in his tracks, suddenly embarrassed by his untamed energy. He waited in front of the desk, shifting his weight from one foot to the other until Pastor Jim finished his phone call and turned to him. "Hello again, Kevin. I see you've done your homework. Have a seat."

Kevin put his folder on the desk as he plopped into the chair. He pulled it close to the desk. Feeling really silly, he apologized for his rude intrusion. He cleared his throat, attempting to regain some dignity. He opened the folder, shuffling the papers into some order.

The pastor waited for him to continue. Kevin found the page in his notebook marked II Kings 20:19 and paraphrased. "Hezekiah said, 'Well, that's good. At least it won't happen before I'm out of here,'" He chuckled again. "I had never thought about how human those Bible characters were."

Pastor Jim took his Bible from the shelf and opened it as he spoke. "That's part of our problem, Kevin. We can become so familiar with the stories that we slip over the details of the humanity of these people—people just like you and me. In fact, too often the Bible characters become so familiar that we have a tendency to think they're just storybook characters—like Superman, or Dino, the dinosaur!"

The pastor scratched an imaginary itch behind his left ear. "I must confess, this week I had to do some 'dusting off' of those familiar stories, too. As I did, I reminded myself that these men and women were real people, living real lives and having all the physical, emotional, mental, and spiritual sensitivities as we have today. Two thousand years ago, James had to remind his readers that 'Elijah was a human being with feelings and passions just like us.'[1] So this is not a new problem."

Kevin nodded as he thought for a moment of being in Hezekiah's shoes.

"So Kevin, in your week of study, what character first came to your mind?"

"No, Pastor Jim. You go first."

"No, you go ahead, Kevin."

"No, you... OK, I'll start with Jonah. Poor Jonah. He always catches it. I don't know why."

The pastor smiled. The story of Jonah and the whale really came alive for his children after they watched the DVD, *Finding Nemo.*

Kevin got up and walked to the window, looking out at the custodian sweeping the courtyard. "Poor Jonah," he said, shaking his head. He glanced back at the pastor, who had moved to a small side table to pour himself a cup of coffee. "Maybe, because we love fish stories," Kevin suggested, trying to answer his own thoughts.

"Yes, maybe that's it," the pastor said, turning back to Kevin. "Would you like coffee?"

1 Read James 5:17

Kevin held up a hand. "No, thanks. So God said, 'Jonah, go to Nineveh! Tell them I am going to destroy them in 40 days.' But Jonah says, 'No way!' He heads in the opposite direction. Three days later, after being vomited from the belly of that great fish—his now hairless skin bleached white from the digestive juices and with seaweed wrapped around his head—Jonah says, 'Oh, now I remember you, Lord.'"

Pastor Jim crossed his arms. "Such insolence."

"Man, I can't even imagine such a response," Kevin said. "So a second time God says, 'Go to Nineveh.' But this time his answer is different. This time he says, 'Okay, okay, I'll go.'"

Kevin went back to his folder and traced a finger over a line from the Bible. "'So Jonah arose and went to Nineveh,' Scripture says. What a sight he must have been. What a smell! So this angry prophet proclaims judgment on the great city. He doesn't tell them about a merciful God. Oh, no. He just says, 'Forty days and you're toast!' It took him three days just to walk from one end to the other of that huge city.

"Well, amazingly, they repent! From king to pauper. Even the animals were wearing sackcloth. But is Jonah happy at what God did through him? No! It displeases him—big time. He's despondent. Jonah says, 'I knew it! I knew it! God, You are so merciful. I told you before I fled to Tarshish that You would forgive them. For I know that You are a gracious God, and merciful, slow to anger, and of great kindness. Now, O Lord, let me die. I would rather be dead than alive.'"[2]

Kevin's tearful cry as he played the part of Jonah almost sounded real. "Kevin, have you ever considered acting?" Pastor Jim asked, trying to talk and laugh at the same time.

2 Read Jonah 1-4

"No, I haven't. But just think of it," Kevin said, looking back out the window. The gardener was gone now. "How's that for a response to revival? Would anyone of us consider Jonah good enough to go? Good enough to be chosen by God? But I can sort of identify with Jonah's not wanting to go to Nineveh. They were attacking Israel, and their method of executing their enemies was to skin them alive! Literally! Jonah spent the rest of his life being reminded of his relationship with the Ninevites by his hairless, bleached skin."

Pastor Jim chuckled again. "God does have a sense of humor."

"Jonah was a real piece of work. Yet God used Him for His purposes. You know, Pastor Jim, I got some of my information about Jonah from *Halley's Bible Handbook*.[3] That little book is crammed full of historical stuff about the Bible and the people of the Bible."

The pastor took his seat again and leaned back. "I like to use that book, too. I like the archeological information in it. But don't get me going on that! They're still making amazing discoveries that lend credibility to the absolute accuracy of the Word of God. Take Hezekiah's tunnel, for example. They...."

"Ahem...! Bible characters?" Kevin wasn't sure if he should have steered Pastor Jim back to the subject.

"OK! You're right." The pastor stopped, glancing at the wall clock. "Another day, maybe. Now back to our Bible. One of the men I read about is Barak in the Book of Judges. He's quite a character as well. The Bible says, 'And the children of Israel were again doing evil in the sight of the Lord.' So the Lord sold them into the hand of Jabin. And the children of Israel cried out to the Lord. In His mercy, God chose a man to accomplish His purposes.

3 *Halley's Bible Handbook,* Henry Halley, Zondervan, 1993.

"But Barak wasn't doing anything about it. Not until a prophetess named Deborah came a-calling. 'Hasn't the Lord God of Israel commanded you to take ten thousand men of the children of Naphtali and of the children of Zebulun to Mount Tabor? And didn't God further say to you that He would bring Sisera, the captain of Jabin's army to you with his chariots and that He would deliver them into your hand?'"

"Busted!" Kevin said, intent, as he listened.

"But what does this 'wimp of a man' say to Deborah? 'I will only go if you will go with me. But if you won't go, I won't go!' Does that sound like Barak would be chosen to be God's man for that hour? Yet, again, God used him for His purposes. Even though the real victory—the killing of Sisera—came through a woman."[4]

"I read a story from the Book of Judges too! The story of Gideon." Kevin ran a large hand through his hair. "Pastor Jim, do you think Gideon was good enough to go? I mean, according to his own testimony, he was a three-time loser as far as self-esteem."

As if Kevin was suddenly transported to the cave where Gideon crouched, his voice became hushed. "Gideon's hiding in a cave for fear of the Midianites. He's threshing a bit of wheat that the enemy hadn't burned. He's startled by the Angel of the Lord: 'Hello! You mighty man of valor! GO! I have sent you.'"

There was such power and strength in his voice as Kevin spoke the words of the angel that Pastor Jim jumped. Even the secretary at the receptionist desk was startled as Kevin boomed the Angel's announcement.

She came down the hall and poked her head through the open doorway. "Is everything okay in here?" she questioned with a quizzical look.

Pastor Jim waved a hand of reassurance. "Kevin

4 Read Judges 4

was just getting a bit dramatic in telling his story of Gideon. I'm wondering if he should be an actor."

"Sorry," Kevin said, grinning sheepishly, his cheeks now flushed.

"Don't be. It's good to be excited about the Lord. It's good to see these people as real human beings. Go on."

"Well Gideon replies: 'Oh, my Lord, how can I save Israel? My tribe is the least in Israel;[5] my family is the least in Manasseh; I am the least of my family.'" Kevin paused, thinking the pastor was going to say something. "Pastor Jim, just think of it. If you stacked up the whole nation of Israel, Gideon saw himself on the bottom of the pile." Now the pastor shook his head in agreeing disbelief.

"And what was God's answer?" the pastor asked Kevin, though he, too, knew the story well.

"'I have sent you. Surely, I will be with you.' But Gideon needed a sign. So one consumed sacrifice, one wet and one dry fleece, and two reductions of his army later, Gideon routs the enemy and is used by God to fulfill His Plan. But wait! Talk about being human—go back. After all of those signs, God is giving him the instruction of battle strategy: Do it at night, on three sides of the camp; the weapons will be lamps, pitchers and trumpets; and the battle cry will be *The Sword of the Lord!'* But as his 'mighty' army of three hundred men go running down the hill toward the 144,000 Midianites, what do we hear them shouting? 'The Sword of the Lord, *and of Gideon!'* What a guy! God had done that double reduction of the army for the very purpose of not allowing Gideon to take any of the glory! Yet, there is his attempt. If that's not human, I don't know what is."

Pastor Jim nodded his head in agreement.

---

5 Manasseh was one of the "half tribes." He was the elder of Joseph's two sons. When Jacob (Israel) placed his hands on the boys' heads, he gave his right hand of blessing to the younger brother, even though Joseph tried to set his father straight..

"So there they are. The battle's won," Kevin said.
"The people want him to judge Israel. 'No! No! Neither I,
nor my sons will rule over you. On second thought,'
Gideon replies, 'just give me the earrings you have tak-
en off the enemy.' And with the gold he makes an image
of an ephod[6] and sets it in the town square to be worshipped." Kevin looked directly at the pastor. "What's
with that? Emboldened by God, he had pulled down the
grove to Baal. And now he sets up another image to be
worshipped. So what on earth made Gideon good
enough to go?"

The pastor waited for Kevin to think it out on his
own.

Kevin looked down at his notes. "It's just crazy.
Here's a guy who goes from self-deprecation (I'm a nobody. I'm not good enough to go.) to trying to claim
some of the glory. A guy who goes from destroying one
grove, to setting up another object of worship. This man
doesn't seem to me to be quality material for God's Plan
of the Ages. Yet, God evidently did. It seems that God is
willing to use ordinary people to accomplish His extraordinary goals."[7]

"Right on! Kevin, that's a brilliant flash of insight.
Say it again."

"What?"

"What you just said."

"What did I just say?"

The pastor smiled. "You just said, 'It seems that
God is willing to use ordinary people to accomplish His
extraordinary goals.' I think we're moving toward a solution to your dilemma. Now you say it, Kevin."

"Ordinary people, under God's direction, do extraordinary things." Kevin said it slowly and deliberately, emphasizing each word. "Yeah!"

6 An ephod was a linen vest-type garment that was worn by the High Priest.
7 Read Judges 6 and 7.

"Kevin, I think we can go on."

"Sure, but let me say it again, first: Ordinary people, used by God, can reach extraordinary goals."

Excitement was mounting. It seemed that each one was trying to tell his story with greater emphasis.

"Let's look at Isaiah," Pastor Jim said, flipping to a marked page in his Bible. "He's one of my favorite Bible characters. His prophesies begin with the words, 'Woe unto you...! Woe unto you...! Woe unto you...!' Pastor Jim tried to make those "woes" sound dramatic.

Kevin interrupted. "No! NO, you have to say it like this." Again, Kevin's bent for character impersonations gave it the correct emphasis.

Deciding to just tell the story and forget the dramatics, Pastor Jim continued. "'In the year that King Uzziah died, Isaiah saw the Lord, high and lifted up, and His train filled the temple. Then he said, 'Woe is me...!'"

Bringing his steaming second cup of coffee to his lips, the pastor blew before taking a sip. "With the live coal touching his lips, his iniquity is taken away and his sin purged. Then he heard the Lord say, 'Whom shall I send? Who will go for us?' Isaiah's reply is, 'Here am I; send me!'"[8] The pastor sipped gently, squinting from the heat, then set his cup down on the desk. Kevin watched every move as though there was a lesson in the very act of drinking coffee.

"Now at this time," the pastor said, "God sent Isaiah to His own people. So, Kevin, it really isn't a story—as it's often used—to encourage people into cross-cultural ministry. The lesson is about humility. But the humility that comes when we see the Lord—when we really have a personal encounter with Him—is certainly applicable to cross-cultural workers, as well."

Kevin stood up and stretched, then wandered over

8 Read Isaiah 6

to the coffee table. He had hoped to find some herbal tea and hot water. But in this coffee-drinking culture, not much attention is given to non-coffee drinkers. He wondered about other cultures in the world— specifically, the culture he would be going to. Looking back at the pastor and the subject at hand, Kevin said, "Look what happened to Peter. He even saw the Lord, in person! He walked with him daily. Talked with him. Ate with Him. He was both commended and rebuked by Him. Years later Peter is in Joppa, in the house of Simon the tanner, he's up on the roof patio."

The pastor nodded.

"Actually, he went up there to pray. It's about noontime. So he gets hungry and sleepy. How human is that, I ask? It was time to pray, but instead he gets sleepy. As he smells the food cooking below, he dozes off. Three times in his trance he sees the sheet of unclean animals. 'Arise and eat, Peter.'

"'But, Lord! I have never eaten anything unclean!'

"'Peter, don't call anything common that I have cleansed.'"

Kevin did a masterful job of booming the voice of God. So loud that the secretary from down the hall shouted a question in response, "Do you want me to order ham sandwiches for you two from the deli?" If the truth would be known, she was listening to this entire story-telling session.

The pastor's eyes twinkled. "You've been listening to our stories," he teased, as she came to the door.

"Well, a little." she acknowledged sheepishly.

"Yes, ham and cheese. That would be nice. Thanks, Karen."

Kevin's stomach growled from the talk of food. He was glad for the interruption. When the secretary left, he jumped back into his story. "The messengers of 'common' Cornelius arrive. He brings them into the tanner's house. The next day they head off to Caesarea.

"Peter is welcomed into the home of a Gentile. But how gracious is he? He pulls his robe tightly around himself so as not to touch or be touched by any person in this crowded room. He says, 'You know it is against the Law of God for me to be here! But God said I shouldn't call you unclean!'"[9] Kevin rolled his eyes. And his head, in utter disbelief. "Would you have chosen someone who would make such an insensitive cultural goof? Yet, God did. I hope my training in cultural sensitivity won't allow me to make such a mistake."

"Kevin, did you hear what you just said?"

"Not again!"

"No, really. You just acknowledged that you're looking forward to further training. I think you're overcoming your uncertainty about 'Who's good enough to go.'"

Kevin took a seat again, encouraged by the pastor's observation. He really had said that! Yes, he then also realized that he was thinking about cultural differences as he had looked for the herbal tea.

The mood seemed to take a more serious tone as Pastor Jim began talking about our Lord. He came around the desk and faced Kevin. "Kevin, because Jesus was fully God and fully man—a truth that is impossible for us to understand—we are often reluctant to focus on His humanity. But even Jesus, when pressed to the limit of His human endurance, cried out: 'Father, if it is possible, let this cup pass from Me!' But out of the agony of Gethsemane, obedience, the supreme submission came as he said, 'Nevertheless, not My will but Thine be done.'"[10] They both paused to contemplate the

9 Read Acts 10   10 Read Matthew 26:36-46

awesomeness of God's plan of redemption. Pastor Jim continued, "Yes, the incarnation is a mystery kept secret for eternity. Yet, somehow as Christ, our Lord was also fully man, we see that humanness showing its limitations. But, 'despising the shame, He endured the cross, for the joy set before Him.'[11] What an example of obedience for us today."

Kevin looked up.

"Kevin, I just used a new word. One that we had not yet considered. Did you hear it?"

"Yes, I think I did. I was just thinking about Mary. What simple, submissive words she said: 'Behold, the handmaiden of the Lord. Be it unto me as you have spoken.'[12] I don't think there could be a more beautiful expression of willing obedience."

"There, you said it too. *Obedience.* I think we're finding the answer. The question of 'Who's good enough to go?' doesn't seem to be the right question to be asking."

The pastor reached across the desk for his Bible, then held it in front of him. He quickly flipped through the pages to a familiar passage in Exodus. "I want us to look at one more guy: Moses. From each of these characters, and others who were called of God to do the bidding of His sovereign will, lessons can be learned. But, to me, Moses is classic."

"Pastor Jim, before you talk about Moses, let me mention Esther. No way was she going to go into the king's court. She didn't want to lose her head. But when Cousin Mort reminded her of the sovereignty of God, she said she would go. And her attitude was, 'If I perish; I perish.'[13] This hits me smack between the eyes with the awesome sovereignty of God. And our privileged opportunity to participate in His Plan."

"Good. Keep that perspective. Never let it go. It will

11 Read Hebrews 12:2   12 Read Luke 1:38   13 Read Esther 4-6

help you over a thousand hurdles that you'll face in this marathon race you're entering."

"I just want to thank you," Kevin said. "I really got into this study. There were so many others—Samson,[14] for one! Man, what a wild guy! Rahab, a prostitute![15] But, let's hear about Moses."

Pastor Jim took his seat once more and launched into his favorite Bible character. "It was a planned rescue from certain death. His older sister watched from between the reeds. 'Moses, don't capsize your little ark of safety with your stirring and crying.' Then Pharaoh's daughter discovers the baby Moses. With a heart of compassion she has her maids bring him out of the basket. His sister steps forward. 'Should I find a nurse for you among the Hebrew women?'[16] And when he is weaned, he is returned to the palace, to be raised as the Pharaoh's grandson.

"The child grows. When Stephen is standing before the Sanhedrin, he says of Moses, 'He became learned in all the wisdom of Egypt and was eloquent in speech.'[17] Moses took positions of leadership.

"Then at the age of forty, grieving in his heart at the despicable treatment of his kindred, he slays an Egyptian and hides him in the sand. The next day, in trying to break up a fight between his brethren, he realizes that his murder has been discovered.

"He flees to Midian. To a shepherd's tent. He spends forty long years pondering his miscalculated and misinterpreted deed. He lives the life of a nomadic sheepherder. The mighty heir apparent to the throne of Egypt spends his days picking the larvae of flies out of sheep's nostrils; trying to keep the herd together for fear of the wild animals; breaking a sheep's leg if he was given to running away, then having to carry that sheep on his

14 Read Judges 13-16   15 Read Joshua 2   16 Read Exodus 2:3-10   17 Read Acts 7:22

shoulders until the leg mended; keeping the herd from eating too much so they don't roll on their backs and suffocate.

"Kevin, do you remember when our pastor encouraged us to read Philip Keller's classic book, *A Shepherd Looks at Psalm 23?*[18] Have you read it?"

The sudden question brought Kevin back to the present. He had been on the mountainside with Moses. "Huh? Oh, no, not yet. College textbooks have been my 'bedtime' reading for the past four years."

"Well, now would be a good time to pick it up. It sure gave me a different perspective on the Good Shepherd than our Christmas manger scenes give. And it contains excellent lessons in spiritual leadership. But back to Moses. So one day, roaming through the backside of the desert, he comes to Horeb, the mountain of God. His attention is arrested by a bush that is burning, but isn't being consumed. He approached. A Voice spoke: 'Moses! Moses! Take off your shoes. This is holy ground on which you are standing. I am the God of Abraham and Isaac and Jacob.'"

"He must have been scared," Kevin said, imagining himself in that position.

"That's putting it mildly. He hid his face. The Voice continued: 'I have seen the affliction of My people in Egypt. I have heard their cry. I know their sorrows. I have come down to deliver them. I am going to bring them up into a good land flowing with milk and honey. And, by the way, Moses, I am sending you to Pharaoh that you may bring My people out of Egypt.'

"However tuned his ear was to know it was God calling his name, Moses missed a very important pronoun in God's message: *I.* God clearly outlined His plan and purpose for that time. And He had chosen Moses to ac-

18 *A Shepherd Looks at Psalm 23,* Philip Keller, Zondervan, 1970.

complish His goal. But is Moses good enough to go? His five excuses are classic. Some of them might ring a bell."

Kevin smiled, then shifted in his seat and listened.

"His first excuse is exactly what we've been talking about. 'Who am I that I should go?' I can only imagine how those forty years as a sheepherder had affected Moses' state of mind. Had the zeal for his people demonstrated on those desert sands so long ago dissipated? Had thoughts of 'I'm a nobody' overwhelmed him? Or, had he possibly pondered schemes of going back to help his families? Or was he so consumed with himself that he didn't even hear Who was going to do the delivering? What were his first words in answer to the Lord? 'Who am *I*...?' Moses plaintively cried."

Kevin looked down at his lap, feeling suddenly ashamed at having thought the same question when he felt his calling.

As if the pastor knew what he was thinking, he added, "And that's an okay question, Kevin, if there's an appropriate follow through. His question is the same one you're asking: Who am I that God would want to use me? There are two perspectives. On the one hand, you are God's 'most finely crafted work of art; His poem; His workmanship, created in Christ Jesus to walk in those good deeds that He beforehand planned for you to walk in.'[19] You're an ambassador of Christ.[20] You represent His Kingdom to those entrapped in the kingdom of darkness. What a high and awesome calling."

The pastor picked up his coffee mug. "On the other hand, you and I are just clay pots," he said, pointing to the mug. "Our bodies are bags of dirt clods! And did you realize that even the 'bag' (our skin) is just made of

19 Read Ephesians 2:10   20 Read II Corinthians 5:20

the elements of the earth? But He's made each vessel precisely designed for His use. Some of the vessels are of gold and silver, but some also of wood and of clay; and some to honor and some to dishonor. As we cooperate with God in the working out of our salvation,[21] we'll become vessels of honor, inspected and approved of God, and prepared for every good work.[22] And He has put the glorious Message of salvation in these vessels of clay so that 'all the excellency of its power will be of God and not of us.'"[23]

Kevin's eyes went wide again, and his head was now nodding adamantly to everything the pastor was saying. "I just remembered something that happened a couple of years ago."

The pastor set down his cup and smiled, thrilled that Kevin was so eagerly entering into this discussion.

"Classes were about to start. Many teams had just returned from their summer of service experiences. As various members of the teams were sharing their stories, it began to sound like they were getting into a one-up-man bragging session. You could almost hear them saying, 'Even the devils were subject to us.'

"At the height of our revelry—you see, I was getting into it also, even though I had not been on one of the trips—one always-quiet young lady, said, 'Professor Jones, when the disciples came back from a short term trip, didn't Jesus say to rather rejoice that our names are written in the Book of Life?'[24] Well, we all looked at one another. It was time for repentance, in a big way!"

"You're right, Kevin. Our God is a jealous God.[25] He will not share His glory with anyone," Pastor Jim confirmed. He shook his head. "I don't know about you, but I shudder at the enormity of God's Plan. I can't wrap my brain around the many facets of His Story."

21 Read Philippians 2:12-13   22 Read II Timothy 2:20-21   23 Read II Corinthians 4:7
24 Read Luke 10:17-20   25 Read Exodus 34:14

Again a silence filled the room. After a brief moment, the pastor continued.

"And in my thinking, it is even more awesome that He has determined to incorporate the likes of us to accomplish His eternal purposes. But we need to see ourselves 'seated in the heavenly places with Christ Jesus,'[26] so we can observe the affairs of this world from His perspective, and not from ours."

"We see things more and more from His perspective by meditating on His Word, I remember our pastor telling us," Kevin observed.

Pastor Jim smiled at Kevin's insight, and continued. "The more we stay in that humbling, but rightful place next to Him, the more we will be able to think the thoughts of Christ. 'For, we who are of the Spirit of God have the very mind of Christ.'"[27]

"That in itself is a mind-boggling thought!" Kevin added. "I remember when Jesus had to rebuke Peter for saying he wouldn't let the priests and the mob arrest and kill Jesus. He clarified with these words: 'Peter, you are looking at things from man's perspective and not from God's.'"[28]

Kevin and Pastor Jim were obviously together in their thinking, as they each built on each other's statements.

"Another thought," Pastor Jim added. "When we ask someone to do something and they begin with a statement of self-deprecation as Moses and Gideon did, how do we respond? We pat them on the back and try to build up their ego. 'Hey! Sure you can do it. I wouldn't have asked you if I thought you weren't up to it. Come on! Give it a try! You might like it!'"

"Isn't that what you started to do last week when I first spilled this on you?" Kevin interjected.

26 Read Ephesians 2:6 27 Read I Corinthians 2:16 28 Read Matthew 16:23

"Okay, okay! Lesson learned," the pastor said sheepishly.

Were his ears burning a little bit? Kevin thought he saw them a darker shade of color.

Pastor Jim ignored the stare, and continued. "And how did God answer Moses' attitude of belittlement? Not a word of bolstering. Not a compliment of his ability. God simply says, 'Hey, Mo! No problem! I'll be there! Surely, I will be with you.'"

The pastor came to Kevin and put a hand on his shoulder. "So Kevin, as you sense the call of God on your life to be a missionary, here's a critical lesson: Don't look to your adequacies or inadequacies. Recognize that if it is truly God calling you, He will be there. He has work that He wants done. And He wants you to do it. He will be with you as you are His hands and feet and mouth to accomplish His will. As it says in Matthew 28:20, 'He will never leave you, nor forsake you. He will be with you always, even to the end of the age.'"

"But Moses sure wasn't ready to go," Kevin quickly acknowledged, being quite familiar with this story.

Pastor Jim shook his head. "No. He was not satisfied with God's answer. He had another excuse: 'But God, I messed up so badly forty years ago, by what authority would I go to them now?'

"God's response: 'I AM THAT I AM! Tell them that I AM sent you. The Lord God of your fathers, the God of Abraham, of Isaac and of Jacob, has sent me to you. Tell them that I have visited them and have seen what Egypt has done to them and I will bring them up out of their affliction.'" Pastor Jim emphasized that passage of Scripture with such conviction, Kevin felt the power of God's Word in his pastor's voice.

"Kevin, no matter where you go or what you do, you are going in the authority of the only One True God. It would be good for you to review that series of sermons our pastor did on the attributes of God. He is an awesome God, isn't He? Creator of the universe. All-powerful. All-knowing.

"God knows everything," Pastor Jim reemphasized. "I look out over our beautiful lake and realize that He knows the size, the molecular structure, the composition and weight of every drop of water in that lake and, for that matter, every ocean, and of every grain of sand on the seashore. More than that, He knows the thoughts and intents of the hearts of the six-plus billion people who currently inhabit this world. But the real mind-blower to me is that this great and mighty God says, 'You may call Me, Father.' So personal; so intimate. So available to me.

"When you receive the confirmation of the church that it is His will for you to go, you can be sure that it's the great I AM—the eternally self-existent, all-sufficient God—who is sending you. Absolutely awesome!"

Kevin was beaming now.

"But here is why I place Moses as the classic example of human hesitation to do God's will. Here he is talking with God. Imagine that—talking with God! Yet he comes up with another excuse. Evidently he was thinking about going because he says, 'But God, they won't believe me.' Again, God answers that excuse with His own all-sufficiency. He uses that which is in our hands.

"That was God's answer to Moses. 'What's that in your hand?' A shepherd's staff; a rod. For forty years now, that once delicate, pampered hand of a royal grandson has held a staff of wood. It was nothing special. Probably worn quite smooth. Maybe he had put some carvings on it as he sat with the sheep. Yes, it was used well in tending the sheep and fighting off the predators. 'Moses,' God says. 'Look what I can do with something that you regard as a common piece of wood. Throw it on the ground.' It became a snake! 'Pick it up by the tail, Moses.' It became a rod again. 'If they won't believe that, forget the rod,' God might have said. 'Moses, look at your hand. Put it inside your cloak. And pull it out.' Leprous! 'Put it in again, Moses. And pull it out.' And now it is normal. 'And, Moses, it is possible that they won't believe either of those signs. Then, go down to the river. Pour the water upon the dry ground. It will become blood.'"

"The power of God is awesome. This is exactly what happened when he went to Pharaoh," Kevin interjected.

"Yes, but back on that mountain, Moses' head must have been spinning. His thoughts might have been, 'This is ridiculous. A bush burning? A Voice talking to me? And I'm answering It! Where are the sheep? It's getting late. Zipporah probably has dinner waiting for me. The children are hungry, asking where is Daddy? But I'm here. The bush isn't being consumed. There's power and authority in the Voice. But, no, this is not for me.'

"Kevin, get ready for his next excuse. It's wild. 'Jehovah, O my Lord, I am not a man of words. Furthermore, You have never before spoken to me. I just don't have it in me. I am slow of speech and I have a slow tongue.' As we said, by Stephen's testimony before the Sanhedrin, we know this was an outright lie!"

The pastor put down his Bible and tugged at his ear, eyeing Kevin. "Of course, we've never lied to God, have we?" No answer was required.

"Moses still didn't get it!" Kevin added in disbelief.

The pastor sighed. "That's right. He was still focused on himself. But God then directs his attention to Himself. 'Who made man's mouth? Have not I the Lord made it?' Uh, oh—it looks like he might be in for the same kind of battle Job got into with the Lord![29] But God then continues, 'I will be with your mouth and teach you what you should say.'

"Incidentally, years later Jeremiah came up with the same excuse. God's answer to him also directed the attention away from Jeremiah and onto Himself. 'Whatever I command you, that is what you will speak.'[30] He also assured Isaiah, 'My Word which goes forth from My mouth (using your lips that were purged by the coal of fire off of My altar) will not return void, but will accomplish that which I please.'"[31]

"Do you think man will ever get it?" Kevin asked, frumping the hair on the back of his head. "I mean, do you think we'll ever learn that life is not all about us! That life is all about Him?"

The pastor smiled gently. "Do you think by now Moses is ready to say, 'Yes, Lord, I am your willing servant'? Nope! Sidestepping all logic and that lie, he says (in good King James English), 'Send by the hand of whom Thou wilt send.' In simple 21st Century English, he said, 'Let George do it!'

"'And the anger of the Lord was kindled against him!' Can't you just see the fire crackling? Maybe tongues of flame reached out to grab Moses. Whether or not the fire was hot, Moses is now in the hot seat! And then he finally says, 'Okay! Okay! I'll go!'

"Now Kevin, I'm not trying to put Moses down or anything. You know, sometimes people think that if they make someone else look bad, it'll somehow makes

29 Read Job 38-41   30 Read Jeremiah 1:6-7   31 Read Isaiah 55:11

them look good. That's not it at all. It was no small assignment to which God was calling Moses to be committed: Convincing 2,000,000 people who had been
entrenched in a culture for over four hundred years to
pack up and move out to—where? Then there was the
impossibility of the Pharaoh letting his slave labor force
leave the country. Not to mention just the logistics of it!
But finally, as reluctant as he was, Moses mobilized
God's people and led them out of Egypt. He became
God's mighty man for that young nation of people."[32]

Kevin needed to change positions. He stood up,
stretched, and then crossed his arms.

"So what can we learn from all of this?" Pastor Jim
asked.

"A lot," Kevin voiced enthusiastically, leaning
against the wall and crossing his long legs.

"That's right. Whether its the reluctance that we
saw in Moses or the willingness we saw in Mary's obedience, arguing 'Who's good enough to go?' is a moot
point. It's just not the issue. Rather, the question we
need to ask ourselves is this: What is my degree of submission to His will? Will I be obedient to His voice? Will
I follow in the footsteps of Jesus and say, 'Nevertheless,
not my will, but Thine be done.'"[33]

The pastor looked at the clock on the wall. "I know
this is getting kind of long—maybe even a bit preachy,
but I think it would be good to add just one more perspective."

"I'm not going anywhere. This is what I asked for—
what I needed. To see that it isn't all about me. To realize that obedience to His will is the key. This has been
great!"

"Well, just a minute now. This last thought comes
from one of those passages of Scripture that I wish

32 Read Exodus 3-4   33 Read Luke 22:42

wouldn't be in the Bible. It's really a tough one. Jesus was quite blunt in His illustration of this point of 'Who's good enough to go.' Listen to it from the words of Luke's Gospel. It's such a wild thought that I'm not going to paraphrase it. I'll just read it straight from the Good Book."

He picked up the Bible one last time and found the page, then read aloud. "If any of you have a servant plowing or looking after the sheep, are you likely to say to him when he comes in from the fields, come on in and sit down to your meal? Aren't you more likely to say, get my supper ready for me: change your coat and wait while I eat and drink, and then, when I am finished, you can have your meal? Do you feel particularly grateful to your servant for doing what you tell him? I don't think so. It is the same with yourselves—when you have done everything that you are told to do, you can say, we are not very good as servants; we have only done our duty."[34]

"Guilty! Yes, I'm guilty. I, also, too often skip over uncomfortable passages." Addressing this particular one, Kevin said, "That hurts! That rubs against my very nature! We're all striving for significance. I want to be somebody. I want to do something I'm good at. I need recognition!" Kevin ended that confession on a higher pitch than he had expected.

"I thought you'd have that reaction. But Kevin, Jesus also said, 'Do you want to be great in My Kingdom? Learn to be the servant of all.'"[35]

"But, didn't Jesus say He would no longer call us servants, but friends?" Kevin was still looking for a way to lessen the impact of that Scripture.

"Yes, He did. And I am so grateful that He would look on me as His friend. However, my attitude, I be-

34 Read Luke 17:7-10   35 Read Mark 10:44

lieve, must be the attitude of His First Century follow-ers. Look at the writers of Scripture: James, a servant of God; Paul, a bond slave by choice; Jude, the servant of Jesus Christ. Peter was there when Jesus said that He would call them 'friend', yet he introduced his Letter with: Simon Peter, a servant. Sorry! But you can't wiggle out of this. In any kingdom, no matter how high a position to which the king might call you, you are still his subject. And certainly, in the Kingdom of God, there is only one King!"

Kevin gave a great exhale and stood solid before the pastor, staring down at his feet. "This is a lot to digest," he said, still looking at the floor. He looked up into the eyes of the pastor, realizing there were yet more lessons to be learned from him. "I need some help. Can you help me summarize these lessons so I can review them? I need to know that I can sort through this issue and walk in Christ's victory."

"I am your servant," the pastor said with a grin.

Pastor Jim and Kevin sat for another hour, eating sandwiches and making a summary of the lessons they learned from the lives of the people in Scripture who lived so many years ago.

SUMMARY OF ISSUES

The following summaries highlight the many issues that were raised in the conversation between Kevin and his pastor. There is no suggestion that you will face all of these issues. However, it would be good to take each one into your closet of prayer and ask God, the Holy Spirit to assure you of those that are resolved in your life and to touch your heart with those that need to be dealt with long before you say, "Good-bye."

Kevin and his pastor explored the lives of people

that God used in Bible times to help him realize that "Who's good enough to go?" is not the question at all. Check out these summary statements as they may apply to your life.

• Finding the right person—a person of understanding and encouragement—to share with initially, will lay a good foundation to the process of missionary preparation.

• There has been an information explosion in our day. Everybody has an opinion about everything—almost! Yet, it is the Bible, the Word of God, which still holds the answers to life and godly living. It is this age-old, yet ageless Book that provides standards and models for every generation.

• There is an enemy. Every aspect of spiritual warfare is vital to missionary preparation.

• Ordinary people at God's direction are able to accomplish extraordinary things.

• A tight, personal relationship with the Lord is a critical prerequisite to missionary service.

• Pre-field preparation is vital to thriving on the mission field. It must include at least the following: Cultural training, interpersonal relationship skills, spiritual warfare, contingency training (What to do when something goes wrong.), primary health care, and skills for language learning. This training is, of course, in addition to the preparation for the specific mission task and a solid Biblical understanding.

• It is a privilege to be about our Father's business. This puts the spotlight on Him and His Plan of the Ages, instead of "me, and I how I helped God out!"

• These few thousand years carved out of eternity that we call time is all about God and His Story. I am not the center of the universe.

• Spiritual leadership skills and experience must also be a part of pre-field preparation.

• Humility is a basic requisite to servanthood.

• Don't lie to God. It insults His creativity.

• God's response to Moses and Jeremiah and Isaiah: *"I will be there!"* David's statement to Goliath: "You come with sword and spear. But I come in the Name of the God of Israel."

• Who am I? On the one hand, I am His highest creation, created to walk in the plans that He has designed for me. On the other hand, I am only a vessel through which His life is to be seen.

• Don't say "no" to God. He may sidestep your opportunity to minister as he uses another to do His will.

• When God taps you for an assignment, it is best to not run away. You can run but you can't hide!

• In the final analysis, "Who's good enough to go?" is an irrelevant question. Whether the assignment is as "easy" as Barak conquering the armies of Jabin or as impossible as Jesus dying on Calvary; whether one is as reluctant as Moses or as willing as Mary, obedience—submission to His will—is the real issue.

For your own summary, place all the people talked about in this chapter on a line from reluctant to willing obedience. Then, after some serious soul-searching and prayer, place yourself on that line!

Suggestion: You might want to read back through the chapter and find the context to which each of these summary statements refers.

As the Lord leads you in this study, you will probably be able to gain further insights from the lives of other in the Bible. Think beyond the "box."

PERSONAL NOTES:

2

BUT I DON'T FEEL CALLED!

The tires squealed; the brakes grabbed. On the spur of the moment Helen had made a decision. It was time to tell someone. For several weeks now she had been meaning to talk to the missions pastor. But each time she tried, someone else was talking with him, or she just didn't know how to say it.

Unfortunately, at the moment she neared the church and slammed on the brakes to enter the parking lot she had failed to notice the police car in her rear-view mirror. By the time the officer had written the ticket, handed it to her, and left with a warning, her emotions had quieted down enough to pull her car into one of the parking spaces marked, "Visitor." She prayed a silent prayer, thanking God that the officer had not hit her car. She also asked for a calm spirit, hoping to fulfill her intended visit with the missions pastor.

Helen was familiar with the layout of the church complex of buildings and easily went to the church office.

Betty, the receptionist, looked up from her computer. "Oh, hi, Helen. What a happy surprise to see you. Ooh, you look a bit—ah—upset."

"Oh, Betty, I thought I was calmed down. But it still shows, huh?"

"What happened?" Betty positioned herself to listen more intently. After hearing Helen's story, the receptionist buzzed the missions pastor's phone. "Pastor Dan, there's a young lady here to see you. She says it's quite urgent." Betty smiled and winked at Helen.

Helen felt a pang of nervousness as she anticipated what he was saying. Betty heard him shuffling through a stack of papers and then he answered. "Betty, you know I have that staff meeting in just fifteen minutes. Who is it?"

The receptionist flashed a polite smile to Helen, but grew serious when she addressed the pastor again. "It's Helen Walker. I know you have the staff meeting shortly." She said this as much to prepare Helen for a very brief meeting, if at all, as to acknowledge Pastor Dan's frustration. Betty continued, "She was driving by the church and felt that she should talk with you. She's a bit upset. She had slammed on the brakes and a cop car almost rear-ended her. She couldn't talk him out of a ticket."

Pastor Dan's voice softened, but the annoyance in his tone was still evident. "Well, what does she want?"

Helen watched the receptionist for any positive sign. *Maybe I shouldn't have stopped in at this time*, she thought. Helen put up her hands and started to back away from the desk. But Betty stopped her, motioning her to stay. Firmly, she spoke into the phone, "Pastor, are you going to see her? Or must I send her away?" She had learned from years of experience how to handle the pastors.

"All right, send her in. But, Betty, let her know I only have a few minutes."

Helen tried to read the receptionist's face as she listened to the pastor's response, hoping it was positive. When the brows of the receptionist furrowed, she prepared to turn and leave.

"He said he'd be glad to see you. But he has only a few minutes."

"Great!" Helen said, and then a little softer, "That's just great. Thank you."

When Helen entered Pastor Dan's office, all signs of irritation instantly dissipated from his face. He stood up from his desk. "Helen? Helen Walker! How great to see you! We have a staff meeting in about ten minutes. But what seems so urgent? Sorry about that ticket. Are you okay?"

"I'm fine, thanks. I should have looked in the rearview mirror. I had no idea he was following so closely. I saw the church. I thought you would be in. It was just a spur of the moment decision." Helen blushed at that thought. It wasn't like her to make that kind of decision. She continued, "I just have something I've wanted to say to you for a while now. I thought this was the right time."

"Please," he said, "sit down."

Pastor Dan was not a short man, but no one would think him tall, either. Maybe a little wide around the middle, but fit. As missions pastor, he spent a great deal of his time in the field, and knew the rigors of cross-cultural missionary work. He had seen much of the world, but the suffering he had witnessed didn't harden him; instead, it motivated him in his work. He was generally light-hearted and smiled easily.

Helen took a seat and stared at her hands that so easily glided over the keys of her piano and organ but were now shaking with a good bit of nervousness. "Pastor Dan, it's so difficult to say this out loud." It was such an awesome thought. How could she put it to words? Before she had time to carefully formulate the right words in her mind, they just tumbled out. "*I think God wants me to be a missionary!*"

Pastor Dan raised his burly arms in a gesture of praise. He opened his mouth to speak but Helen quickly continued. "I was sure you would give your hearty, 'Praise the Lord.' And I thought it would be good to get a taste of ministry in another culture before I go on to college."

Pastor Dan was again ready to say something, but...!

"But, Pastor Dan—" And now the words just tumbled out. "There's a problem. A big problem! I don't feel called. How do I know this is God speaking to me, and not just some human desire? Or a pizza and Pepsi nightmare? Or the strong emphasis of our church on missions? Or my folks so involved with internationals who live here? Or my desire for adventure? Or...."

"Helen!" the pastor said, putting up his hands again, this time to stop her. "Slow down. Let's take this one step at a time." Just then he spotted the report he had been searching for that he needed for his meeting. He picked it up and held it in front of her. "I have a meeting to go to in five minutes. Do you really want me to try to give you an answer to those questions now?"

"No. When I drove up I didn't know you had a staff meeting to go to. I do appreciate your letting me see you. But I'm just so confused. The books I read about missions...." She hesitated, then rephrased her thought. "Missionaries seem to be in a different category of person than I am. And if I'm going to be one of 'them,' I want to make sure it's God calling me and not my own—or worse—someone else's desires."

"First of all, Helen, missionaries are just ordinary people called to do extraordinary things for God. Everybody who's doing His will is doing the 'extraordinary thing' God has called him to do. But listen, I'll tell you what. I wrote a paper on that very subject of knowing God's will for one of my seminary classes. I think I can find it here. Why don't you let me give it to you. You can read it here in my office, and then we can discuss this awesome subject when I get back."

Helen wondered how the pastor could find anything in the heaps of paperwork on his desk. If his shelves were as disorganized as the rest of his office, she wondered how he would ever find the paper.

But the pastor surprised her. He walked right over to a shelf and pulled down a neatly bound report. "Here it is. Make some notes if you wish. We can discuss it after the meeting."

Helen opened the first page and saw a professor's large check mark giving the paper an okay. Her eyes widened. "You only got a check mark for all this work? My mom and dad make comments on their comments. When they're finished with my papers, I can barely see what I have written."

Pastor Dan chuckled, privately appreciating that his wife was doing such a good job at homeschooling their children as Helen's parents had done for her. "I think the professor only checked to see that we did our assignments. I don't think he ever read any of them. But it sure helped me to put the thoughts down on paper. I've got to go. Happy reading." He closed the door behind him, leaving Helen alone.

She turned the first page and read the title:

"BUT I DON'T FEEL CALLED
by Dan Harris"

She began to read aloud, as she usually did in her room when she did her homework.

"Paul, the Apostle, said, 'Don't be unwise (vague), but understand (firmly grasp) what the will of the Lord is.'[1] Volumes have been written on the subject. Yet, before they go out of print, others have taken their place. And we still want to read more about this elusive something known as 'God's will for my life.'"

Helen nodded to herself. She needed to be sure what God's will was for her. She sensed that if she kept reading, she might find out.

She read the next title that began the Introduction:

"A HANDFUL OF STRAWY GRASPS.
"A drowning person will reach for even a straw in an attempt to stay afloat. Without the emotion of the moment, he would know that that straw would not support him. But in the frenzy of panic, any attempt becomes worth a try. Unfortunately, this is the method often used in discerning God's will. Not having learned and practiced listening to the still, small Voice of God, many people in their desperation to know God's will, may grasp for one or another of these very 'strawy' methods:"

Naturally following the good study skills she had learned, Helen paused to grab a pen and began to take notes on the methods described.

"1) *The Lord Told Me To Tell You...* Not knowing how to discern God's will on their own, some may listen to the many voices of men. And so they take other people's word as the word of God and begin preparation, until...something goes wrong. Or it becomes too hard. Or,

1 Read Ephesians 5:17

it isn't happening like they had been told that it would. Then, what do they cry out? 'God changed His mind!' No, no one would say that. It sounds... so... unGod. What they do say is, 'Well, I guess He closed that door on me!' Which is saying the same thing. And they have brought God down to the same capricious level as finite humans.

"A word of wisdom, a word of knowledge, a prophecy; wise counsel: Yes! But since God wants to guide you, any word from another, at best, should be a word of confirmation to what God is already telling you."

That's my question, Helen thought. *Is it God telling me? Or is it just the voices of others?* She continued to read aloud.

"2) *Finger Pointing & Promise Card Dealing...*Out-of-context-Scripture is a dangerous game to play in decision making. However, I do know of a man who was seeking the Lord for a wife. (This is good.) As he was reading in Peter's letters, 'Grace be unto you' became God's promise of his wife's name! It 'worked!' But one could also 'finger point' to this combination: 'Judas... went and hanged himself.'[2] 'Go thou and do likewise.'"[3]

Helen smiled. How many of her friends did the same thing, taking passages from Scripture out of context to use for their own arguments. *I have been guilty on one or two occasions—probably more,* Helen thought, deciding to be honest with herself.

"Regarding promise cards: I have come to realize that though all of the promises of God are 'Yes' and 'So be it,' most also have a contingency. *If* you are My people, *if* you call yourself by My name, *if* you will humble yourself, *if* you will pray, *if* you will seek My face, *if* you will turn from your wicked ways, then I will....[4] *(If you)* Give, and it shall be given unto you....[5] Usually, prom-

2 Read Matthew 27   3 Read Luke 10   4 Read II Chronicales 7:14   5 Read Luke 6:38

ise cards leave out the 'if' clauses—a very dangerous thing, often with a misguiding result. Or, in discussion, they are minimized as we get excited about the promise. The promise is God's doing; ours is the contingency, the '*if.*'"

Helen copied the last sentence down and underlined the words 'promise' and 'contingency.' *That is a concept for me to consider more seriously as I read the Word,* she thought. She shifted in her chair and continued.

"3) *You Seek For A Sign...* Signs have been used in God's guidance of men, as He did for the wise men. Gideon was at a very low spot emotionally. God accommodated him with several signs.[6]

"I know of a man who, in his opinion, had been cruelly dismissed from his ministry position. (At the least, it was handled in a most unprofessional manner.) One had come to his pastor and had convinced him that he could run the ministry with greater success. Thus, the dismissal. Yet, in the next year, they all watched that ministry fall apart and completely shut down. Unfortunately, this brother was not ready spiritually or emotionally to handle this series of events.

"However, through eight months of very wise counsel and encouragement, he came to accept that there was 'life beyond that lost ministry.' Wanting to believe the counsel he was hearing, he put a wild, three-part fleece before the Lord. And in due time (one more month), the Lord graciously fulfilled that request. The new ministry he now directs has far exceeded the challenge and fulfillment he ever thought possible."

Helen had recently read a beautiful poem titled: *Beauty for Ashes. This man's story is certainly an example of God's grace,* she thought. She read on.

"A fleece? Yes, perhaps—as an accommodation for

6 Read Judges 6 and 7

the weakness of our soul. Or as a confirmation of His will, as in Gideon's situation, granted. Yet, guardedly, for our vulnerability to natural or supernatural phenomena causes them—if used by themselves—to be a very non-conclusive source of guidance. Thus, in this gentleman's situation, it was also the godly counsel of several friends and a deep sense in his own heart that this was to be his new direction that accompanied that fulfilled fleece."

For a moment Helen paused, remembering the good counsel friends and family had given her through her pre-teen and teen years and how it has strengthened her faith through tough times—like right now. She breathed deeply, confident that God was with her. She also paused to reflect and identify with that deep sense in the young minister's heart in the report, for she too carried an urgent sense that she was being shown a new direction. She read on—another 'strawy grasp.'

"4) *Lord Bless My Plans...* We in America, regard individualism as a highly valued ideal. Though our heroes of Buffalo Bill and Babe Ruth have been replaced by the latest movie star or popular singer, it is still the unique 'only I did it' nature of the hero that makes them stand out. Is it any wonder, then, that a Christian approaches God with his 'very own plans'?

"The focus of God's calling is not me and my plans, but His perfect purposes, and my participation in His Will. Esther struggled over the issue of losing her head when she was challenged to fit into God's Plan: 'The king hasn't called for me for over thirty days....' Mordecai, however, put the situation into perspective: 'Esther, God will save His people. But who knows but that this is the time that He wants you to participate in that salvation?'[7]

7 Read Esther 4

"Abraham had a plan for his son's life when he said to God, 'May Ishmael stand before You.' But God said that His Plan would flow through a yet unborn son of Sarah, Isaac."[8]

Helen took a break to stand up and stretch. She wanted to straighten the pastor's desk for him. She despised clutter. Her own room was neat and tidy, with everything in its proper place, a value instilled in her by her Swedish mother. Best leave it alone. If she organized it, the pastor would probably never be able to find anything again.

She returned to her seat and continued to read.

"5) *Do Your Own Thing. After all, God isn't that interested in your plans.* Unfortunately, others have capitulated and have fallen prey to the spirit of this age, saying, 'He has given you some guidelines in the Good Book. But beyond that, use your own judgment.'

"It is impossible for me to understand or believe that the One who attends the funeral of every sparrow[9] and keeps track of the number of hairs on our head...."[10] Helen stopped and laughed out loud. She wondered if Pastor Dan had included that reference because of his balding head! She realized that was a totally irrelevant thought, but it amused her. She had to go back and reread: "It is impossible for me to understand or believe that the One who attends the funeral of every sparrow [9] and keeps track of the number of hairs on our head[10] does not have a greater interest than that in the plans of my life! It is true that about 90% of His Will for our life is found in the Word of God—that is, regarding our lifestyle. But I believe He is also very interested in our personal decisions, those decisions that make me a unique expression of His creative genius."

Helen added that last thought to her growing pad of

8 Read Genesus 17   9 Read Mathhew 10:29   10 Read Luke 12:7

notes. She liked the idea of being an expression of God's creativity.

"Well. Enough about those 'strawy' grasps at His will for our lives. We sincerely want to walk in our day-by-day decisions as Christ did, Who said, 'I work the works of the One Who sent Me.'[11] And again, 'I do nothing of Myself, but that which My Father has told Me.'[12]

"In a sequence of three *'calls'*, I would like to present a 'firm grasp' and a precise answer to this issue: *But I Don't Feel Called.*"

Now we're talking, thought Helen, looking forward to a precise answer. She turned the page on her note pad. Not that there wasn't more room on that page, but she turned the page as a deliberate decision to put those "strawy grasps" behind her. She prepared to write as she began reading the next section:

"CALL TO THE BODY OF CHRIST.
"For many, salvation is a very personal, one-on-one commitment to Jesus Christ. 'I have been brought back into a right relationship with the Father through Jesus Christ, drawn by the Holy Spirit of God.' Granted. However, it is an anomaly for a Christian to remain isolated. Scripture is clear in its every analogy that we are to unite with others: As brothers and sisters—as children, in the Family of God; as 'lively stones' in the building of God; as functioning members in the Body of Christ.

"I believe that each local fellowship (the people, not the building) is to be a microcosm of the Body of Christ universal. Thus, the life of the Church universal, and that of each local fellowship, is worship. And that is more than the one hymn and three choruses sung on Sunday morning. It encompasses all that is discovered—and discovered again and again—in the con-

11 Read John 9:4   12 Read John 8:28

cept: My spirit is alive unto God through Jesus
Christ![13] As we cry out, 'Our Father...,' we sense the
unity of the family of God. Our spirits have broken
through the dimensions of time and space and we are
able to touch the eternal. We are alive—really alive! No
matter how 'good' we were before our salvation, it is different now. I was five years old when I trusted in
Christ. Oh, I sang the song, 'I was sinking deep in sin,
far from the peaceful shore....' How deep in sin can a
five year old sink, I ask? But my later theological training taught me that it is a sin nature that needs to be
dealt with. We were 'dead in our trespasses and sins.'
But we are now alive. (If I were preaching this as a sermon, I would expect at least one 'Hallelujah!')."

"Hallelujah," Helen whispered with a smile. She remembered when she had trusted in Christ—she had
been just seven years old. She suddenly had a new appreciation for Pastor Dan. Through the paper she was
reading, he had become not only more accessible, but
also more human. It was that humanity that she as-
sociated with the most—with regards to her current dilemma.

"The growth of the Church, then, is nurture—
nurture from the Word of God. Yes, milk to the young
and meat to the mature.[14] Again, this is more than the
Sunday morning sermon. It includes every meditation
on His life-giving and life-sustaining Word, whether in
private tutoring by the Holy Spirit, our Divine Teacher,
or in a Bible study with others.

"When these two things, worship and nurture, take
place in a fellowship of believers, the 'lively stones' of
First Peter 2:5 really become energized. Or, to change
the analogy, the Body parts are healthy and want to
function within the tasks for which they were created."

13 Read Romans 6:11b   14 Read Hebrews 5 and 6

She could feel it! She could feel that energy as she read. Even now, in this meditation of hers on these passages from Scripture, she could feel the Spirit move within her. It was warm; it was exciting; it was strong.

She read aloud faster. "All Christians are called to exercise some function in the local fellowship of believers. The Spirit distributes—as He chooses—a diversity of gifts. As the individual 'exercises' within the Body, it becomes evident to him and the Body which gift(s) he has been equipped with by the Holy Spirit. As he continues to function within that Body, those spiritual gifts are developed, just as muscles in our physical body develop when they are exercised. (Need I suggest what happens to them without exercise? I will: They sit in atrophy, not knowing where they fit in Body life.)"

Helen wrinkled her nose at the analogy.

"It happened to Joseph, whose name means 'increaser', in a most dramatic way. He had joined himself to the Body of believers in Jerusalem, having come from Cyprus. When his gifting was recognized, he was given a new name, Barnabas, which means 'Son of consolation, exhortation, encouragement, comfort.' Quite a gift. Thank You, Holy Spirit! 'Barney,' they might have said, 'You never go out to do street evangelism. You aren't an 'increaser.' But now we see how your gift of consolation sure helps you to bring peace into situations when people are rankled. Let's give you a name that more reflects your gifting.'"

Helen thought of her own given birth name. Her mother had told her it was Greek in origin, and meant 'beacon' or 'torchlight'. Did her name reflect her God-given nature? Would she become a beacon in the darkness for the spiritually atrophied—also for the many who are dead spiritually? Could she one day help light the way like Pastor Dan was doing for her right now?

She continued reading out loud, jotting down notes from time to time as she read. "Scripture is also clear that—from God's perspective—the gifts that man looks on as the more prominent, are less honored. And the less honorable, more feeble, uncomely parts are to be given greater honor. That there should be no division in the Body.[15] Now He places certain apostles, prophets, evangelists, pastors and teachers, each with their gifting, in the Body to equip and train the saints for the work of the ministry.'[16]

"The end result is that every believer is 'perfected' to fulfill some function in the Body of Christ. Some become mouths; some, listening ears (a much-needed, but lacking function in the Church); the noses, the 'smellers' of trouble; the pituitary gland. And even the appendix that seems to be just 'hanging on' to that lower intestine! All are needed for their respective function. Current medical thinking still declares some organs 'vestige', left over from some pre-human existence. It is interesting that as they are learning more and more about how the human body functions, fewer and fewer parts are called 'vestige'!"

Vestige or no, Helen secretly wished that her destiny was not to become an appendix, just hanging on to the lower intestine!

"Do I have to draw out the parallel? I will. Some pastors look over their congregation, declaring this member or that one—vestige! But as they learn more about how the Body functions, fewer and fewer parts are 'hangovers' from another life.

"When we trusted in Christ as Savior, we were called to the Body of Christ, with a specific function within that Body. At this very critical time in the growth and development of the Body, wise leadership must di-

15 Read I Corinthians 12:1-24   16 Read Ephesians 4:11-12

rect the people toward the true mission of the Church."

"What's the true mission?" Helen asked aloud, quickly flipping the page to get to the answer. She found a new heading:

"CALL TO MISSION," and began reading with vigor. "Just what is the mission of the Church? God reveals Himself in the Word as an outgoing, missionary God. 'For God so loved the world....' 'He is not willing that any perish....' 'Whom shall I send? Who will go for Us?' 'Tell them, I AM sent you....'[17] He is involved in the lives of people; all may call Him Father.

"Jesus reached out to all sorts of people. The children sat on His knees; the prostitute washed His feet with her tears; the religious leader sought His counsel by night; he touched the leper; He talked with the woman of Samaria and with the Syrophenician woman.[18] He refused to be bound by human social barriers.

"To a nation that did not call on My name, I said, 'Here am I. Here am I.' All day long I have held out My hands....'[19] God is a Person who reaches out to people."

Helen was happy that her church reached out to people. She recalled a few months ago when a woman came to their church. She sat far in the back. Her hair was oily, her clothes stained and torn. She smelled. No doubt she was homeless—destitute. The ushers quickly called for Mary to come. She and her husband were the leaders of the ministry to the homeless. She soon was receiving help from the church.

After reading the passages above, the meaning of reaching out to that woman really struck home. She more clearly saw Scripture in the context of daily living. *"This is good,"* Helen mused. *"I am sure glad I stopped at the church today."* Ugh! She just remembered the

17 Read John 3:16; II Peter 3:9; Isaiah 6:8; Exodus 3:14   18 Read Mark 10:16; Luke 7:38; John 3; Matthew 3:3; John4; Mark 7:26   19 Read Isaiah 65:1-2

near accident! And the ticket! Oh well, "Don't cry over spilt milk," her grandma always said. She continued reading.

"We have been created in the image of God. There-fore, deep within the spiritual 'DNA' of every individual who has been brought back into a right relationship with God through the salvation of Jesus Christ, is the 'stuff' to cause us to be 'reaching out' people. I say it again, the individuals that the Reaching Out God calls and chooses, then, have within themselves the ability—the zeal, the compulsion—to become reaching out peo-ple, also. Jesus said it succinctly: 'As the Father sent Me, even so send I you!'[20] As the life of Christ is vibrant within us, it will be as natural as life itself to reveal Him through our lifestyle.

"The mission of the Church, then, is Outreach."

There it was. The answer. Outreach. Yes, Helen thought, *reaching out. Helping others find their way to the right path, to His path. To be a light for those lost, even in the darkest of places.* Excitedly, she continued.

"Once the newly formed church, or movement of churches, gets over the initial euphoria of 'I'm saved!' it needs to get down to the business of the Kingdom. Since God is a missionary God, His Church must be a missionary Church. Every Christian 'accepted' a 'call to mission' when he became a follower of Christ—whether he realized it or not!

"The Church of Jesus Christ is a militant Body. There is no room for detente; no allowance for 'peaceful coexistence' with religions. True Christianity is not just another religion. The Gospel of Christ is an all-inclusive message of hope—'Whosoever will, may come.'[21] But it is an equally all-exclusive mandate—'No man comes to the Father but by Me.'[22]

20 Read John 20:21   21 Read Revelation 22:7   22 Read John 14:6

"Jesus said, 'All authority in Heaven and earth has been given to Me. Therefore, go and make disciples of all nations...'[23] These marching orders have never been rescinded. The Church does not need to wait for additional guidance before it goes out to make disciples. Both in your local sphere of influence (Jerusalem), and in the surrounding counties or states (Judea), and to the most hated and despised of all people (Samaria), and to all ethnic peoples of the world. A healthy church will be reaching out to people in all the world in contrast with the totally erroneous idea of first here, then there, then there, and then there.[24]

"In this general sense, then, every committed Christian, as a disciple of Christ, is called to the Mission of the Church: Outreach. But...! Where in the world?"

Wow, thought Helen. *This is powerful stuff.* Knowing that every Christian is called made her own apprehension at wanting to be a missionary less intense.

Helen nearly jumped out of her seat when Betty opened the door and called her name.

"I'm sorry; I didn't mean to startle you, dear. I just wanted to check in on you, to see if you needed anything. A soda? Water?"

"No thank you, Betty, but may I ask you a question?"

The receptionist came in and took the seat next to Helen. "Sure."

"Have you read this paper by Pastor Dan?"

The receptionist looked at the paper sitting half read in Helen's lap. "No, I don't believe I have."

Helen noticed her lunch bag in her hand. "I was wondering if you wouldn't mind staying with me. It helps me to read aloud to someone."

"I would like that. I was just heading to the lunch

23 Read Matthew 28:18-19   24 Read Acts 1:8; Also, study the Greek words, *te* and *kai*.

room, but if you don't mind my eating while you read, I would be happy to stay." Betty spread a napkin on her lap and unwrapped her sandwich.

It seemed like she was over anxious for this invitation, Helen thought, as she watched Betty take her first bite. *Maybe I should have asked for something,* Helen mused, as the sight and smell of lunch was now in front of her. She swallowed the extra saliva forming in her mouth. Looking at her notes, she briefly reviewed what she had read for Betty's benefit. Then she began reading the next section, titled:

"CALL TO A LOCATION.

"Everyone is born to live somewhere! (Not a very brilliant declaration; but it had to be said somehow.)"

The receptionist chuckled at the pastor's humor.

"We grow up and become a part of that culture. We experience our counter-cultures, certainly. It is interesting that Plato, several hundred years before Christ, wrote a scathing essay on the deplorable state of the youth of his day! Somehow, the rebellious of one generation become the citizens of the next. They settle down in their 3.4 bedroom houses in the suburbs, or urban townhouses, with 1.3 children and 3.1 cars, etc! Enculturization always does its work for the perpetuation of society.

"And some will become a part of the Body of Christ. But they will remain in that location only until the leadership begins recognizing their gifting in relating to people of other cultures; their facility with language; their ability to communicate the simplicity of the Gospel; their heart beating with God's, 'not willing that any perish.'[25] Though we don't change a person's name anymore (like Joseph to Barnabas), wise leadership will

25 Read II Peter 3:9

give a word of encouraging challenge: Do you think that God might want you to be a missionary? And the church will provide an 'exercise room'—a missions fellowship through which they can exercise their cross-cultural 'muscles'.

"Thus, we have all been called to function within the Body of Christ; we have all been called to the mission of the Church; we have all been called to live in a particular location."

"Hallelujah!" the receptionist said. "I like my location—right here in Middletown!" Helen looked at her as she wiped a bit of mustard from the corner of her mouth with her napkin. She had been careful to keep the sandwich in her lap rather than on the pastor's desk. Mustard on Pastor Dan's stacks of papers would not have looked good. "Helen, keep reading," Betty encouraged.

Helen came to the next section:

"MISSIONARY CALL.

"As these three calls are merged into one, they constitute a missionary call. Thus, a missionary, as a Christian, is called to the Body of Christ, just like all others. And, as the Body of Christ is called to make disciples of all nations, a missionary has also received this call. Thirdly, as he manifests the social, professional, and spiritual gifts appropriate to bridging cultural distinctives, and he is open to the call to a change in location, he is quite possibly ready to consider that God has placed on his life the missionary call.

"It is at this point that many lose out, for they have somehow been trained to think: 'Not until I hear a voice from Heaven!'[26] Or, 'When I see the handwriting on the wall!'"[27]

26 Read Acts 9   27 Read Daniel 5

"I don't ever want to see the handwriting on the wall that Belshazzar saw that evening!" Helen declared emphatically. Betty agreed, with a nod of her head and the final slurping sound of her juice through the straw.

Helen looked sideways at Betty's manners and continued reading. "When it comes to cross-cultural outreach ministry—missions—it seems that there must be some 'special' call. To stay at home doesn't seem to require that call."

Helen looked up. "Did you ever feel a special call or hear an inner voice that you were supposed to work here at the church?"

The receptionist shook her head. "No. I love my church. I love God. And I figured if I could do some computer work, file a few papers, photocopy the bulletins and set up appointments, then so be it. We each work with the gifts we're given. Mine happen to be a knack for organization and a love for people. *And* putting up with the pastor's idiosyncrasies," she added with a grin, looking at Pastor Dan's desk.

Helen reread that last sentence as she continued. "When it comes to cross-cultural outreach ministry— missions—it seems that there must be some 'special' call. To stay at home doesn't seem to require that call.' This should not be. Each person should know that where he is, is exactly where God wants him to be. It should be as natural for the 'feet' to move at His direction as for any other member in His Body. I regard the feet in the body of Christ as those who go to the fields of the world. For, as Isaiah said, 'How beautiful on the mountains are the feet of those who bring Good News.'[28]

"But where should they go? We can't counter that question with a simplistic: 'Go where the needs are.' For

28 Read Isaiah 52:7

there are thousands of needy ministries around the world asking for workers to come alongside of them to help.

"How, then, does a missionary get from 'here' to 'there'? From where he is at the moment to where God wants him to be? A look at the Book of Acts with this question in mind will give us at least six different ways that call to location occurred, and could occur today."

They were interrupted by a phone call, and Helen waited for Betty to return, happy for the fact that she had joined her for this reading. She just hoped Betty wouldn't get in trouble for being away from her desk so long. "It's okay for you to be taking this time with me?" Helen asked, wanting assurance.

"No problem, Helen. We are here to help people."

"Okay, so here are the six different ways," Helen said, then continued to read.

"1) *Supernatural Direction:* In Acts 13:2, it is clear that the Church heard the Holy Spirit say, 'I want Barnabas and Saul.' Later, Paul had a vision of the Macedonia man appealing, 'Come over and help.'29 These are examples of clear, supernatural direction. And when that clear Voice is heard it does give strong assurance of His will.

"A friend several years ago was attending Prairie Bible Institute in Canada, a school with a strong crosscultural vision. Direct supernatural guidance came to his friend the first night he was there: He had a dream. A plane appeared in a cloudless sky. It began skywriting! One word: NEPAL! Through an amazing set of circumstances, upon graduation, he was invited by nationals to this otherwise difficult-to-get-into country!"

Helen looked up again. "Wow. I wish something like that would happen to me. It would be much easier."

29 Read Acts 16:9

"Not necessarily," the receptionist said. "Other issues could come to frustrate you. What's another way?" she asked, seeming even more interested now in Pastor Dan's paper.

"2) *'Sanctified' Common Sense:* Paul's second journey, however, seems to have been initiated by a sensible, responsible plan to go back and check up on how the brothers were doing in the cities they had previously visited. Some days later, after the First Church Council sorted out the issue of circumcision, Paul spoke to Barnabas; 'Let's go again and visit the brothers in every city where we have proclaimed the Word of the Lord and see how they are doing.'[30]

"A vast number of unreached people groups have been identified in recent years—even delineating their degree of openness to the Gospel. In prayerfully looking over this long list, a friend of mine made a logical determination to prepare himself to minister to one of them. He, and his family, will be leaving within the year with a prayer team in agreement and fully supportive."

"I think I know the friend he's talking about. We had a great commissioning service for them," Betty remembered. "And, you know, I think 'sanctified common sense' is why I work here." Helen continued reading.

"3) *Circumstantial Guidance:* There wasn't a Christian in Jerusalem following the martyrdom of Stephen who cried out, 'I don't feel called!' When the persecution came, they split![31] Also, when Claudius commanded all Jews to leave Rome, Aquila didn't 'go into a season of prayer' with Priscilla over it; they left![32]

"A Pastor friend in central California had established a good ministry among a group of 'field workers'—they were illegal aliens. When he heard they had been picked up and bussed back across the border, his

30 Read Acts 15:36   31 Read Acts 8:1; 11:19   32 Read Acts 18:2

first response was disappointment. When I pointed out that he had just sent out his first missionaries, his countenance brightened. Circumstances caused by authority or physical calamity can, without doubt, make guidance decisions for you."

Helen set the paper down in her lap and looked up. "I never thought of it that way. I like that. I just pray those new 'missionaries' going back home are strong in the Lord and can share the Good News boldly."

The receptionist nodded with a smile.

"4) *Invitation By Nationals:* It appears the Macedonia 'man' turned out to be a woman! One Lydia, a seller of purple, from the city of Thyatira! And when she and her household were baptized, she 'constrained Paul and his team to stay there.'33

"Paul had experienced this 'constraint' many times. As he was returning to Jerusalem, he wanted to have one more visit with the elders of the churches in Ephesus. But he knew that if he went there, they would insist on his staying longer. So that he could keep his schedule to arrive in Jerusalem for the feast, he had the elders meet him in Miletus, instead.34

"Third World Christians, today, are standing—so to speak—on a 21st Century Macedonia shore. They are crying out a new Macedonia Call: Come over and help us. Teach us the Word so we can go out and teach others.35 And as God has raised up Third World Christians as a new missionary force, one of the very best things we in America can do is respond to their invitation!"

The room went silent as Helen stopped reading. The receptionist looked over to see Helen's eyes fill with tears.

"What's the matter, sweetheart? Are you okay?"

Helen nodded, then dabbed at her eyes with the cor-

33 Read Acts 16:14   34 Read Acts 20:17   35 Read II Timothy 2:2

ner of her sleeve. "I was just really affected by that—by the thought of those Third World Christians in need of teachers. We're so blessed to be so well taken care of; it's so easy to forget about how others struggle without good teaching and teaching materials."

"Well, that's why Pastor Dan is here, to remind us," Betty said, smiling sweetly.

Helen nodded and kept reading.

"5) *Sent By A Church:* When the church in Jerusalem heard of the revival going on in Antioch, they sent Barnabas to 'check it out.'[36]

"A key to responsible action and accountability is the church's initial involvement with those who sense a missionary call. Too often, the church leadership is the 'last to know' when one or another of their 'members' goes cross-culturally.

"Church leaders must become involved in identifying, training, sending, and supporting those parts of their Body 'gifted' in ministry to the uttermost parts.

"Even young churches can participate in God's will of guiding missionaries. The brothers of Thessalonica and Berea, sensing the danger of persecution, sent Paul away for his own safety.[37]

"I must declare that no church is too young or small to send out their first missionary, particularly after hearing about this church: A one-year-old church in a country which a few years before had been declared a totally atheistic nation, with twenty adult members, sent a worker into cross-cultural ministry, fully supported by the remaining nineteen members!"

"I wonder what country that is," Helen pondered.

Betty brightened. "I remember that a Mr. Hoxha claimed that his country of Albania was a totally atheistic nation. Maybe Pastor Dan is referring to Albania."

36 Read Acts 11:22   37 Read Acts 17:10,14

Helen was really surprised at the secretary's knowledge of that fact of history. *How did I miss that one?* Helen wondered, but made no outward reference to her lack of knowledge. Instead:

"Wow! A one-year old church with twenty adult members sending out a fully supported missionary." Helen was amazed. She continued reading. "Over the past eight years I have related with many individuals wanting to go to the fields of the world. Without exception, those who have a strong sense of their church sending them go with a greater confidence. Though some have gone without the church's blessing—and have done well in the field, there is always an 'emptiness', realizing their need for moral support."

Helen turned the page. "Okay, here's the last one."

"6) *Sent By Missionary Leaders:* It is clear from Luke's writings that as Paul's ministry team grew (at one point eight men were traveling with him), it became his responsibility to send them here or there. Timothy he 'left in Ephesus.'[38] Another time Timothy and Erastus were sent to Macedonia from Ephesus.[39] Titus was sent to Crete to 'set the churches in order....'[40]

"A fellow student in this class..."

Betty interrupted, "Pastor Dan must be referring to the seminary class for which he prepared this paper."

Helen surprised at the interruption, started that sentence over again. "A fellow student in this class related his family's call to a particular location: 'My wife and I had been on a short term trip. In addition to our main goal in Chile, we visited a number of ministries asking for help. When we returned home, we prayed and then applied to New Tribes Mission. Naturally we requested to be sent to Colombia. We had been there; we had talked with the principal; he had given us an

38 Read I Timothy 1:3   39 Read Acts 19:22   40 Read Titus 1:6

open invitation; we had a good 'feeling' about the place. But most importantly, we had a deep sense that we could do this. When the mission board decided to accept me as a missionary teacher, though, they saw a greater need for us in Bolivia. We allowed them to guide us in this way.'"

Once again they were interrupted by a phone call. When the receptionist came back, she said, "Pastor Dan should be through soon."

"Do you have to get back to work now?"

"No, go ahead and read. I want to hear how it ends. I love a good ending," she said, giving Helen a wink.

"Okay, the last part is titled:

"ONE FINAL THOUGHT.

"In an essay of this length, it would be futile to think we have covered the enormity of this subject—all the ramifications of knowing His will:
- The integrity of the upright shall guide them;[41]
- Conditional (if/then) guidance;[42]
- The sovereignty of God;[43]
- The will of satan;[44]
- Let this mind be in you;[45]
- A voice behind you saying, 'This is the way';[46]
- Thy Word is a Lamp to my feet.[47]

"Subjects as these, and more, bring us the whole Counsel of God. But one final thought that I believe encompasses all considerations of His will for our lives:

"'*Let the peace of Christ rule (act as an umpire continually) in your hearts—deciding and settling with finality all questions that rise in your minds....*'"[48]

"'My peace I give to you: not as the world gives, give I to you.'[49] The peace that Christ gives is not pictured in the calm, pastoral scene of sheep by still waters, nor is

41 Read Proverbs 11:3   42 Read II Chronicles 7:14   43 Read Psalm 46:10
44 Read Isaiah 14:13   45 Read Philippians 2:5   46 Read Isaiah 30:21
47 Read Psalm 119:105   48 Read Colossians 3:15 AMP   49 Read John 14:27

it seen in the newborn infant, warm and safe in the arms of its mother."

Helen exhaled heavily. "I thought he was going to say that," she said. The receptionist chuckled.

"The peace of Christ is rather seen in a picture of a raging river of life coursing between its banks, now through a mountain gorge, now across the open plains. Mile after mile, there is a deep-flowing, sure current that keeps surging forward in spite of any surface splashing of trouble. The winds of adversity can whip up the waves to white-cap ferocity. The speed of life down through the passes can dash the water forcefully against the rocks. The reeds along the riverbank can cut or fallen logs can swirl the water into small whirlpools, spinning the water in dizzying circles of uncertainty of direction."

"I feel like my life is like that sometimes," Betty said.

"Me too!" Helen was glad she had invited the receptionist to listen. She kept reading. "Yet the river keeps moving by the force of the current.

"His peace in my heart is that current, assuring me that I am in the flow of His will. —Daniel Harris"

"Amen," the receptionist said quietly when Helen had finished. She put a hand on Helen's shoulder. "I have to get back to my desk now. Thank you for inviting me to listen."

"Thank you," Helen said, still filled with emotion from the text. She waited until the receptionist had walked back down the hall, and then bowed her head: "Dear Lord, You are a faithful God. I am sure that You are more interested than even I am that I should walk in Your ways—to do Your will. May I know Your peace in my heart. Thank You, Jesus. Amen."

Just then Pastor Dan returned to his office. "Hey,

you didn't fall asleep reading that paper, did you?"

Helen turned to look. "No. I was just praying. How come you're back so soon?" Helen asked.

Pastor Dan grinned, "Pastor Joe had a luncheon to attend. That report I was looking for when you first got here—I didn't even get a chance to share it." He approached Helen and took the seat next to her where the receptionist had been. "Tell me, did that paper help?"

"You know, I think your professor did read this. There's a really positive comment at the end," Helen said.

"No. That's not from the professor. I showed it to our pastor. That's his comment. How about what I wrote? Do you have a firmer grasp now on how to sense His call on your life?"

"Well, you cleared up some of the ways to not determine His will. Did that friend of yours really marry a girl named Grace?

"I thought that would catch your attention. And, yes, he did...happily married, with kids and a ministry. But, I'm so sorry, Helen." A twinkle filled the pastor's eyes and his wide cheeks rounded out with a smile.

"About what?" The paper she had read had brought a seriousness to her mood, and she was not expecting to be teased.

"I don't think there is any mention in the Bible of the name, Harold!" Pastor Dan laughed aloud.

"Why you...! That's not fair, Pastor Dan. Harold and I are just 'friends.'" She grew serious again. "Unfortunately, that 'promise card dealing' is a method I've tried using before. I never came away feeling very confident, though." Her brows furrowed at the memory.

"I know exactly what you mean," the pastor said. He saw his paper still open to that final thought about

Christ's peace. "Another verse in that Colossians 3 passage that I think is as important as 'His peace' is where Paul says, 'Let the Word of Christ dwell (take up residence) in your hearts, making you rich in wisdom.'[50] It's the 'whole Counsel of God' that more clearly gives His perspective on all issues of life. Reading bits and pieces of the Word is like the blind men describing an elephant. Each one grabs a different part and assures his friends he knows what an elephant looks like. Letting the whole Counsel of God take up residence in your mind and spirit makes it easier to be at peace with the direction He gives you. I really should have included that verse in my paper," he added.

"Furthermore..." Pastor Dan continued. It seemed like he was on a roll now that the staff meeting was over. "Furthermore, when Paul was writing to the Christians at Rome, he again emphasized the importance of getting the Word deep in our hearts. He said, 'Don't let the world around you squeeze you into its mold, but let God renew your minds from within so that you may know what is the good and acceptable and perfect will of God for your lives.'[51]

"Do we really want to know God's will?" The pastor answered his own question: "Let God renew our minds from within. How do we renew our minds? By meditating on the Word of God. Getting in the Word, in the Word, in the Word.

He's not going to let go of this thought, Helen realized. *It must be vital to his own life.*

Pastor Dan kept going. "As each Scripture sheds new light on our thoughts, more of the Light of Jesus, who is the Living Word, is directing our steps.[52] Solomon said, "The spirit of man is the candle of the Lord searching all the inner rooms of our soul—all of those

50 Read Colossians 3:16   51 Read Romans 12:2   52 Read Psalm 119:105

thought and feelings that give us direction.[53] Then, put that together with the Psalmist's statement: 'The Lord will light my candle; the Lord will enlighten my darkness,'[54] and you have a powerful recipe for God directing your life through the Word. As I said, 'In the Word! In the Word! In the Word!'"

"Pastor Dan! That thought really lit your 'fire!'" Helen surprised herself at her boldness. She continued, "Would you believe, some friends of our family were over for dinner the other evening. I was surprised at an amazing testimony the father shared. He said that he'd not read the whole Bible through until he was—well, older than my dad. Although he was saved as a child, grew up in the church, went to Bible College, taught and administered in Christian schools, he regretfully admitted to a very sketchy knowledge of the Word. One day, he said, he was given a guide to read through the Word systematically. Though he had looked at many others, this one seemed to click with him. Year after year, now, he says the Word is 'dwelling' more and more richly in his heart."

"Unfortunately, Helen, that's not unusual. Though we in America have Bibles and more Bibles, and with translations of all sorts, it's a Book left unread in many Christian homes. Whereas in China, where an average of ten people share one Bible, they can quote whole passages that they've committed to memory."

"I know China is on your heart, Pastor Dan. Since you've been back from that Bible delivery trip, I've seen a difference in your passion for the world—not that it wasn't there before. It's just more noticeable now. I really appreciate your help today."

"Of course. Were there any other questions?"

"Oh, yes! Do you mind?"

53 Read Proverbs 20:27   54 Read Psalm 18:28

"Not at all. Your interest in knowing God's will has inspired me, also."

"Well, another real confusing issue is that first 'strawy' grasp. I asked a friend how his plans were developing. He had shared how excited he was about what God was helping him to do. Then, a week later, with a disappointed look, he said the very same words you wrote in your paper, 'I guess God just closed that door on me.' 'What happened?' I asked. 'Oh, things just didn't seem to be working out. Road blocks at every turn.'"

The pastor's smile faded into disappointment as he shook his head. "As I said, Helen, this paper barely scratches the surface of this enormous issue. In the first place, that God would be so interested in each one of us—personally—to have a specific plan and purpose for our lives.... That alone is enough to make me say, 'What an absolutely awesome God!' There are a couple of thoughts I can add here. What's your time schedule?"

"Pastor Dan, I have the time, if you do. This is important to me. I'd like a copy of your paper, though, especially to follow up on the other aspects of your 'One Final Thought.' I took pretty good notes on the other sections."

"Okay, we can get it copied. Let's see, what was I saying? Oh, yes. Paul is in Ephesus. He's writing a letter to the Church in Corinth. He's making plans for his next visit. Says he might be there by winter. Might even spend the winter with them. But for now 'I am going to stay in Ephesus until Pentecost because a great door of opportunity to minister has been opened before me.... I can just see Paul dictating those words to Fortunatus. So passionate. So grateful for God's call on his life. 'The chiefest of sinners,' he called himself. And God has given him this great opportunity in Ephesus. But as he comes back to his letter writing, he might have said, 'Fortunatus, you had better add to that statement, "...and there are many adversaries—strong enemy forces—opposing me.""55

The pastor turned to face Helen full on. "Helen, with every open door of opportunity there are powers working against the Plan of God. Whether in discouraging thoughts only in your own head, or from people— maybe even well-meaning friends—there will be spiritual forces trying to thwart the will of God for your life. It's hard to swim upstream."

Helen pictured those salmon fighting their way upstream to spawn. She had watched them struggle once when her family vacationed in Washington.

Pastor Dan saw her far-away look. "Are you with me, Helen?"

"Oh, yes. I was just thinking of the upstream feeling I am already experiencing."

"Helen, I assure you, the effort builds 'muscles' of character in your life. But back to your friend. The misunderstanding he had was that when the going got tough, he thought it was God 'closing the door' when it was probably the enemy trying to oppose the work of God. And God gets 'blamed' for it!"

"You're right!" Helen said, thinking back on her friend.

"On the other hand," Pastor Dan was quick to add, "this can also happen. I've done it a time or two—or more! I develop some fabulously wonderful plans, praying as I go. And that 'open door' looks more and more inviting every day. It's been painted in such glowing colors; it looks so real. But as I go to walk through it, I

55 Read I Corinthians 16:9

bang my 'emotional/spiritual head' against a solid brick wall! It was never a door being held open by my Master. It was a door that I had convinced myself was there—and that it was being opened by Him; but there was no door there at all. I tell you, that hurts! But even that provides a lesson in life that makes us more sensitive to His voice saying, 'This is the way. Walk in it, when you would turn to the left or to the right.'"[56]

Helen smiled at the thought of Pastor Dan bumping his head. *Would she ever find herself painting a doorway on a solid brick wall?* she wondered.

"I like what Jesus said to John as He was giving His Revelation to the seven Churches," the pastor continued. "To the Church of Philadelphia, He said, 'I hold the keys of David. They can open doors that no man can shut and shut doors that no man can open.' Then, to this Church of brotherly love, He said, 'Before you I have set an open door and no man can shut it!' Pretty powerful words, I'd say. I believe we're members of that Church, Helen. Jesus continues: 'Though your strength is small, yet you have obeyed My word and have not denied My Name.'[57] Oh, how we deny His Name by saying we are His followers, yet do not do His will."

"Actions speak louder than words," Helen said, again echoing her grandmother's words.

"But that's another subject for another time. Helen, are you with me?"

"Yes, this is good. Things look a lot clearer when we see them through Scripture. I'm glad you're placing such an emphasis on the Word. It just seems so right."

"Now, I don't want to complicate the issue. But you'll hear it sooner or later, so let me point this out right now. And I'll admit that I don't understand this one."

56 Read Isaiah 30:21   57 Read Revelation 3:7-13

Helen leaned forward to listen. What could it be?

"Paul, the Apostle. I really like this guy. He's so radical; yet so human. He was a traveling man. This time his face was set to reach Jerusalem by Pentecost. As I said earlier, not wanting to get stuck in Ephesus, he met with the elders at Miletus. After his fabulous farewell address to them,[58] he and his team sailed to Coos, and to Rhodes, to Patria, passed by the island of Cypress and landed at Tyre. 'And finding disciples, we tarried there for seven days.' During that time, they said to Paul, 'prompted by the Holy Spirit, that he should not go up to Jerusalem.'[59] He must have ignored that warning or argued that he had to go—some reason prompted him to not follow that guidance, because Luke records that after seven days they went on their way.

"Next they came to Caesarea, to the house of Philip, the evangelist who had four daughters who prophesied. Now a prophet named Agabus showed up. He took Paul's waistband and bound himself with it, and said, 'The Holy Spirit says, "The man who owns this belt will be bound by the Jews in Jerusalem and handed over to the Gentiles."'[60]

"I don't like the sound of that!" Helen said. "Did the first group not hear correctly what the Holy Spirit said? Or is it because Paul didn't heed their word that Agabus had to give another word by the inspiration of the Holy Spirit?"

"Helen, only eternity will answer that one. One way or the other, it speaks to the human element that's always a factor in this business of knowing God's will—His call—His direction in our lives."

The Pastor put a hand on his stomach. "Wow! What happened to lunch time? I'm hungry!"

"You should be. It's three o'clock already," Helen

58 Study Acts 20:18-38   59 Read Acts 21:4   60 Read Acts 21:11

said, looking at her watch. "Can I buy us a couple of bagels down the street? It's the least I can do."

"No, that's okay. I think there are a few donuts in the staff room. Do you want one?"

"No thanks. But I do have one final question: Was it God's will for me to get that traffic ticket?"

The pastor stood up and grinned. Then, with a sympathetic look on his face, he said, "That's one you're going to have to answer for yourself!"

SUMMARY OF ISSUES

Helen's impetuous action almost cost her more than just a ticket. But it was good that her pastor had written that paper. See if these summary statements are issues that you have already dealt with or if there might be some work to do before you go to the field.

• It is good to be actively involved in a church before going to the field. There are several reasons:

1) You can learn the discipline of commitment in a context not too unfamiliar to you.

2) You give the church an opportunity to see you— your strengths and weaknesses, giving them a better understanding to offer you the support needed.

3) It gives you a family and ministry to come home to. Paul and Barnabas returned to Antioch after their two years venture. I believe their reentry was made easier because they had a ministry to which to return.[61]

• Missionaries are just ordinary people called to do extraordinary things for God.

• It is God's desire that we have a firm grip on His will for our lives.

• Five "strawy" grasps at how to know God's will:

1) Others—often very well-meaning Christians—

61 Compare Acts 13:1 with Acts 15:35

telling us what God wants us to do.

2) Using Scriptures out of context.

3) Fleeces as guidance, rather than for a confirmation, due to the weakness of our soul.

4) Bringing our plans to God for His blessing.

5) Yes, God set the world in motion, but He is not too interested in the details of our plans.

• We are a unique expression of the creative genius of God. Thus, our lives will be a unique expression of His will.

• When we trust in Christ as Savior, we become a part of the Body of Christ. Each local fellowship is a microcosm of the Church universal.

• The life of the Church is worship. This includes all that is encompassed in the statement: My spirit is alive in God through Jesus Christ.

• The growth of the Church is nurture. This includes every meditation in His life-giving and life-sustaining Word.

• When worship and nurture are happening, the members of the Body of Christ are healthy and want to function within the tasks for which they were created.

• The mission of the Church, then, is outreach—reaching out to all peoples, whether over the back fence or around the world.

• Scripture must come alive in the context of our daily living.

• Every Christian (not only a missionary) is called to the Body of Christ, to a specific function within that Body, and with the purpose (mission) of reaching out.

• A missionary call, then, occurs when one is qualified for cross-cultural work and is willing to change his location of living to fulfill that purpose.

62 Read Acts 13:2   63 Read Acts 15:36   64 Read Acts 11:19   65 Read Acts 16:15
66 Read Acts 11:22   67 Read Acts 19:22

• There are six ways in the Book of Acts that missionaries were called to change their location:
1) Supernatural direction;[62]
2) Sanctified common sense;[63]
3) Circumstantial guidance;[64]
4) Invitation by nationals;[65]
5) Sent out by the Church;[66]
6) Sent by missionary leaders;[67]

• The vast subject of knowing God's will encompasses many aspects:
1) The integrity of the upright
2) If/then guidance
3) The sovereignty of God
4) The will of satan
5) The mind of Christ
6) The voice of God
7) Your Word is a Lamp to my feet; a Light to my path. It must dwell (take up residence) in me richly.
8) The peace of Christ, likened to the ever surging current of a river, not affected by the surface waves and eddies, ruling in our hearts.

• With every open door of opportunity, there are many adversaries. But Christ has promised to hold open the doors of opportunity that He has designed for us to walk through.

• It is possible for us to paint beautiful "open doors" on solid brick walls.

• There will always be the human element of missing an opportunity. When that happens, we change direction and go on.

Suggestion: You might want to read back through the chapter and find the context to which each of these summary statements refers, particularly for those about which the Holy Spirit has nudged you.

PERSONAL NOTES:

3

NOW WHY DID I DO THAT?

It was a hot, sultry day in Middletown. You could fry an egg on the sidewalk. But who would eat it? *Would there be any relief from this heat wave? Maybe at the beach,* thought Jason. *Yes, on the Boardwalk. Hopefully there would be a breeze there.*

The wind in his hair brought some relief as he raced his ten-speed bike down the steep hill toward the water. Once the bike was parked and locked, he gave the seat a pat and walked away. He looked both ways—up and down the Boardwalk. Man! The whole city had the same idea. It was wall-to-wall people. No relief here. Any breeze was lost in this crowd. And not a familiar face in the bunch. But wait, who was that? Could it be? Yes, it was!

"Pastor Steve! What are you doing here?" Jason had never seen Pastor Steve outside the context of a church activity. It was strange to see him in such a common setting.

"Oh, Jason. Hi! I might ask you the same question!"

"The heat, man! I thought I might catch some breezes, but it looks like everyone in Middletown is here." Sweat was beaded on Jason's forehead, running down in rivulets of water.

"Yeah, that was my thought, too. Before you showed up I was about to go home. It was just such a lazy Saturday afternoon with nothing to do," Pastor Steve said.

Pastor Steve—a tall, lanky man with big bones—reached up and wiped the sweat from his neck with a handkerchief. His pale cheeks were now pink, and the freckles across his nose a shade darker from the sun. But he was still in stark contrast next to Jason's ebony skin. "Not sure why I came down. I suppose I hoped for some relief from this heat."

Jason gave the pastor a sly grin. "Man, I don't believe it. I thought you always had a reason for everything you did. You always seem to have everything together. That's why I made an appointment to see you next week. Didn't the church secretary tell you?"

"No, I haven't looked at that schedule yet. But, there—you see—maybe this is our divine appointment."

"Get outta here," Jason said, crossing his arms and cocking his head. "Are you saying that God brought this heat to get both of us down here so we could meet?"

"Something like that. There are no circumstances in life that are just by chance. God uses everything—I mean everything—for His purposes. But, enough of that. We're here now. Together." The pastor leaned against the rail and faced the beach. "What did you want to talk with me about?"

Jason joined him, grabbing the bar with both hands. "I'm not so sure, anymore. I've been all intense about this and, well, you seem so casual. Maybe it's not a good time, Pastor."

The pastor turned to Jason and straightened. "Give me a try."

"Well, all right then. Here goes. **I think God wants me to be a missionary!**"

One of Pastor Steve's bushy brows lifted high above his eye. "You know that I am aware of that. We are processing your application. It's a great idea. So what's the problem?" Although the staff had not yet confirmed Jason's call to missions, Pastor Steve felt sure they would. He seemed to have a God-given ability to read people. But Jason thought otherwise.

Oh, brother! This guy doesn't have a clue about what's on my mind, Jason thought, as he searched for the right words to express himself—not his usual pattern. But this was serious business.

"Well, let me just set my mind straight and talk out loud," Jason said. He put a foot on the rail and leaned his elbows on the top bar. "You know, my generation has grown up on some pretty worldly motivators: 'Do your own thing.' 'If it feels good, do it.' 'Are we having fun yet?' You name 'em. There's not a godly thought in them. So, now I'm seriously considering a major move, and I'm not sure what my motives are. Even the literature put out by some of the mission agencies is appealing to those worldly motivators. I remember one ad saying, 'Be sure to bring your sunscreen. We'll have plenty of beach time.' It's scary. I thought you would have a good answer for me. But when you admitted you didn't even know why you were down here, now I'm not so sure!"

"Whoa! Wait a minute. I don't need to defend myself, but like I said, it was a lazy Saturday. It was hot. Do I need a better reason to be here?"

Jason bit his lip. It was an inconsiderate thing to say, but he had a hard time knowing when to clam up and think, and when to talk. It was always getting him into trouble, and people often took offense at his unchecked honesty. *Such ignorance,* he chided himself.

"Let's start again, shall we?" the pastor said.

Jason relaxed his shoulders and nodded.

"But first, let's get into some shade."

Pastor Steve and Jason found a curb to sit on under a tree that would provide some shade. They would have fewer distractions there, also.

The pastor crossed his long legs and started in. "Do you remember several weeks ago when Pastor Chapman encouraged us to do a personal, in-depth study in a Book—in addition to our regular Bible reading?"

Jason nodded.

"Well, I chose the Gospel of Luke. So far I've read it through only a couple of times. But there's a paragraph about this issue that caught my attention." The pastor took out a small Bible from his back pocket, then slipped on a pair of reading glasses. "Let's see, I think it's in Chapter 10...maybe 11.... No, here it is in Chapter 12. Listen. Jesus is talking. He's talking about responses of servants to their masters. Then, verse 47: 'And that servant, who knew his master's will, but did not prepare himself for the task, neither did he do according to the master's will, shall be severely punished.'

"There are three distinct steps. I like that linear logic. That servant knew the master's plan for him, but he didn't prepare himself to do it. He didn't even make an attempt to carry out those duties. I believe we can use that trilogy and turn it into positive phrases of instruction, without violating Scripture."

Jason swatted a mosquito, which was so overcome by the heat that it didn't even try to escape. "Well, I'm not like that servant. I believe I know its God's will for me to be a missionary. I'm still waiting for the church leadership to confirm that personal call. What's holding you up?"

Pastor Steve looked down over his glasses at Jason. "Your petition has come up at two staff meetings. We're still praying. But the sincerity you're showing in checking your motives is certainly a positive move in the right direction. Unfortunately, many young people..." Pastor Steve hesitated—thinking. "You know, it is not only young people.... Too many, young or old, grope about, wasting years of their lives trying to 'discern' God's will. They act like it's a cosmic hide-and-seek game. And because God is a better 'hider' than they are a 'seeker', they can never be sure of His will.

"Why, just the other day I saw a guy I hadn't seen for many years. Excitedly, I approach him. As he shuffled towards me with his shoulders slumped, I already knew the answer to the question coming out of my mouth. 'Hi, Allen! What's going on?' I asked.

"'Oh, nuttin' really. I don't know. Just sorta moving on,' he mumbled.

"I groaned inside. This was exactly what he had said to me years before. How sad. What a waste to just wander from one thing to another, never being sure of anything."

Jason shook his head. "Bummer, man. That is a waste. I don't ever want to be like that. That dude has to live with himself 24/7! It must be depressing. Well, I'm passed that. I do believe that God has called me. So, I guess I'm in the preparing stage now. Right?"

"That's right, Jason." The pastor removed his glasses and carefully folded them and put them back in his shirt pocket. "In the very early stages, may I remind you," he said, raising his one brow again. *Why did he always raise that one brow?* Jason wondered, as the pastor continued. "That's not to discourage you, but to help you realize that we as a church plan to send you out *very* well-prepared."

"Then you've confirmed it?"

"No, I didn't say that. Don't get anxious on us now. Unfortunately, that second phrase is where a lot more people get 'lost'. There are two directions people take: Some just say, 'God has called me. I'm outta here! The Holy Spirit will guide me. I don't need any training.' And off they go. Others become professional students, going from one degree to another. 'Just this one more class....' 'Maybe I should study more. I heard about a great seminar....' 'Someday I'll be ready to go. There's always so much good teaching. I think I could learn a bit more, then I'll go.'"

"But," Jason urged, "that trilogy you read continues. The time has to come when we start doing it. Pastor Steve, I'm ready now! It's James who says we must be 'doers of the Word, and not hearers only.'"[1]

"That's right, Jason. When did you read that?"

Jason had a slight smirk on his face. "I chose the Letter of James for my in-depth study." Jason wondered if the pastor would catch on as to why he chose James—how he thought it would help him to keep his mouth in check.

"That's great! It's a privilege to be about our Father's business," Pastor Steve said. "I've been youth pastor now for two years. And I'm still amazed—I think I always will be—that He chose us, earthen vessels, in which to place His treasure.[2] Or, as Paul says, we are 'living epistles known and read among men.'[3] And yet, as I read e-zines on missions, the cry around the world today is the same as it was 2,000 years ago. Jesus said it: 'The harvest is plentiful; the laborers are few.'"[4]

The pastor uncrossed his legs and turned to Jason. "Do you realize that we still haven't gotten to the gut is-

1 Read James 1:22   2 Read II Corinthians 4:7   3 II Corinthians 3:2
4 Read Matthew 9:37

sue of motivation? What motivates us to action? What gives us the fuel to run our motors? What ignites the fires in our spirit to *do* 'those good deeds that He beforehand has prepared for us to walk in'?"[5]

Jason flashed another sly grin. "You don't really know the answer, do you? Naw—I'm just giving you a hard time." He wiped the beads of sweat now forming rivers running down his face and stinging his eyes. "Pastor Steve, I'm sure you could go on and on, and I don't mean any disrespect or anything, but I need to get back home. This heat is killing me! Can we get together again—soon? I still need to check my motives."

"I'm sure we will, Jason. Let's keep that appointment you set up for next week. Take care."

Pumping his bike back up the hill was hard work. But Jason's brain was working even harder. He was surprised at how personable a guy Pastor Steve was. He had never really talked with him one-on-one before. He just hoped the pastor could help him with this issue. His thoughts kept returning to one single conviction: *I do believe God wants me to be a missionary.* But why?

By the time he reached the top of the hill, heat overtook his thoughts. All he could concentrate on now was that ice cold Gatorade waiting for him in the fridge. Other issues would have to take a back seat. *There was no 'back seat' on his ten-speed.* He smiled as his own quip.

MONDAY

The heat wave had broken, and the temperature was now a livable 80 degrees. The last time Jason saw Pastor Steve since their discussion on the Boardwalk, was across the auditorium on Sunday. Had he forgotten about their discussion? Had the heat addled his brain?

5 Read Ephesians 2:10

No, I'm sure he remembered. I should call him.

These were the thoughts going through Jason's head when the phone rang on the table next to him, causing him to jump.

Jason answered the phone in his usual way, "Hey!" But, being startled by the loud ring, the tone of his voice was an octave higher in pitch.

"Jason, is that you? What's wrong?" Pastor Steve asked.

"Nothing's wrong. I was just deep in thought when you called. I was actually thinking about you. Man, that's weird."

"I didn't see you yesterday. Were you at church?"

"Yeah, of course, I was there. I saw you, but you seemed pretty busy." *Why am I being so defensive?* Jason wondered. *He was only asking a question.*

"Well, I'm calling because I wanted to tell you that yesterday I found out that the adult Elective Sunday School class is devoting a full week to that subject we started to discuss at the beach. I think it would be good for both of us to attend. I got special permission since we're not regularly signed up for that class."

"That would be great! Awesome. Next Sunday?"

"Yeah, next Sunday. Be there."

"So we won't meet this week, then. Huh?"

"Good thinking. Yeah, we should probably wait until after next Sunday, if that's okay with you."

"Sure." *This is great,* Jason thought. *They're going to allow me into the adult class. Way cool!*

SUNDAY

As Jason observed the adults walking in, he watched them gather in small circles, as friends and family recognized one another. On the one hand, he was glad his parents had not chosen this elective. He would feel more adult without them. However, they would have provided him some security right now. He had been nervous about coming, but there were only a few sideways glances at him, fewer than he thought there would be. They were probably wondering why he was there.

Jason straightened his collar and stared back. *They better not be dissin' my hair....* He scowled, not at anyone in particular, mostly at himself for feeling so awkward.

"Oh, hi, Pastor Steve!" Jason shouted out across the room, just as the moderator was about to speak. The room went silent and the moderator glanced at Jason. Jason punched a fist into his palm. "There I go again," he muttered under his breath.

The moderator cleared his throat and began. He spoke clearly, and from his tone Jason could sense the excitement and anticipation. "We have a number of people who are going to share this morning. As calls came in this week, I realized that many of you were doing your homework on this vital subject of motivation. I'll give a bit of an introduction, and then five people have come up with 'worldly motivators' which Christians sometimes use. And five others called me with 'godly motivators.' This should be a stimulating presentation.

Jason nodded, never taking his eyes off of the moderator. *You got that right!* He made a mental note that he had better concentrate—this is adult stuff.

The moderator continued. "Abraham Maslow, founder of modern humanistic psychology, though not a Christian, had some interesting thoughts on motivation. He suggested a scale of motivation from involuntary to voluntary: Duress, compulsion, coercion, duty, obligation, expectation, desire, self-fulfillment. He further stated that the higher your motivation, the more rewarding it is and the more likely you'll stick with the activity.

"Dr. John Brewster, U.S. Department of Agriculture, in a paper titled, "The Cultural Crisis of our Time," theorized that the cultural universal, the highest motivation of man, is his striving for significance—the desire to be somebody—within the framework of his culture, of course.

Dr. James Dobson, founder of Focus on the Family, places 'to love and to be loved' high on his list of godly motivators."

To love and be loved, thought Jason. In the context of his family this was absolutely true.

"Motives—the intents of the heart, as the writer of Hebrews says—are very deep. More often than not our thoughts on motivations are reflective: Now why did I do that? How often when somebody asks us, 'Now, why did you do that?', do we shrug our shoulders and say 'I dunno!'? The question suggests that after an action is done, we (maybe) evaluate the motivation, and too often conclude that probably we weren't properly motivated, or that we just didn't give any thought to what motivated us. 'Oh, well, things just happen,' we might say.

"And that plays right into the enemy's hand of condemnation. Up come the replays of regrets of the past. 'It could've, it should've, it might have been, if only!' And as long as we continue to be reflective in our evaluation of motives, the cycle continues."

Jason thought about how he should have done his math homework last week instead of reading motocross magazines. He might have gotten an A instead of a C on his math exam.

"Rather, our thoughts on motivation need to be determinative. Before we act, we must ask ourselves, 'Why am I going to do this?' Yet, even regarding motivation as determinative rather than reflective, we can fall prey to the 'wiles of the enemy' and apply worldly motivators to our work for the Lord.

"Well, I have said enough for now. Let's have the people who are going to share come forward. I'll let you each introduce yourself. Who's first?"

"Pssst! Jason! Are you following all this?"

Jason turned to find Pastor Steve sitting right behind him.

"Yeah, Pastor. But I hope that they're taping it. I know I'll want to hear this stuff over a few times to give it more thought."

A trimly-dressed woman stepped up to the podium. "I'll be first. My name's Mary. I see 'peer pressure' being used in the church as a motivator."

A listener up front interrupted. "But Mary, doesn't the Bible say 'to provoke one another to good works?'"

"Yes, Bill, that's the exact Scripture where I was going. Hear me out, please. It actually says 'to provoke unto *love* and good works.' Culture through the years changes—maybe not the basic meaning of a word—but the current usage. I like the King James translation. I think it's rich as literature and very accurate in consistency and theology. But some of the meanings of words have changed through the years.

Let's look at another word that is probably more easily understood as to its change. In the King James Version, Jesus said, '*Suffer* the little children to come unto me.' We know that the word 'suffer' has completely changed it's meaning over the years."

Some in the audience nodded.

"Well, I'm not a Greek scholar but I did do a bit of Strong's concordance and Greek dictionary work on the word, provoke. There are several Greek words for which we have only the one word, 'provoke'. Some are only negative. The one used here in Hebrews 10 can be negative or positive, depending on the rest of the thought. Certainly 'love and good works' are positive, so 'stimulate, arouse, encourage' are some of the words more modern translations use.

"Now, peer pressure, in a generously broad sense, could encompass the thought of a culture's mores exerting pressure on the whole population. But this also could be for good or evil, in God's eyes, depending on the particular mores—or values—of that culture. Certainly the Sawa Indian of Irian Jaya who deceived his enemy into thinking he was a friend for a whole year before he roasted him and ate him, was exalted in his society for his great ability in their highly esteemed value of deception. But I don't think God (nor, do I think we) would applaud him."

Jason shifted in his chair. *Roasted and eaten! Man, what a way to go! Am I going to see this sort of stuff on the mission field?* Jason wondered.

"And, I believe, one of the reasons our culture is in such turmoil is that we have 'outlawed' the Judeo-Christian moral fiber in our society. So there are as many negative 'cultural mores exerting pressure on the community' as positive (if not more).

"But back to peer pressure. I believe that in the current usage of the term, peer pressure is a negative motivation. The generation of my parents yelled, 'Yellow!'— a negative slur against the Japanese Kamikaze pilots. Today we hear: 'Come on.... Everybody's doin' it! What's wrong? Are you chicken?' And they add insult by 'clucking' around and flapping their arms until the person gives in to the peer pressure.

"What the next generation will chide, I don't know. But the intent is to embarrass the person into an action about which he is hesitant. I've said enough. Peer pressure, in the current context of our culture, is not a godly motivator. Though sometimes used by Christians, it originates in the pit of hell! It should never be used to motivate us into action. Thank you."

"Whoa!" Jason said, turning to the pastor. "She's good!"

Pastor Steve nodded. He was about to make a comment when the next speaker began to talk.

"Thank you, Mary. I just realized that the expectations of this class (peer pressure) are heavy on me to give as good a presentation as you did. His eyes were directly on Mary.

There was some light laughter as the audience understood the complexity of these issues.

"My name's Peter," the speaker continued, as he looked back at the group of listeners. "As I gave thought to this subject this week, I realized that 'achievement' has been a strong, driving force in my life. My dad hammered into my head, 'You've got to make something of yourself! Be all that you can be! The Horatio Algier—the self-made man.' I was pushed to be a Who's Who in the Zoo--only to discover that there are thousands of 'zoos'.

We climb the corporate ladder to success—only to realize the pain and frustration that awaits us in that upper echelon of society. This is a powerful capitalistic motivator, but one that allows for shady deals, cutting corners, insider information, using questionable materials in products, hostile takeovers, lawsuits, and a host of other business and corporate ills.

"Yes, we should run the race to win, as Paul said in I Corinthians 9:24. But with our eyes fixed on Jesus, the source and goal of our faith,[6] we will obtain an imperishable crown of righteousness,[7] not the common laurel wreaths given at the stadium that wither and die.

"Jesus gave a very pointed illustration recorded in Luke 17:10. 'After working in the fields all day, after fixing the master's meal, after eating the leftovers, we still say, "There is no merit in this, I have only done what I ought to have done."'

"We sing the chorus, 'If you want to be great in God's Kingdom, learn to be the servant of all.' That thought is actually in the context of James and John wanting to achieve greatness by sitting on the right hand and on the left of Jesus in His Kingdom. To this Jesus said, 'The Gentiles exercise despotic powers over men. But it must not be so among you. If you aspire to be the "chief executive" you must be everybody's slave.'"[8]

Now this is getting interesting, thought Jason. *Learn to be the servant of all. Do I have the stuff in me for that?*

"Now, here's a difficult perspective: Jesus also said, 'In like manner (like a city set on a hill so that it can't be hid), let your light shine in the sight of men, that they may see your good works (your achievements, your accomplishments—the good that you do)....' Now, if Jesus had stopped there we could all do that with ease. As another Scripture says, 'Most men will proclaim their own goodness to everyone....'[9] But Jesus adds the punch line: Do it in such a way that they and you will bring 'glory to your Father in Heaven.'[10] And that's the tough part. All that I am, all that I ever will be, I owe to Him. He holds in His control the very breath that I breathe. He has beforehand planned the good deeds in

6 Read Hebrews 12:2   7 Read II Timothy 4:8   8 Read Mark 10:35-45
9 Read Proverbs 20:6-8   10 Read Matthew 5:16

which we should walk, for we are His most finely crafted work of art."[11]

There is that Scripture again. Must be really important, Jason noted. He glanced back at Pastor Steve, who smiled in return.

"One last thought: In the final analysis, our achievement must be considered in the godly perspective of Colossians 3:23. Let the Word speak for itself: 'Whatever you do, put your whole heart and soul into it, as though you are working for the Lord, and not merely for men—knowing that your real reward, a Heavenly one, will come from the Lord....' Thank you."

"Guilt!" a man shouted, as he arose from his chair. The class, still contemplating what Peter had said, jumped at the intrusion of this ugly word.

"Guilt!" The speaker shouted it again. He definitely wanted their full attention. And he now had it. Speaking more evenly, he continued. "Yes, 'guilt' is a powerful motivator and unfortunately it is used in some churches. In fact, it was the 'final straw' that led me out of a particular church, which I will leave unnamed. By the way, my name is John. As I was saying, we Sunday School teachers had been challenged—harangued might be a more accurate word—to do better: more kids, more money, more, more, more! The superintendent then asked the assistant pastor to close in prayer. He reiterated in his prayer the whole litany of 'challenge' that had already been given to us. But it was his final sentence that did it. It still rings in my ear: 'And God,' he said, 'make us feel *guilty* so we will get out and work harder for You!'"

Some of the group members chuckled a nervous laugh and shook their heads; others just gasped at the thought.

11 Read Ephesians 2:10

"People raised on the 'never quite good enough' philosophy, find themselves easy victims to guilt motivation. Now, I agree, guilt is of God. It's a device of our conscience that, when sensitive to the Holy Spirit, will convict us of sin, yielding to a godly sorrow that leads to repentance. When not in tune with the Spirit, however, guilt triggers the condemnation of satan, resulting in a worldly sorrow which is a very deadly thing.[12]

"'Enlightened' cultures through the ages have made their attempts at ridding us of guilt. Never. But, though guilt is here to stay, let's not allow it to drive us, compel us, motivate us to do the good works that He has planned for us to do. Use it to help us quickly go to God and others for forgiveness when we sin, but never as a motivation in our work for the Lord. Thank you."

Another person quickly went to the speaker's podium. "Hello, my name is Amber. I gave some thought to the things that I let motivate me. Yes, I had thought of peer pressure and guilt, but the one that seems to trouble me more is 'money'. Money's a neutral commodity, but as the saying goes, 'Money talks!'" She paused. "Just a minute, why did it get so quiet in here? I'll tell you why. Because when money talks, we listen!" There was a round of nervous laughter.

"My point—exactly! Whenever anyone starts talking about money, it becomes very personal. 'Don't touch my money,' we protest. Oh, how it motivates. 'Every person has his price,' they say. Scripture puts it this way: 'A bribe (or gift) is as a precious stone in the hand of its owner; it gets him whatever he wants.'[13] But when Simon, the ex-sorcerer, tried to buy the power of the Holy Spirit, Peter was motivated to say, 'You will go to hell with your money if you don't repent of your wickedness.'[14]

12 Read II Corinthians 7:10   13 Read Proverbs 17:8   14 Read Acts 8:20

Jason smiled. *That's clear enough! These speakers are great,* he thought.

"In other words," Amber continued, "now that you are a new believer, you need to have a different attitude toward money—like Zacchaeus, the tax collector. He promised Jesus that he would give 'half of my goods to the poor' when he became a believer."[15]

"God's Spirit says, 'He who had gathered much, had nothing left over; he who gathered little had no lack.'[16] 'Godliness with contentment is great gain.'[17] 'That there may be equality....'[18] But even here, the context of that verse takes us at least back to verse 12: 'But first, there must be a *willing mind.*' Yes, we are to be wise in our use of the wealth of this world so that we can be entrusted with true riches.[19]

"Peter, in talking to the elders of the churches, said, 'Accept the responsibility of looking after your flock of God willingly and not because you feel that you can't get out of it, nor from the motive of personal gain, but freely.'[20] Yes, a workman is worthy of his hire.[21] But today we aren't talking about pay scales. What we're talking about is our motivation. Money shouldn't be used as a motivation to work the works of the One who sent us.[22]

"There's so much more. Jesus talked more about money and its use and misuse than any other one subject. But I think enough has been said to conclude: Money talks, but we had better rather listen to the Lord for His thoughts on godly motivations. Thank you."

The next speaker stood up. He looked at his watch, then at the moderator, who gave him a go-ahead nod, and then at his audience. "Hi, my name's Arnold. I'll try to make this as brief as possible. I know we're running out of time. I agree with the other four speakers. We

---

15 Read Luke 19:8   16 Read II Corinthians 8:15, quoting Exodus 16:18
17 Read I Timothy 6:6   18 Read II Corinthians 8:14   19 Read Luke 16:11
20 Read I Peter 5:2   21 Read Matthew 10:10   22 Read John 9:4

would do well to proactively—before the action is taken—check our motives in these four areas: peer pressure, achievement, guilt, and money. But I believe there's another worldly motivator that is the 'granddaddy' of them all. I believe it could even be considered the motivation behind these other motivators."

That got their interest, thought Jason, looking at those around him. *And mine!*

"A couple of Scriptures that I planned to use have already been quoted, but I think there's no harm in repeating them. You might have noticed that I still haven't stated what I think this powerful motivator is. Of all motivations, this one's the most insidious. It has worked its way into every aspect of life, probably in every culture in the world. And when one would even suggest that it is ungodly, rebellion is at hand. So I must go carefully here. Let's start with a question. What was the very first sin?"

Immediately someone answered. "That's easy. Eve eating that apple!"

"No, it was a papaya!" said another, followed by laughter.

Arnold smiled but shook his head. "No. The eating of the fruit, whatever kind it was, was the *action* of her motivation. What motivated her to eat the apple?"

The audience grew serious again. Someone else said, "Believing that she would be like God."

Again Arnold shook his head. "No. She was told by satan that that would be the *result* of her action. Let me help us move forward on this. Eve was not the first being to sin—to miss the mark set by God. I believe her motivation was the same motivation that caused Lucifer, son of the morning, to say, 'I will be like the Most High God.'[23] One word says it all: 'Pride'."

23 Read Isaiah 14:12-17; Ezekiel 28

A chorus of objections rose from the adult students. They protested and whined as if they were little children who were just told that there is no Santa Claus. Jason looked at Pastor Steve. He was just shaking his head. Jason shrugged his shoulders and turned back to the speaker.

"Hold it! Hold your objections! I know we're taught from infancy that pride is okay. What parents aren't 'proud' of their baby when it is first born—no matter how it looks? What child isn't made to feel proud at his first accomplishment—of anything? Of everything! Face it, that word is woven into the fabric of every aspect of life.

"But, be that as it may, as I said, it still is not of God. 'But,' you may say, 'I take an *honest* pride in my work for the Lord.' Sorry. There is no 'honest' pride in the Bible. The words pride, proud, and proudly are used ninety-seven times in the Old Testament and nine times in the New Testament (KJV). In every case they are used in the context of evil and negativity. A proud look is one of the seven abominations of God.[24] God hates pride.[25] In fact, in the Book of Proverbs, these words occur 14 times. I cannot find any support from the Bible to feel proud.

"Think of it, if anyone had reason to be proud of His accomplishments, it had to be God when He created the heavens and the earth. Can you find any hint of pride in those first chapters of Genesis? I can find affirmation in the repeated words, '...and it was good.' But that is not pride.

"James tells us that God 'resists the proud but gives grace to the humble.'[26] Our work for the Lord is to be done in humility and meekness (strength of character under control)."

24 Read Proverbs 6:17   25 Read Proverbs 8:13   Read James 4:6

Despite the reference to Scripture, there were still grumbles from audience members. Arnold ignored them as he continued. "An interesting meaning of the root word of pride in Greek is 'to inflate with smoke.' Another way to put it is that pride is just a lot of hot acrid air!

One last Scripture. First we must realize that a person 'wise in his own conceit' in King James English means a proud person. Now let's look at Chapter 26 of Proverbs. In 10 verses Solomon is painting the hopelessness of a fool: 'Giving honor to a fool is like binding a stone into a slingshot.' 'Sending a fool with your message is like cutting off your feet or drinking poison.' 'As a dog returns to its vomit, so a fool returns to his folly.' 'A rod is for the fool's back.' A pretty dismal picture is painted with each of his many illustrations. Then he says, 'Have you seen a man wise in his own conceit (proud)? There is more hope for a fool than for him!'"

The audience had grown oddly silent. Arnold looked from face to face. He could not 'read' their attitude, now masked by silence. He continued, speaking softly, yet firmly. "Pride. I believe it's the most basic negative motivator. It's deadly. It's as subtle as that serpent that deceived Eve. It is from the pit of hell! May God help us to recognize when we allow pride to motivate us into any action."

As Arnold sat down, hands of objections popped up, followed by mumblings of disagreement. The moderator took the front and tried to gain control of the class.

"Class, Class! Please, settle down." When they quieted again, he continued. "Well, that's a heavy note to end on, Arnold. But it obviously was something that was spoken from your heart. By the reactions to your placing pride as a negative motivator, I think you can expect a lot of phone calls this week."

"Yeah, Arnold, what's your number?" one student asked, irritation in his tone.

"I want his home address," another shouted. "So I can come over personally. We'll see how proud he is after what I do!"

Jason thought, *Whoa! I'm not the only one who speaks before putting his brain into gear!*

"Okay, class, now that was the negative," the moderator said, trying to ignore the disruptions. He wanted to dismiss the class as quickly as possible without further outbursts. But when he noticed that the class had sobered following the last inappropriate comment, he continued. "Very well presented. Thank you all for your research and sharing. There's a lot to consider in all that was said. I would encourage each of us to take these thoughts into our closet of prayer and allow the Holy Spirit, our Divine Teacher, to sink His thoughts on these issues deep into our hearts. Well, we're also going to get to the positive. But, folks, our time is gone. We're going to have to save the positive for next Sunday. We did tape this session. It will be available in the bookstore after the morning service. Let's pray."

The same class that moments before had been divided, joined together in prayer.

"Father," said the moderator aloud, "You are an awesome God. We love Your Word. It is a Lamp to our feet and a Light to our path. And today, Light has been beamed on our pathway regarding motivations. Help us to guard against the use of any of these or other worldly motivators in our daily Christian living. Thank You for Your faithfulness, Your mercy and Your grace. Amen."

He looked up. "We'll see you next Sunday."

The discussions that followed the people out of that

room were more animated than any in a long time.

"Pastor Steve, am I ever glad that you had me come to this class." Jason said. "These people really did their homework. I'm sure going to look up those hundred and six references on pride. My parents are so proud of my accomplishments. Man, it's embarrassing some-times. And I've fallen right in line with our culture. There are times—too many times—when I really like the attention. You know, pride is used in a lot of com-mercials. It is the motivation of most sports activity. It's everywhere! It's so ingrained in my life, how will I ever reverse it? 'From the pit of hell,' no less, he said!"

"Jason, I think we'll have to hold our thoughts in re-serve until next Sunday. I think the best policy here is what's called 'replacement' therapy."

"What? Wait a minute! I'm not sick or nothing. What's with this 'therapy'?"

Pastor Steve chuckled. "I didn't mean to scare you with that term. It simply means that often to rid our-selves of something bad, we have to replace it with something good. You must have read that already in your study of the Letter of James, Chapter Four."

Jason looked down. "Well, I have to admit, Pastor, I haven't gotten that far yet."

"Well when you get there, you'll see a clear two-part action: In an attitude of submission to God, we resist the devil. Scripture declares: He has to flee! But we can't just stop there. We replace his presence in our thoughts of temptation (for example, to be proud of our accomplishments) with God's thoughts. Scripture con-tinues: 'Come close to God, and He will come close to you.'[27] One way we come close to God is by thinking His thoughts. And we find His thoughts on this—and on all issues of life—in His Word. You will have to hear

---

27 Read James 4:7-10

from the Holy Spirit yourself on this, but a good 'It is written...' might be the one in James 4:7 that Arnold shared: 'God resists the proud, but gives grace to the humble.' So, we don't try to drive 'pride' out of our lives, we simple focus on replacing it with humility."

"Yeah, I get it. Whew! A lot to learn. I'll be here next Sunday, no doubt about it."

During the week, Jason listened to the tape a couple of times and spent some quality "closet" time to try to digest the thoughts on all five of the speakers regarding ungodly motivation that some Christians use. But the one he chose to discuss with his parents was pride. He now wished that he hadn't. They hit the roof when he mentioned what Arnold had said. Jason feared that the brief discussion they had was only a fuse to light a greater fire building in their minds.

He had to talk with Pastor Steve again. He found the pastor in the church hall.

"Pastor Steve, do you have a few? I really need to chat with you."

"Sure, Jason. Do you want to come to the office?"

"Naw. Just a short pep talk would help. Check this out. I looked up those Scriptures on pride. Arnold was right! There's not a single positive reference to pride in the Bible. I couldn't believe it! I thought I had this concept worked out in my mind. So I decided it would be good to share what Arnold (and the Bible) said about pride with my folks. Whoa! Did I get blasted! Man, they came unglued. 'Heresy,' they shouted. They said they were going to call the church."

"Jason, guess what? They did. But Pastor Chapman thinks he got them calmed down enough to look at the Scriptures themselves. But I'll tell you, we haven't heard the last of this. A lot of people are calling. There's going to be some shaking of ideas before this is settled."

"But for all their hollering, I think it was just a final straw, or an excuse to say what came next. They may have been putting up a front of support for what I'm doing, but they actually admitted that they were just going along with me, hoping, even praying—Pastor Steve, they were praying—that this whole 'thing' (as they called it) would go away! What's up with that?"

Pastor Steve had reached his office. "Jason, are you sure you don't want to come in?" It was obvious that he was quite upset about this change in his parents' attitude.

"No, man. Can you just give me a thumbs up that I am on the right track?"

"Jason, Scripture is correct when it says that children are to honor their parents. So you want to go very slow in what you say to them. You're emerging into adulthood. So, more and more you're going to experience thoughts independent of your folks. They'll always be your parents. And you'll always honor them. But the time may come when you will honorably disagree with them."

Jason leaned against the wall and absently stared out a nearby window.

"Jason, are you still there?"

"Yeah, I'm cool. Just disappointed. I thought they were backing me up on this two-year commitment of mine before going to college. I remember them even saying that it would broaden my worldview before I entered formal higher education. I don't know what to think, now."

Pastor Steve breathed a silent prayer to give him the right words to guide Jason. This was not a simple issue. When is a child old enough to disagree with his parents? "Jason, didn't you make a clear declaration just a few days ago that you believed this calling was from God?"

"Straight up. And I still want to believe that."

"Jason, we haven't talked much about the spiritual warfare."

Jason looked from the window to the wall to the floor. Everywhere but at the pastor. His eyes were on fire! "Whoa! You aren't going to say that my parents are being used by satan, are you?"

"Jason, this would go a lot better if we were looking at each other, eye-to-eye."

"I don't think so. I'm glad I didn't come in. I gotta' go now. I'm outta here, man! Bye."

"Jason. Jason!" Pastor Steve called after him, but Jason did not turn as he hurried down the hall and out the front door.

The pastor bowed his head. "Dear Lord, what did I say wrong?"

He was sure he heard a voice answer, "Now, son, don't you get tripped up by the enemy. Let Jason cool down. He respects you. He'll be back."

THE NEXT SUNDAY

But Jason didn't call back—didn't even call to cancel his appointment. Pastor Steve anxiously watched the door to see if Jason would show up for class. *He has to hear the positive,* thought the pastor. But he knew that Jason was also struggling with how well-meaning people such as his own parents could possibly be used by the enemy to put doubt in his mind.

"Good morning," the moderator said, bringing the class to order. "By the increased size of the class today, obviously last week's lesson must have provoked some discussion. That's good. For those of you who weren't here, we considered five 'worldly motivators' that Christians sometimes use. We don't have the time to review them today, but a tape was made and is available in the bookstore. In fact, if today's presentations are as thought-provoking as last week's, we might make it a package of two sessions for wider distribution.

"Well, today we have five more speakers who will share their thoughts on five 'godly motivators'. Again, I'll let them introduce themselves as they come up."

"Hi all. I'm Samantha. Some of you know me as Sam. I've written out what I plan to say today. This is an emotional issue for me, and if I wander from what I've written, I'm sure I'll start crying. So I'm going to stick to what I've written." She unfolded her paper, her hands trembling slightly, and began to read.

"I can't pick up a Christian periodical that's even remotely concerned with the peoples of the world without being confronted by one after another statistic of need. There's a large unreached people group—15 million culturally Muslim people—living under an oppressive, dictatorial atheistic government. There are only 15 expatriate Christians working among them who have a grasp of their language. Simple math says the ratio is one to a million, literally. 'They need me!' is the cry that comes from that statistic. AIDS, orphans, sex slaves, malnutrition—each give their cry for help. And those are just physical needs. Emotionally, depression is the number one disease in the world. Pills are being dispensed for everything from sleeplessness to sweaty hands! And yet, even more seriously, we live in a sin-sick world. False religions are deceiving millions. Maybe the most deadly 'religion' is materialism. A recent Asian news magazine declared materialism as the new religion of the youth in Asia. Compile any statistic and you will hear the plea, 'They need me.'

"Jesus established 'need' as a godly motivator when He said, 'the sick need a Physician.'[28] 'I have come to seek and to save the lost.'[29] The appeal to Ezekiel was for a man of intercession to stand in the gap.[30] Isaiah responded to God's call for someone to go to the lost children of Israel.[31] The appeal of Jesus is, 'the harvest is great; the laborers are few. Pray, therefore....'[32] Holy Scripture through Solomon's lips says, 'Open your mouths, judge righteously and plead the cause of the poor and needy.'[33]

I'm not sure if I have a very good grasp on the needs of the world, Jason wondered. *I guess I should read more—other than motocross magazines! I didn't really think that, did I?* he questioned. *Maybe I'm learning!*

The speaker continued, "A godly motivator to action is a realization of the tremendous physical, emotional, and spiritual needs in our world. Coupled with all the ability in the world to meet that need, the Church should spring into action. If not, there's a sobering statement from the Word: 'If you do nothing to deliver those on the verge of death, and those ready to be killed; if you say, "Look, I didn't know anything about it," does not He who ponders the heart, consider it? And He who keeps your soul, doesn't He know it? And shall He not render to every man according to his works?'[34] I don't need to harden, nor will I soften those words. May the needs of a sin-sick world motivate us into action.

Pastor Steve wondered if this speaker was going to arouse the same feelings as Arnold did last week. But her next words did soften her tone, though not the import of her subject.

28 Read Matthew 9:12   29 Read Luke 19:10   30 Read Ezekiel 22:30   31 Read Isaiah 6:1-9
32 Read Luke 10:2   33 Read Proverbs 31:9   34 Read Proverbs 24:11-12

"I was once reading 'The Gospel According to Peanuts.'" Sam had to pause. Snickers were being muffled behind hands that admitted that they, too, were familiar with Charlie Brown's theology. She continued, "All of his truths may not line up exactly with the Bible, but I thought this particular cartoon was appropriate to my subject. Charlie Brown is walking along the proverbial brick wall. Lucy is on the sidewalk. Charlie says, 'I think God wants me to be a missionary.' Lucy is excited with agreement. In the next two pictures Charlie is telling all of his objections: 'There are strange foods and difficult languages and different cultures. There are wars and famine and suffering and starvation and danger out there.' The final picture shows Charlie on the sidewalk, flat on his back. A Voice is booming out of Heaven: 'Isn't that reason enough?'

Chuckles and muted laugher tried to cover the conviction of truth they just heard in that cartoon.

When they had quieted again, Samantha sat down and Harry stood up. "Good morning. It might be appropriate to stop right here. Sam has already given us a lot to think about. But I've been given the nod to continue. My name's Harry. I've been fascinated by the word 'fear'. It's a powerful motivator. And it can be either positive or negative, depending on to whom you direct your fear. The fear of man is a very deadly thing. Scripture says it brings a snare—a death-trap.[35]

"But today we're looking at the positive. Thus, we must direct our fear towards God. I realize there are some who try to 'water down' the word fear in the Bible. 'It just means awesome respect,' they say. I agree that the fear of God motivates me to have an awesome respect for Him. Jonathan Edwards, at age 38, knew the fear of God when he preached his sermon, *Sinners in*

35 Read Proverbs 29:25

the Hands of an Angry God, based on the Scripture, 'It is a fearful thing to fall into the hands of a living God.'[36]

"The fear of the Lord is the beginning of knowledge, wisdom, and understanding. The fear of God is to hate evil.[37] In fact, in the book of Proverbs alone there are twenty-three references to fear; seventeen of them direct our fear toward God."

Some of those in the audience turned to the Book of Proverbs as Harry spoke.

"The children of Israel were told to choose judges who fear God; they would make wiser judgments.[38] Exodus 18, by the way, is the foundation for our whole judicial system in the USA. Our problem today is to find judges who fear God! I read recently about one judge who did—fear God, that is. An atheist was bringing a charge against Christians and Jews for the holidays that they observe, which celebrate their religions. The atheist complained that atheists have no holidays. The judge dismissed his case by saying that he did have one holiday: April 1st! 'For,' said the judge, 'the fool has said in his heart that there is no God.'"[39]

The comment brought some laughs from the audience. One person said, "Are you sure that really happened? Or is it just one of those interesting 'forwards' that flow through the Internet?"

The speaker, deciding to ignore the comment, continued. "Joseph's fear of God kept him from doing his brothers in![40] The fear of God motivated the midwives to save the Hebrew children alive rather then to obey Pharaoh.[41] Paul said, 'knowing therefore, the terror (solemn fear) of the Lord, we persuade men....' The 'therefore' refers back to the previous verse. What does it say? 'For each one of us will have to stand without pretense before Christ's judgment seat, and we will be rewarded for

36 Read Hebrews 10:31   37 Read Proverbs 1:7; 9:10; 8:13   38 Read Exodus 18:21
39 Read Psalm 14:1   40 Read Genesis 42   41 Read Exodus 1:21

what we did when we lived in our bodies, whether it was good or bad.'[42]

"We don't have the time for it now, but after reading all of Chapter 12 of Luke's Gospel, come back to verse 5. Jesus is talking: 'But I will forewarn you Whom you should fear: Fear Him, Who after He has killed, has power to cast into hell. Believe Me, He is the one to fear.'"

The room became so silent you could hear a pin drop.

"All of this 'fear stuff' could get quite heavy. Let me lighten it a bit. I think this is a reasonable parallel. My sister had been having a good deal of trouble with her oldest daughter who was forging her way through the teen years. Last week there was a monumental break-through. My niece called me and said, 'Guess what, Uncle Harry? I just realized that if I obeyed my mother, I wouldn't be on restriction all the time!' It worked."

Once again there were chuckles from the group.

"Guess what? If we obeyed our Heavenly Father, motivated by the fear of who He is and what He can do, we wouldn't be on restriction all the time, either! In fact, as we move closer in our relationship with Him, that intimacy allows love to become a stronger and stronger binding force. And one day we will experience the truth that 'perfect love casts out all fear.'"[43]

There were nods of approval and understanding from the group.

Harry finished up. "One last thought: Because fear is such a strong motivator—powerful in emotions—it can sometimes be difficult to differentiate between the fear of God and the fear of man. But God has not left us stranded. The answer is found in Proverbs 2:1-5. If you do these things (eight in all), 'then you will understand

42 Read II Corinthians 5:11, then verse 10   43 Read I John 4:18

the fear of the Lord.' Oh, let me share just one more thought—another one of those in Proverbs: 'The fear of the Lord is a fountain of life. It causes (motivates) us to depart from the snare of death.'[44]

"Fear is a powerful motivator, whether it's fear directed toward man, or God. When that fear is directed toward God, it is a positive motivator."

Harry looked at his watch. "I'm 'afraid' my thoughts were very brief this morning. Is that because of a fear of God, or a fear of our time constraint? Or neither? Thank you all for listening."

Harry sat down. Jason didn't quite get the pun intended. He had some strong fears working in his thoughts since his folks had made their new position clear. And now they wanted to talk with him—over dinner—after church. His attention was brought back to the present as the next speaker began to talk.

"I hope you didn't fear that we'd go to sleep on you, Harry. Those are powerful thoughts," said a woman as she stood up and faced the class. "The motivation I thought of is a valid godly motivator, but it doesn't get quite as technical as Harry's, although he did reference my first verse. Oh, by the way, my name's Alice. At the Judgment Seat of Christ, 'rewards' will be given for the good we've done in this life. Have we built our house (our life) with gold, silver and precious stones?

"This is a long passage of Scripture, but it gets the point across: Paul is talking: 'In this work, we work with God, and that means that you are a field under cultivation, or if you like, a house being built. I, like a master-builder who knows his job, by the grace that God has given me, lay the foundation; someone else builds upon it. I say only this, let the builder be careful how he builds! The foundation is laid already, and no

44 Read Proverbs 14:27

one can lay another, for it is Jesus Christ himself. But any man who builds on the foundation using as his materials gold, silver, and precious stones, or wood, hay and stubble, must know that each man's work will one day be shown for what it is. The day will show it plainly enough, for the day will arise in a blaze of fire, and that fire will prove the nature of each man's work. If the work that a man has built upon the foundation will stand the test, he will be rewarded. But if a man's work be destroyed under the test, he loses it all. He personally will be safe, though rather like a man rescued from a fire.'"[45]

Alice looked up. "It's interesting how few words we need to use when the Scripture speaks so clearly."

"True," Harry said, and others nodded.

Alice continued. "Paul said of his own life, 'I have finished my course.... There awaits for me a victor's crown of righteousness—for being right with God and for doing right.'[46]

"The writer of Hebrews says, 'Jesus, for the joy (reward) set before Him, endured the cross, despising the shame....'[47]

"To be aware that there is reward for good works is okay. However," she added, holding up a finger of warning, "if we start focusing on that reward, we've lost this as a godly motivator.

"While I was on vacation, I visited a church. That morning, a young lady sang two songs. The first one was quite lively. Applause seemed okay. However, her second song was very serious—definitely not one to be applauded. But there was a smattering of applause throughout the audience. Then she said, 'Go ahead and applaud. I like it. I sing better when you do.' Either in her nervousness she had a slip of the tongue, or she

45 Read I Corinthians 3:9-15   46 Read II Timothy 4:8   47 Read Hebrews 12:2

really enjoyed the applause. I hesitate to judge, but it sure sounded like hearty applause was her motivation. And, if so, that applause is all the reward she probably received.

"There are satisfactions of the soul—though temporal—that give us a sense of accomplishment. I don't think there's anything wrong with encouraging a person with 'Good job!' Or, 'That's a fine piece of work!'

"Affirmation, on a human level, is sorely lacking. We would do well to spice our conversations with a bit more of it. But all earthly reward will be eclipsed by His one statement: 'Well done, thou good and faithful servant. Enter in to the joy of the Lord.'[48] This is the reward that I trust all of us are working toward. Thanks."

Pastor Steve took this moment to scan the classroom, hoping that he would see Jason. Had he come, or not, was his concern.

Jason saw Pastor Steve looking around, but teasingly decided to not identify himself. The search was cut short by the next speaker.

"Hi, my name is Bill. Bill Fry. I love God!"

"We all do, Bill," someone broke in. The interruption momentarily lightened the seriousness of the atmosphere.

"You're right. We would be fools to not love God. So, our 'love' for God definitely is a motivator," Bill said. "Jesus said, 'If you love Me, you will keep My commandments.'[49] I couldn't find Scriptures that talk about us initiating a love for Him. It seems clear that our love is a response to His love. Scripture says, 'We love Him because He first loved us.'[50] It's with gentleness that Jesus tried to draw out Peter's love for Him in John 21. And then His firm command: 'Feed My sheep!'

"It was Peter's love for Christ that motivated him to

48 Read Matthew 25:21   49 Read John 14:15   50 Read I John 4:19

pull out his sword that night in Gethsemane. But on that same night in the shadow of the palace of the High Priest, his love dissipated into a trilogy of denials. With cursing and swearing he declared that he didn't even know the Man.[51] How often in the crush of daily living do we find ourselves in a similar dilemma?"

Many in the audience lowered their eyes in thought.

"My personal commitment love to the Lord is solid. But my action love, i.e. my love as a motivation, is a real area of struggle. I too often find myself in Paul's dilemma of putting his commitment love into action love. In Romans Seven, Paul graphically described his (and our) struggle. He might have awakened one morning to say, 'A great new day. I have done my morning Scripture reading. I know right from wrong. I am determined to do right today.' He stretches, blinks his eyes, lets out a yawn and gets out of bed determined to do right. The day starts out okay, but, sure enough, he finds himself doing wrong!

"The next morning he wakes up with a (commitment) love to not repeat that wrong. But he finds himself doing it again. He continues. He moans, 'Oh, wretched man that I am! Who will deliver me from this body of flesh?' He likens his sinful nature to the decaying body of one murdered tied to the body of the murderer."

A woman sitting next to Jason wrinkled her nose. "Oh, yuck! Did he really just say that?"

"Yes, that was one way of executing murderers in Paul's day. They would tie the body of the one murdered to that of the murderer—face to face, torso to torso, arm to arm and leg to leg. And from the looks on your faces, I don't need to go into further detail for you to get the picture. As I was saying, Paul likened his sin-

51 Read Matthew 26:69-74

ful nature, tempted by satan and drawn away by the lusts of the world, to a dead, decaying body clinging to him."[52]

There were more looks of disgust, but with them came nods of understanding.

"Well, I didn't mean to get so graphic. But this is the struggle we too often have with our love for Him as our motivation. We say we love Him. And we do—with a commitment love. But, sometimes when push comes to shove, our love as a motivation fails us.

"One last thought: In I Corinthians 13:4-8, we are given eight positive things God's agape love through us does and eight negative things it doesn't do. This should be our focus. But, even then, that is Christ's love flowing through us. Let's face it: most often human love is very selfish. Or it's tied to conditions, and that isn't even love at all. I'll stop here. But I'd like to recommend a very good book on this subject. It was written by C.S. Lewis titled, *The Four Loves*.[53] Excellent reading. Thank you."

"We love everything from motherhood to apple pie. The word has lost its meaning," one thoughtful student offered as Bill sat down.

I love my mother and her apple pie, Jason thought. *I am so glad I decided to come to hear the positive motivators. There is Pastor Steve looking around again. He will really be surprised when he sees that I am here.* His thoughts were interrupted by the next speaker. *She looks too young to be in this senior adult class!* Jason thought.

"Hello, my name is Sarah. It's interesting to me that three of the four speakers this morning pointed out that although the motivations they spoke of were Biblical, these godly motivators in themselves, can fall short,

52 Read Romans 7:15-25   53 *The Four Loves*, C.S. Lewis, Harcourt Brace Jovanovich, 1960.

each of them having a margin of human failing. And even what Samantha spoke about—that the needs of the world being a godly motivator—there can come a margin of human failure. If we focus on the fact that *I* am needed, we can develop a 'messiah complex,' a very dangerous and deadly thing. There are already over 2000 self-proclaimed 'messiahs' in America waiting for their time to be revealed. This world doesn't need another one. I trust you didn't mind my adding that thought, Sam."

"Not at all, Sarah."

"There's one motivation, emanating from God, that stands on no human force for strength. It's the powerful dynamo—the motivating force—of a man who said, 'I can do all things through Christ who is my strength.'[54] God said, 'I have loved you with an everlasting love.'[55] There is no greater motivation than this: 'God loves me.'"

There were a few "Amens" uttered from the group.

"To comprehend the depth of His love for us;[56]

"To understand that while we were yet sinners, Christ died for us;[57]

"To appreciate that nothing can separate us from the Love of Christ;[58]

"To experience the redemptive work of His love.[59]

These are the Scriptures and thoughts we must take into our closet of prayer. And let the Holy Spirit deal with us; let Him assure us of God's love.

"I can only say it again: There is no greater motivation than this: God loves me. It is true: We must come to that understanding and we must experience His love to use it as a motivation. But that love is solid whether or not we appropriate it. It comes from God. It's the love from which there is no escape. As the Psalmist said,

54 Read Philippians 4:13   55 Read Jeremiah 31:3   56 Read Ephesians 3:18
57 Read Romans 5:8   58 Read Romans 8:35, 38-39   59 Read John 3:16

'Where can I hide from Your presence...?'[60]

"Scripture is without end expressing God's love for me. 'My thoughts toward you are for good and not for evil,'[61] comes from His heart of love. 'Consider the incredible love that the Father has shown us in allowing us to be called "children of God"—and that is not just what we are called, but what we are.'[62] How about the simplicity of 'God is love'?[63] In fact, the whole Book of First John speaks of His wonderful love for us. I hope this excites you as much as it does me."

Almost everybody in the group nodded.

"Another person, thought to be insane, attempted to describe the expansiveness of God's love. Penned on the wall of his room in a mental institution, discovered only after his death, were these words:

Could we with ink the ocean fill
And were the skies of parchment made;
Were every stalk on earth a quill
And every man a scribe by trade:
To write the love of God above
Would drain the ocean dry;
Nor could the scroll contain the whole
Though stretched from sky to sky!

"Here is motivation at its ultimate: God loves me! When we grasp the significance of His love for me—better yet, when we have this Love, who is literally, Christ, alive—really alive—in us,[64] then we, too, with Paul will say, 'The love of Christ constrains me—motivates me—compels me—leaves me no choice—is the very wellspring of all my action.'[65] All praise to His Holy Name."

The room was hushed as Sarah sat down. In fact, no one moved for several minutes. Each student was in deep thought of what had just been said. Yes, God's

60 Read Psalm 139:7   61 Read Jeremiah 29:11   62 Read I John 3:1
63 Read I John 4:16   64 Read Galatians 2:20   65 Read II Corinthians 5:14

love for me should be my highest motivation.

Quietly, almost reverently, the moderator took his place in front of the class. Not wanting to interrupt the silent meditation, he stood for another long moment. He cleared his throat and spoke softly. "This has been good," he said, still not wanting to interrupt the atmosphere of awe that had fallen over the room. "A big 'Thank you' to all ten of you—from last Sunday and this one—who did such a tremendous job. Your use of Scripture in each of the areas gives us a foundation for further study on this inexhaustible subject of motivation.

"Pastor Steve, our youth pastor, called me this week. As we talked, he thanked me for letting him and Jason, one of our youth, join this class for these two weeks. Jason is about to graduate from high school. He believes God wants him to do a two-year mission before starting college. He told Pastor Steve that he really needed to check his motivation. So, Jason, have these lessons helped?"

When Jason called out from the back of the room, Pastor Steve beamed to see him, overjoyed that he had come after all.

"After today, I can definitely say, 'Yes.' Last week left me with some real questions—particularly that last one about pride. But with these positive motivations, I can more clearly see that my motivations are right."

"Thank you, Jason. We're really prou—" the moderator stopped himself. "Let me rephrase that."

Laughter rippled across the classroom as they recognized the lesson. How difficult it is to break bad thought patterns.

"Jason, we rejoice with you in the privilege God has giving you to minister cross-culturally. As a class, maybe we could be a part of your support team. Class, let's pray. I would like to ask Pastor Steve to close our time with prayer."

Pastor Steve stood and smiled. "I would add my thanks for letting us join you," he told the moderator. "I'm impressed with the solid research your speakers did. I trust many others will listen to the tapes that were made last week and today. Let's pray now.

"Father, how good it is to know with assurance that we are in Your presence. You have given us Your Word. It is rich in all Truth. Give us Your wisdom and understanding to apply these truths to our daily living. And give us the grace to forgive those who would disagree with these interpretations of Your Word. In Jesus' Holy Name, Amen."

Jason sided up to the pastor. "Pastor Steve," he said quietly, "was that last phrase of your prayer directed at my relationship with my folks?"

"Jason, it could apply to that. It could also apply to our last conversation."

"Oh, that. Yeah, I really don't have a strong grasp on the subject of spiritual warfare."

"Well, it's a lot more than just a subject. It's more deeply a part of a Christian's life than most people realize. Survey statistics are only generalities, but I just read that although 78% of those surveyed believe they are Christians, only 24% strongly believe that satan is a real being, not just an 'evil force.'"

"Oh, don't get me wrong, Pastor Steve, at least I believe that much. The Bible says he's a fallen angel. How can anyone be a Christian and not be on the same page with that?"

"I don't know, Jason. My dad told me that there was a time when he couldn't believe that the day could ever come when wrong would be taught as right and right as wrong. But it sure is here now!

"Jason, I know that thought of mine about your folks came across as a personal attack. I didn't mean to offend you. But look at good ol' Peter. Just days after he made that powerful declaration that Jesus is the Christ, Jesus had to say, 'Get behind Me, satan! You are an offense to Me. You are seeing things from man's perspective and not God's.'[66] He wasn't calling Peter 'satan'. But He was acknowledging that at that moment Peter was not seeing things the way God does. But that does lead us into the subject of spiritual warfare."

"There! You just called it a 'subject'!"

"You're right, I did. Well, so much for our English language. Jason, are you ready for the good news? Because of all the uproar this week at church over the 'pride' issue, the leadership met a number of times. I told them of your sincerity in checking your motives. I gave them my best recommendation. I encouraged them to give us a final 'yes' on your two-year mission. They really questioned me about your folks. But Pastor Chapman assured us all that he had a good understanding with them."

"You're the man, Pastor Steve! I appreciate it. I wonder if that's what my folks want to talk with me about today? They said they wanted to take me out for dinner after church—to talk."

"Probably so. I'll be praying for you. We better get into the sanctuary. The service has already begun."

SUMMARY OF ISSUES

I had fun identifying with Jason. He is a real person. Honest. Human. Yet, becoming serious as he realizes the importance of knowing his motivations. I trust as

66 Read Matthew 16:23

you review these ungodly and godly motivations, you will find your motivations to be godly.

- God is a good economist; He uses everything for His purposes.
- The Church's prayerful confirmation of a personal call is one of the safest assurances of knowing God's will.
- We must know God's will, prepare to do it, then just do it!
- Striving for significance is a cultural universal. Everybody wants to be a somebody.
- Too often, we look at our motivation after an action. We need to be proactive—determinative—in deciding why we do what we do *before* we do it.
- Five worldly motivators that godly people sometimes use:

1) Peer Pressure: In current cultural usage, it is negative.

2) Achievement can be a driving force. Yes, we should run the race to win, but our focus is on Jesus, the source and goal of our faith.

3) Guilt is a godly motivator to take quick action in asking for forgiveness, but a deadly motivator to get us to work the good deeds that He has prepared for us to walk in. Those who have been raised in a "never good enough" and shame culture are particularly susceptible to this negative motivation.

4) Money talks—and we listen! It is a neutral commodity, yet when it (or what it can buy) becomes the focal point, we're in deep trouble.

5) Pride is the most basic of ungodly motivators. From the very entrance of sin into the cosmos, pride was the insidious motivator. It is behind and undergirds all other negative motivations.

- One of the best methods of avoiding negative thoughts and motivations is to replace them with the positive.
- Well-meaning people can be used by the enemy to discourage godly commitment.
- Five godly motivators we should strive to use:

1) The needs of a sin-sick world call Christians to action. A greater awareness of these needs will serve as a greater motivation.

2) Whereas the fear of man is a very deadly thing, the fear of God brings tremendous wisdom and understanding and motivation to do right.

3) As amazing as it may seem, God gives us gifts, talents and abilities, gives us the opportunity to use them for His purposes and glory, and then He rewards us for doing His will.

4) Our love for God motivates us to action. Understanding all He has done for us leaves us no choice but to give our entire beings back to Him. Yet, though our commitment love for the Lord may be solid, our action love can be an area of struggle.

5) When we experience His Love—Christ—alive, really alive in us, then we too, with Paul will say, "The love of Christ constrains me—motivates me—compels me—leaves me no choice—is the very wellspring of all my actions."

- Being prepared for the spiritual warfare involved when one is aggressively engaged in the battle for lost souls is an absolute necessity.

Suggestion: You might want to read back through the chapter and find the context to which each of these summary statements refers. Then, in your closet of prayer, allow the Holy Spirit to affirm or convict you re-

garding each one. He will gently lead you to the Word—
to Christ Himself—to discover the solutions to your
needs.

PERSONAL NOTES:

4

THE CHALLENGE

A mountain of paperwork covered his desk. Teams were preparing for their summer of service. A couple was applying to Frontiers and wanted to know what the church's policy was. Then there was the full In-Box of e-mails from missionaries on the field. There was always more work than Pastor Carl could handle. Although he was the missions pastor, other assignments seemed to find their way to his desk.

Sometimes it was hard to know where to start. But first on the list today was to place a call. He dialed.

"Hello. Kyle? Say, this is Pastor Carl, calling from church."

"Oh, hi," said the voice on the other end. "Yes, I was going to call you."

"Well, the youth pastor said that you had mentioned to him that you thought God wanted you to be a missionary. He said that he told you to give me a call."

"I've been meaning too," Kyle answered after a pause. "I've been so busy with finals, you know. But they're over now."

"How did you do?"

"Okay I think. Physics was hard, but..." There was another pause as Kyle shrugged on the other end. "I'll find out next week how they all went."

"I'm sure you did good. I mean, ...did well. Talking with an English major, I'd better be more careful with my words."

Kyle chuckled. "I know I did well in my major subjects. It's just math that has me a bit concerned."

"Well, when can we get together?"

"I don't go to work until six today. I could come over this afternoon."

"Great. How about two o'clock?"

"Yes, that's a good time."

When Kyle hung up the phone, he felt a knot in his stomach. He had never spoken to Pastor Carl before. The pastor was certainly one of the more visible pastors, what with so much emphasis on cross-cultural ministry. And, for a number of years now, Kyle had inklings—just slight twinges—of interest as teams came forward to be prayed for before leaving on some mission. And then more interest as he heard the reports they gave when they returned. Exciting and challenging, for sure. But college was his current focus. Good grades did not come easily for him. Four years of solid cracking the books had paid off. He was close to graduation. And close to some relief, he had thought.

That changed though one Sunday evening. Miles Dupree had shared his experiences working with national pastors in Kenya. Dupree's words were the catalyst that gave Kyle a thought that he had to share with someone. But who? As he walked into the foyer, thoughts racing through his mind, directly in front of him stood Mike, the youth pastor. Before Kyle knew what he was saying, it just came out of him.

"I think that God wants me to be a missionary!" Kyle blurted. It was a scary, exciting moment for Kyle.

There was that knot in his stomach and wild ideas spinning in his mind. But he had now said it aloud: I think God wants me to be a missionary. To do what, he didn't know. To go where, he didn't know. When? He was even less sure about that. But he felt like he needed to pursue that tug in his heart, placed there when Dupree challenged the congregation to "lift up their eyes to see that the field is the world."[1] Those words spoken by Jesus had a positive, compelling ring in Kyle's ears. And in prayerful consideration, they were growing deep in his heart. It was at that time that the Youth Pastor had recommended that Kyle call Pastor Carl. He told Kyle that the church had a real clear policy leading to ministry involvement.

2:00 PM: A MIDDLETOWN CHURCH

The secretary was cordial as she directed Kyle down the hall to Pastor Carl's office.

Pastor Carl, always kind and neatly groomed, motioned for Kyle to enter. "Hello, Kyle. Come on in."

Kyle looked around the office. Bookshelves lined two of the walls, and they were filled with hundreds of books, some old leather bound ones, but many more current titles. Also placed on a shelf here and there and on the walls were interesting artifacts from around the world. Kyle's eyes quickly took all this in. "This is fantastic! Your office looks like a missions' museum."

The pastor smiled, rubbing a smoothly shaved chin. "Yes, the Lord has privileged me the opportunity to travel quite a bit. Our church leadership believes that it is important for our missionaries to be visited regularly. The joy is mine to see them at their ministry location, and they appreciate the visit. It is nothing special; just a chance for them to connect with home."

1 Read John 4:35; Matthew 13:38

"Pastor Mike said that we have a well-stated missions policy here. I guess I'm about to find out for myself." Kyle was still looking around the room in awe. He gently picked up a hand-painted egg shell.

Pastor Carl chuckled, "You break; you buy! And that would be quite expensive, including a trip to Slovakia, where I purchased those shells."

"I shall do my best," Kyle said as he carefully replaced the egg onto its stand.

Pastor Carl continued, bringing the subject back to Kyle's reason for being there. "Mike said when you came through those foyer doors you had the look of fierce determination in your eyes."

Kyle's head shot up. "Oh? What else did he say?"

"That you are a very serious-minded English major, about to graduate. And that you are a solid Christian young man with a good heart for the Lord."

Kyle was pleased to hear that. He looked thoughtfully at the pastor. Although he sounded formal, his gentle face put Kyle at ease. Kyle could imagine looking like Pastor Carl one day. His dark hair dusted with gray, his once sharp features softened with age. "Pastor Mike said all of that?"

Pastor Carl nodded. "He also said that it was the words of Miles Dupree, challenging us to lift up our eyes to see that the field is the world that was for you the final catalyst in your heart to take the next step. It becomes my privilege to discuss this with you—to help you explore the opportunities of cross-cultural ministry."

"Pastor, it encourages me that you're this committed. I really don't know all the facts involved yet. But I'm glad Pastor Mike directed me to you."

"Well, I sure trust that I can help. I was just looking

over my notes on a seminar I do called, 'For Those Who Go.' I don't remember ever seeing you at one of them. Have you ever attended on a Saturday?"

Kyle shifted his blue eyes around the room, and then brought them back to rest on the pastor. "No, I'm sorry. College has been my last four-year focus. But with my papers in and the last of the finals over, I'm beginning to breathe again."

"I understand. I thought some of the introductory section might be a good starting point for our discussion. It gives a broad perspective of the challenge to missions."

"It's not the same as that Perspectives Course, is it?"

"No, but I was going to mention that to you, as well. There is no better foundation to understanding missions than what that course offers. It is actually entitled 'Perspectives On The World Christian Movement.'[2] They bring the 'heavyweights' of the missions community together to teach it. You can get college credit for it, too. Anyway, they look at missions from four perspectives: Biblical, Historical, Cultural, and Strategic. Churches around the country and around the world, now, sponsor it. It is wonderful."

"Sounds like it. When is it coming to Middletown?"

After Pastor Carl motioned for Kyle to sit down, he took out a folder he had prepared for Kyle and placed in on the desk, sliding it in his direction. He leaned back in his well-worn leather chair, crossed his legs, and answered Kyle, "Well, I have been talking with some of the other church leaders about bringing the seminar to Middletown. I have attended the Course, but you need additional training to be a facilitator. I do hope we can bring it here—soon."

2 Perspectives On The World Christian Movement, USCWM, www.perspectives.org, perspectives@uscwm.org, 626 398-2125

Kyle was anxious to get started. He was curious about what was in the folder. It looked like it didn't hold very many pages. Kyle's training had taught him to not be presumptuous, so he waited. But Pastor Carl did not seem in a hurry. He acted like he would just as soon just keep talking. Finally Kyle said, "Let's take a look at your notes," opening the folder. "What! Only one page?"

The pastor smiled wide, crows-feet spreading out from the corners of his eyes. "Kyle, I could talk for six hours from that one page. Notice all of the Scripture references. I rarely teach anything that does not have a sound Biblical foundation."

"Six hours? I have to be at work at 6:00!"

"Not to worry. I'm not going to give you the whole cabbage. Just a few leaves. We will follow this simple outline. When you fall asleep, I'll quit!"

Kyle laughed. "So, where do you start?"

"With God."

Kyle looked up and grew serious.

"This whole business of world evangelization is His plan. He is sovereign. He has a purpose. So we can start with the foundational truth that whatever He says is going to happen is going to happen.

"Psalm 46:10 is where we go first. Many people, when they hear the first two words of that verse, think they know the whole of it. 'Be still...'"

"'...and know that I am God,'" Kyle finished.

"Yes, go on."

"Go on? Is there more?"

"Of course. This is a strong verse expressing the sovereignty of God in relation to missions. In this verse, He is telling us to slow down, to be still, to get quiet before Him. He is saying, 'I have something very important to say. First of all I want you to know that I am God. Creator of the universe, all-knowing, all-powerful, all-loving. I am God.' Kyle, I don't know you very well. I have seen you around, but we have never conversed with one another. Do you have a healthy image of God?"

"Yes, I think so. There is sure a lot about Him that I don't understand, but I believe His Word is true. And that speaks pretty clearly about Him."

"If you have the time, I would suggest a book. A little one; I like that kind. It's titled, *Your God Is Too Small*, by J.B. Philips.[3] In the first half, he destroys a lot of images people have about God. In the second half, he then gives a fabulous foundation on the greatness of God." The pastor paused. "By the expression you're wearing, I would say you have doubts?"

"No doubts, Pastor. It's just that I'm about booked-out! But maybe a little one would be an encouragement after all the reading I've done. I'll check it out. Now I can see how you could spend six hours on this one page. We're only one phrase into the first verse!"

Pastor Carl continued on. "Once we have a proper perspective of who God is, and we hear Him say, 'I will be...,' we have no doubt He *will be* whatever He says He will be!"

"What does He say He will be?"

"It is powerful. He says, 'I will be exalted among the heathen.' And to add emphasis, He gives the parameters of that declaration: 'I will be exalted in all the earth.' Revelation 5:9, then, prophetically corroborates that statement: Thousands upon thousands of people are before the Throne of God, singing: 'You (Christ) have redeemed us to God by Your blood out of every kindred and tongue, people and nation.'

3 *Your God is Too Small*, J.B. Phillips, MacMillan, 1961.

"You understand that nowadays we are hearing that that last word 'nation' in the Greek is 'ethnos.' So the thought is 'people group' rather than a politically- or geographically-bound nation."

"Yes, I've taken a course in classical Greek. I got into Biblical Greek from there."

"Great! You could probably teach me, then."

"It sure does help me to understand Scripture better. But I'm sure you had Greek in college, yourself. I was going to go for Hebrew, but my schedule was just too tight."

Pastor Carl cocked his head slightly as he recalled how many years ago he had struggled through Greek in college. He gave his chin a thoughtful rub and scrutinized Kyle more closely. *Intelligent. Straightforward. Dedicated. Good qualities. Hmm,* the pastor mused.

"Let's continue," he said to Kyle. "It is one thing to 'know' God is sovereign. It is another thing to relate and accept His sovereignty in our day-to-day living. Listen to this for example: Peter and John are going into the temple at the three o'clock hour of prayer. A man who is lame asks them for alms. Peter says, 'We don't have any money, but what we do have, we'll give to you.' He takes him by the hand and lifts him up. You know," Pastor Carl chuckled, "I have always wondered what would have happened if John had said, 'No, Peter, I've got a denarius here.'"

Kyle pulled his head back in surprise. "Pastor Carl, forgive me for insinuating, but isn't having thoughts like that desecrating Scripture?"

"No, I don't believe so. As long as I always keep separate my 'supposings' from what is actually written as Scripture. Kyle, what you must remember is that these men were real people. They got hungry, they laughed and joked with one another; they got tired. Don't mis-understand me. I hold Scripture in the highest regard. It is God's Word to us, preserved through the centuries with a greater accuracy than any other ancient writing. I am sure you studied that in college. But sometimes people go overboard in so solemnizing the Bible that they lose sight of the fact that these were real people in-volved in real-life situations."

Kyle heaved a sigh. They didn't study the Bible at his college, not even as a representation of ancient his-tory. In fact, they did everything they could to discredit it in the minds of the students. But that did not stop Kyle. He studied on his own a number of books that speak of the credibility and accurate historicity of the Bible. His favorite was an old one by Josh McDowell, *Evidence That Demands A Verdict.*[4]

"Anyway, John had no coins," Pastor Carl con-tinued. "The man gets healed. They preach in the tem-ple. They get put in the jail. They are then brought be-fore the Sanhedrin. They preach again. This time they are rebuked and released. They rejoin their compan-ions—probably in the Upper Room. They tell them everything that had happened. Then they spend some time in united prayer. And in that prayer they relate present happenings with the sovereignty of God. They are fitting the circumstances of their times into His per-spective. Now, verse 24 of Chapter 4 of Acts—."

Pastor Carl opened his Bible and looked down his hawk-like nose to find the page. "No, excuse me, here it is, verse 28: 'But only to carry out all that Your prov-idence and will had already determined should be done.' Here is the point: These men who had so recently been fighting over who would be the greatest in His kingdom, who had deserted Him in the Garden, who

4 *Evidence That Demands A Verdict,* Josh McDowell, Here's Life Publishers, 1979.

had even denied the Lord—these men were now able to see events of their daily living tying into God's sovereignty.[5]

"With hindsight we can say, 'Simple. Of course! That's easy to see.' But we need to realize that they did not have the New Testament and probably were not great Old Testament scholars, either. We need to be sensitive in the daily affairs of our living to understand His sovereign hand at work."

"Point well taken. God is sovereign in my life today," Kyle verbalized to solidify that thought in his mind.

"Great. As powerful as that is, the next thought will amaze you. God could have chosen any method in His creative imagination to share the plan of salvation with the peoples of the world. But He chose us! You and me! Remember when Jesus was coming into the city of Jerusalem, riding on that young donkey?"

Kyle nodded vigorously. "The people were shouting, 'Hosanna! Long live the King!' The priests told Him to stop the people. He said, 'If they stopped, these rocks would cry out!'"

"Good, Kyle. So you know where I am going with this. Can you imagine me taking you out to the field to introduce you to the 'rock' that led me to the Lord?" Pastor Carl paused a moment, a wry smile twisted his face. "And on that road to Jerusalem, we could have encountered the first 'rock' band!"

Kyle laughed. Just as Pastor Carl, who at first seemed so stoic and formal, had become a man of patience and humor—a real human being right before Kyle's eyes—Kyle was beginning to see that thinking a little beyond just the words of Scripture also gave it some flesh and skin. He could see the benefit of that, but wanted to make sure he knew Scripture well

5 Read Acts 3:1-4:31

enough that he would never change the meaning of God's Word.

"Kyle, God did not choose that plan. He chose us to participate in His phenomenally wild, sovereign will. And James makes it clear that we are to play an active role: 'You are to be doers of the Word, and not hearers only.'[6] What a privilege!"

The pastor's excitement was instantly doused as he changed his thought. "Now you probably read the news as much as I do. There is very little good news in the world today. The physical and emotional needs of the world are overwhelming: AIDS, cancer, circulatory disease, malnutrition, civil wars (Mind you, there is nothing civil about war!), coalition wars, war of the sexes! Depressing news at every turn."

Kyle crossed his legs and leaned back a bit in his chair. "I read the other day," he said, "that depression is the number one illness in the world today. For some it is a chemical imbalance; for most, it's just messed up emotions."

"But even worse than all of that," Pastor Carl said, "is the spiritual state of the world. God's heart is beating to the pulse of Peter's words: 'He (God) is not willing that any perish, but (He is willing) that all come to repentance.'[7] The 'lub-dub' of God's heart: not willing—willing; not willing—willing; not willing—willing! And with the sound of that heartbeat pulsing through Scripture, about half of the six-plus billion people alive today have not heard a culturally relevant presentation of the Good News of Jesus Christ. Millions more have heard and have rejected the Message."

"Whoa! I didn't realize it was that bad." Kyle sat straight up in his chair.

"Oh, there is good news here and there: Tre-

6 Read James 1:22   7 Read II Peter 3:9

mendous growth in the Church in some nations where persecution is rampant. I don't want us to get depressed, but there is some more bad news. What are we—the Church—doing about this situation? Of all the Christian workers, about 90% of them are working in areas where the Gospel has already saturated the air waves and filled the printed page; where churches, crusades and conferences abound. Further, out of what little money is given to the work of Christ (A recent statistic said all charitable giving amounted to only about 2.7% of North American Christian income.), just a fraction of one percent of that 2.7% is being given to areas where the Good News has not yet been heard."

Kyle shifted uncomfortably. He came from a giving Christian family, and the statistic rubbed him the wrong way. "Hold on! That sounds like a real condemnation to those who are doing their part."

"Sorry, Kyle. That is not what I meant to suggest. For sure, we need to be careful not to let satan bring his condemnation on us. But, on the other hand (and according to Papa in 'Fiddler on the Roof', there always is 'the other hand'), a little conviction of the Holy Spirit wouldn't hurt. I only wanted to impress on you the enormity and urgency of the need and how little the Church at large is doing about it."

"I understand now. But Pastor, that brings us to a question that's really been bothering me: I've been keeping up on world news. With all the great needs out there, what opportunity is there for me? What would I do? Where would I start?"

"Well, Kyle, I don't think you're really ready for a specific ministry location, yet. The church leadership is going to want to test your ministry gifts." The pastor saw the expression of horror on Kyle's face, so quickly added, "Nothing like those finals you just took. We're going to want to see you minister within the framework of our church for a time. That lets the people in the church get to know you better—a very good thing as you begin building your support team. And it lets us see your ability to stick to a ministry. Mission work is not just 'a piece of cake!' It places demands on you that you cannot even imagine at this time. But I am confident that all the pieces will come together in their proper place and in the appropriate time. But there are several basic considerations that will provide a solid foundation to the specific ministry and location."

The pastor directed Kyle's attention to the next point on the page. He had led this seminar so many times that he didn't need his notes. "One basic thought is found in Ephesians 2:10. 'We are His most finely crafted work of art, created in Christ Jesus to walk in those good deeds that He beforehand determined for us to go.' We are His highest creation! Now, don't let me get started on that! I am so fascinated by the new discoveries being made in (true) science about the creativity that went into the making of the human body. The Genome Project alone was absolutely mind-boggling. Do you realize...."

Kyle cleared his throat. "Um, Pastor Carl, I think you're getting started."

"Yes, I guess I am," the pastor chuckled. "Okay. The point at this time is especially phenomenal: Before time began—actually, in that God lives outside the dimensions of time and space, it is now—God knows the needs of this present hour. Kyle, in your physics class did they get into the area of nano-technology?"

"No, just the basic stuff."

"Kyle, this is the 'basic stuff' of your generation.

With the accuracy of measurement to the nano-second, there are those theorists who are moving beyond Einstein's determination that the speed of light is constant. In fact, they believe they have observed the same object be in two places at the same time! It is absolutely unbeliev—."

"Pastor Carl—," Kyle interrupted. The pastor had a reputation for going off on current scientific discoveries, although he usually found his way back to the subject at hand, but only after some time of excited deliberation.

"Okay! Okay! Back to the notes. But, Kyle, we really do need to keep abreast of developments in true science. More and more of today's discoveries are pointing to a creative God who—."

"Pastor Carl!" Kyle couldn't keep himself from laughing at the pastor's determination to follow that rabbit trail.

"Yes, yes. Of course. Where were we? God has you in mind, Kyle, to meet those needs. And He, through the years of your life, has been building into you— through your education and experiences—all that will be necessary for you to find success in what He has planned for you to do."

"I can see how that's a basic concept to help me when I get out there. Troubles come and troubles go. Like Paul said, 'I might be knocked down, but never knocked out.'[8] God will not bring to me more than I can handle. I think I've learned that through my experiences these past four years in college."

"Good," the pastor said. "The Bible is filled with such a fabulous variety of figurative language. I love it! Another thought is how our opportunity is expressed in II Corinthians 5:20. We are ambassadors of Christ."

8 Read II Corinthians 4:8-9

"Pastor Carl, did you know that my uncle is a United States ambassador? He lives overseas most of the time. When they're home, my cousins have told me some pretty wild stories. My uncle says he has had some extremely tough assignments representing our government to the leadership of his host country—particularly some of our foreign policy actions."

"You obviously understand this concept quite clearly then. The only difference between your uncle's situation and ours is this: In this world there are about a couple hundred governments trying to understand or control each other. In spiritual terms there are only two governments, or kingdoms: The Kingdom of Light and the kingdom of darkness. And we have the high honor of representing the principles and policies of God's Kingdom to all of those who are ensnared in satan's kingdom. What a privilege!

"Then, of course, Matthew 5:13-16 brings this concept of opportunity into very basic terms of another sort. We are salt and light—salt to make them thirsty for the Living Water, and light to direct them to the True Light, Jesus, our Savior.

"There is one more perspective to this great opportunity God has given us to participate in His divine will. This one should cause us to take serious consideration. Paul was writing to the Church in Corinth, telling of his commitment to all men. 'To the Jew, I became like Jews. To those under the Law, I put myself under the Law.' This was so evident on his last trip to Jerusalem. Remember?"

"Yes," Kyle said. "I think I know where you are going on this point."

"He had hurried to get there for the Feast of Pentecost. He brought a huge offering for the poor Christians. Then," and here Pastor Carl began reading the Scripture: "some of the elders came to him: 'Paul, you know, there is a belief that you teach the Jews living among the Gentiles that they don't need to obey the laws of Moses, nor the customs of the patriarchs. The Jews who are here are going to find out that you are here. So, do this: We have four men here under a vow. Suppose you join them and be purified with them, pay their expenses so that they may have their hair cut short, and then everyone will know there is no truth in the stories about you, but that you yourself observe the Law.'9 I can just see Paul shaking his head in unbelief. 'I thought we got that issue settled back in Chapter 15 of Acts. I mean, right after our first missionary journey,' I can hear him groan. 'Okay, if it might help to win the Jews to Christ, I will do it.'

Kyle wondered at the 'Acts 15' reference. *Acts hadn't been written yet.* Then he realized Pastor Carl was doing his "adding his 'supposings' to the Scripture" thing. *I guess it is okay to do that,* Kyle mused. *I just want to make sure I don't ever "change" the Word of God.*

"'Further,' Pastor Carl continued, quoting Paul, "'When I am with the heathen who are without the law, I agree with them as much as I can, except I have to do what is right by the Law of Christ. To the weak, I became weak, that I might win the overscrupulous.' Now, here is the clincher of this lesson, I believe. Paul concludes, 'I *have been made* all things to all men so that by all means I might win some to Christ.'10 There are at least three major lessons in that conclusion."

With a squeak from his chair, the pastor arose and paced the floor, grabbing a long finger as he counted. "First, Paul was a realist. He acknowledged that only 'some' would be won to Christ. We, too, have to accept

9 Read Acts 21:21-24 10 Read I Corinthians 9:19-22

that fact that broad is the way to destruction, while narrow is the gate to eternal life.[11]

Kyle's eyes followed Pastor Carl as he paced in a large oval around his office. Then he looked to the carpet to see if there was a worn pattern where he paced.

"What are you looking at, Kyle?" Pastor Carl stopped at a shelf and realigned several books.

"I was just wondering if you did this pacing very often." Kyle was a bit embarrassed at his causing this interruption.

"Only when I am wanting to make a strong point. Now, where was I?" He again grabbed a second finger, and continued. "Secondly, I don't know what the 'all means' were that were available to Paul in his day. But, by comparison, today we have multiplied 'means' of sharing the Good News. And because of that multiplicity, you and your support team, as you begin praying, are going to need to hear very clearly the arena of service He has prepared for you—there are so many.

"Let me illustrate. I think this is one of the most creative 'all means' I have ever heard of."

"Of which I have heard," Kyle corrected. He had become so comfortable with the pastor that he decided to correct his English, as he was used to doing with his friends. But after he blurted it out, he wasn't sure how the pastor would react.

Pastor Carl stopped pacing a moment and glanced back at Kyle. "You certainly are a stickler on correct grammar!"

"Sorry," Kyle said. "It's a habit of mine."

"A good one," the pastor said, and continued. "Of which I have heard," he repeated Kyle's words with a smile. "Anyway, a couple who owned a beauty shop—one of those places where they do the fancy manicures

11 Read Matthew 7:13-14

and pedicures—went on vacation to Amsterdam, in Holland. They went to visit a Christian Youth Hostel which was located in an older business district. As they walked down the street, to their amazement, sitting in the store windows where half-clad women, waiting to be chosen for sexual pleasure. Their hearts were broken with compassion for these women. And they learned anew how desperately wicked the enemy is and how low a woman will fall to support a habit or a family.

"They went home. But they could not get those images out of their minds. 'God, how can we be used to help those women,' they prayed. He answered. They turned their business in the States over to others. They took the 'tools of their trade' with them. They made appointments with these women, one at a time. And paid the going rate for their time! While they were fixing the women's nails, they told them of the love God had for them. Those who trusted in Christ were then brought into a home where they learned a different trade. That's right: manicurist! We can never limit the creative genius of God in the 'all means' He might have for us to use in sharing His love to lost humanity."

Kyle was amazed by that story. *All means*, he noted.

"Thirdly...." Pastor Carl grabbed three of his large fingers with his whole left hand and shook them for emphasis. "Thirdly," he repeated, "think of those first four words I so strongly emphasized. *'I have been made...'* suggests to me that all that Paul became was not fun and games: Three times ship-wrecked; beaten with rods three times; whipped the regulation thirty-nine lashes five times (Did you know that some people died from just one of those beatings?); stoned, and left for dead, once. But there's more! You can read the whole list in II Corinthians 11."

Kyle was shaking his head in sad disbelief.

"Here is my point, Kyle. Mission life is not all a bowl of cherries. You are going to face some tough times and hard decisions. But, as with Paul, I am sure the time will come when you will say with him, 'This light affliction, so temporary, is achieving for us a solid, permanent and glorious reward, beyond all proportions by comparison.'[12]

The pastor returned to his seat and rolled the chair up to his desk. "Kyle, you have made it very easy for me to share with you. I see a lot of me in you, when I was younger. But maybe you have had enough to 'digest' for one day. Why don't we set another time to continue?"

"Yes, my brain is getting quite full. Let me download all this onto a memory disc," Kyle quipped. Then I'll be ready for some more. Really, I like to summarize lessons. I'll bring my notes with me next time. Maybe I'll even have some new questions."

"How about next week, Tuesday, about this same time?"

"Great."

"Why don't we say a prayer before we go?"

Kyle led the prayer. "Father, thank You for your love. Thank You for Pastor Carl. Thank You for the wisdom You have given him from Your Word. And for making it so practical. Give me Your wisdom in all the decisions as I prepare for what I believe is Your plan for my life. But Lord, even as I say that, I have to admit it is a bit scary! Give me Your peace. Thank You, Jesus. Amen."

THE NEXT TUESDAY: MISSIONS PASTOR'S OFFICE

The secretary noticed the worry in Kyle's face, and clearly read the look on the face of the young lady who

12 Read II Corinthians 4:17

was with him. She obviously did not want to be there. But the secretary smiled pleasantly at the woman anyway. It was not returned. The secretary wished she had had the time to give Pastor Carl advanced warning, but it was too late. The couple was already entering the pastor's office.

"Pastor Carl, I want you to meet Melanie, a friend of mine."

"Well, hello, Kyle," the pastor said, looking up with surprise. "It is a pleasure to meet you, Melanie." He held out a hand over the enormous stack of papers threatening to spill off of his desk.

Melanie took it weakly and shook.

"Is this one of your questions, Kyle?" Pastor Carl said innocently, flashing Melanie a glance, then looking back to Kyle.

Kyle shifted from foot to foot, unable to look at Melanie directly. "Well, she's just a...."

"What are you two talking about?" Melanie said, staring at Kyle.

"Mel, I told Pastor Carl that when I came back I might bring some questions with me. He was asking me if you are one of them. You know, we've talked about our relationship and the seriousness I feel about being a missionary. I didn't realize it would be the first topic up today. But we did say that we wanted Pastor Carl's counsel."

"No, *we* didn't," she said.

"Excuse me," the pastor said, realizing now that something wasn't right. "Let me back up. You deserve an apology, Melanie. I did not mean to offend you by suggesting that you are a 'problem'. Please forgive me. There is nothing more beautiful than to see fine Christian young people developing a relationship with God at the center of their decisions."

"Thank you, Pastor Carl," Melanie said, her shoulders relaxing a bit. "Yes, we've known each other for years. It's just been this last year that, well—you know—things have gotten a bit more serious. And then Kyle...." Her voice caught in her throat. Slowly, quietly, trying to control her emotions, she continued. "Kyle comes up with this crazy idea, 'I think God wants me to be a missionary!'" Sarcasm edged her words. She paused, sorry she had used that tone of voice. She continued, "I cried for hours! Oh, why...?" More tears flowed down her cheeks and were daubed with her lace handkerchief.

"I guess I don't have to ask you where you stand on this issue," Pastor Carl said soberly, giving her a gentle smile, with one brow raised. "But you came with him today. That would suggest that you are open to consider that this might be the will of God." He was hoping for a way to rescue the direction this conversation had taken. But that was not to be!

"Not really!" was her quick retort. Now her voice was clearly set to make her point—her reason for coming today. "My ambition might be a bit old-fashioned, but I had the idea of settling down in the suburbs, having children, my husband working a *real* job, coming home and playing with the kids and teaching them to ride a bike and build model airplanes and...."

Tears spilled from her eyes again and she held her face in her hands. "I can't believe this is happening to me," she whimpered.

The pastor came around the desk, handing her a box of tissues. She took a few moments of awkward silence to blow her nose and dry her eyes. When she was composed, she looked up red-eyed at the pastor.

There was a more gentle tone in Pastor Carl's voice now. "Melanie, that idea is anything but old-fashioned; it is certainly a very current 'American dream.' Kyle, do you want to talk?"

Kyle sighed heavily. "I think you can see the direction that some of Mel and my most recent dates have taken. We weren't really ready for marriage yet, but we did think, 'Childhood sweethearts marry and live happily ever after.' Then, on your recommendation we went to see that video, *'Beyond the Sun.'*[13] Remember when you announced that in church? And then, Miles Dupree shared about his work in Kenya. Since then I haven't been able to get out of my head a passion for the lost. And the belief that God wants me to be a missionary."

"So," Pastor Carl said, "Where do we go from here?"

"Tell Kyle he can witness to internationals who are living right here in Middletown!" Melanie said, the pitch of her voice high and excited again.

Pastor Carl's voice remained calm and even. "You are right, Melanie. There are many different groups of internationals living here in Middletown. And that is a step we require in our preparation of missionaries. The saying, 'If you aren't going to do it here, you certainly won't do it there' is only too true. There are actually thousands of internationals living in every neighborhood."

Melanie's voice was cold. "That's not what I meant."

"I know, Melanie, I know you must be hurting to the core. Your dreams seem to be shattering before your eyes. You obviously still have strong feelings for Kyle or you would not be here. Are you at least a little bit open to the possibility that God still means for you to be together, but that He has a much more daring and adventurous life for you?"

13 *Beyond The Sun*, VHS, available through Open Doors w/Brother Andrew.

Her answer was definite. "No!"

"Melanie?" Kyle's tone had lost the confidence that Pastor Carl heard the week before. His voice wavered.

For the first time Melanie turned to face Kyle full-on. "I'm sorry, Kyle. It just won't work!" Pain filled her long-lashed hazel eyes that once looked on Kyle with adoration. When she looked away, his heart felt desolate. She got up to leave. With one more look at Kyle, she rushed to the door, slamming it on her way out.

"Pastor Carl?" Kyle said weakly.

"I'm sorry, Kyle. You had better let her go for now. No! Go with her. We can meet again another time. Go!"

ANOTHER TUESDAY: PASTOR CARL'S OFFICE

"Pastor Carl, it was the hardest thing I've ever done. We've decided to not see each other anymore. She just can't get past her dream—even if it means sharing that dream with someone else. I can't believe it. For a while I was even considering denying this passion that God has given me. But since we made the decision of breaking up, the desire to do His will has grown even stronger."

"Kyle, are you sure you want to talk about this so soon? It could be painful for you."

"Yes, go ahead. It might help."

"Human sexuality (and that encompasses a lot more than sex) is a mysterious, yet wonderful part of our personality—our being. Paul tried to deal with it in his day and culture. 'I wish you could be like me,' he said. He was single, maybe divorced, or at least separated from his wife. Scholars think he had to have been married to be a member of the Sanhedrin. Anyway, as he is now a missionary, he is single. Once, when he was defending his apostleship, he said, 'Do they deny me the right to take a Christian wife with me on my journeys as do the other apostles and the Lord's brother and Peter?'[14] So, I'm sure he had his struggles with his singleness. But in the distressful times in which he lived, he was making this recommendation: 'If you are married, stay married. Realize that you have the concerns of this world. But, if you're single, don't try to be married, for you are free to concern yourself wholeheartedly with the affairs of the Lord.'[15]

"We can't even comprehend the distress of that day. Christians were being fed to the lions in the arenas or becoming torches to light the night for Nero's parties of debauchery. Young women were being kidnapped as sex slaves. One did not expect to live happily ever after."

"I never thought about things that that, that these issues would be in Scripture," Kyle said, leaning forward with interest.

The pastor continued. "In speaking from his own experience, Paul wrote some pretty clear words to the Christians at Thessalonica. 'God's plan for your life is to make you holy, and that entails first of all a clean break with sexual immorality. Every one of you should learn to control his body, keeping it pure and treating it with respect, and never regarding it as an instrument of self-gratification, as do the pagans with no knowledge of God. You cannot break this rule without in some way cheating your fellow men. And you must remember that God will punish all who do offend in this matter, as we have warned you how we have seen this work out in our own experience of life. The calling of God is not to impurity but to the most thorough purity, and anyone who makes light of the matter is not making light of a man's ruling but of God's command. It is not for noth-

14 Read I Corinthians 9:5   15 Read I Corinthians 7

ing that the Spirit God gives is called the Holy Spirit.'"[16]

The pastor looked at Kyle. "So what does all of this have to do with us today?" he asked him.

"Well, I must admit, this is an area of my life that I've struggled in."

The pastor raised a brow again.

"No, that's not what I meant!" Kyle said. "Melanie and I have behaved ourselves. Early on, we made a strong commitment to keep our relationship pure. But, personally—"

This was an awkward subject for Kyle. Pastor Carl, sensing Kyle's uneasiness, continued his previous line of thought.

"I think this issue can be best illustrated by this story: A number of years ago I walked through this with a young man we will call Seth. Handsome, virile, every bit as interested in love, marriage, companionship, as any man in his twenties. But as he was preparing to go to the mission field, he realized that relationships and a potential wife could be very distracting from language and culture learning—just the work of getting established in a second culture would be difficult.

"We looked at the words of Jesus. He had been talking about marriage and divorce and fornication and adultery. His disciples came to Him: 'If that is a man's position with his wife, it is not worth getting married, they exclaimed.'

"'It is not everybody who can live up to this,' replied Jesus, '—only those who have a special gift. For some are eunuchs by birth defect. Some have been made that way by men and some have made themselves so for the sake of the Kingdom of Heaven. Let the man who can accept what I have said, accept it.'[17]

"Through much prayer and fasting, Seth came to

16 Read I Thessalonians 4:3-7   17 Read Matthew 19:10-12

the decision to make a vow of celibacy for his first two-year commitment on the field. Sure enough, there were the girls! But he was protected. He had vowed to God. Therefore, he knew that none of these ladies warranted a relationship beyond that of a sister in the Lord.

"He came home after two years. He admitted how freeing that vow was. Again, after another season of fasting and prayer, he made the vow for the next two years. During this time on the field, a single lady missionary even had the forwardness to say that God had told her that they should marry. But Seth was protected by the vow he had made."

"Wow," Kyle muttered, thinking about Melanie.

"Well, two years later he is home again. Though there was no one in his mind, he sensed that God did not want him to make the vow a third time. Back on the field, while he was away, God had brought the woman who was to be his wife to the church where he was working. When he returned to the field, there she was! The rest is history! Together they are now serving the Lord in a fabulous ministry."

"That's a great story."

"This lesson is as valid for a woman as it is for a man. Kyle, I hope this gives you some Scriptural perspective to help you sort through your situation with Melanie."

Kyle eyed the folder that had been placed again on the pastor's desk. "I don't believe all of that was in your one page of notes, was it?" he asked, as he settled himself comfortably in his chair.

"No. But it is sure a very basic area that needs serious consideration by both men and women. Do you feel like getting back to those notes? Or, should we put this off until another time?"

"No, I'd like to go on."

"Good. By the way, were you able to summarize the thoughts from that first day?"

"No, sorry. I do have some notes I took, but the whole issue with Melanie blew up in our faces. Nothing else seemed to matter at the time."

"I understand. Possibly we can summarize these thoughts together. But let's move forward. Scripture tells us to not despise the days of small things. They were talking about the smaller foundation of the second temple. Though it would be smaller than Solomon's temple, it would be the one in which Jesus walked. In a broader sense, we can be assured that no matter how small the beginnings of what we set out to do may be, if we are following His 'blueprints,' it will result in exactly what He desires.[18]

"Or, look at it from another perspective. This story is full of human emotion. In Chapter 12 of Jeremiah, he has decided to have a 'discussion' with God about His judgments. He starts out by saying: 'Righteous art Thou, O Lord, when I plead with You.' Twenty-first Century translation might be: 'I'm sure, O Lord, that You will be very fair with me as I reason my case with You. What I want to talk with You about are Your judgments. I'm not so sure about the fairness of them!' For the next verse and a half, he talks about how the wicked are prospering and God is with them."

The pastor quickly flipped through the pages of his well-worn Bible to the passage.

"Verse 3: Poor me!

"Verse 4: He even brings in the plants and animals that are being consumed because God is not caring for them.

"Verse 5, then, God is ready to answer (not quite

King James English): 'Jerry! If you are going to belly-ache when I have you up against the footmen, what in the world is going to happen when you have to contend with the horsemen?'"[19]

The pastor noted that Kyle was not quick to be amused, and so added, "Well, not quite. Lesson for to-day: Missions is war! God may initially have you doing 'footman' battles, but He assures us that 'horsemen' battles lie ahead. As we become more involved in the battle for lost souls, we can be sure of only one thing: It will be a more heated battle. I realized that I had not yet said anything about spiritual warfare. I hope that state-ment was not too much of a bombshell."

"No, Pastor Carl. I've tasted some of the warfare already. Not only losing Melanie. But my friends are all chiding me for letting her go. It's tough! My mother doesn't know yet. She already had us married—in her mind. I don't know what's going to happen when she finds out."

"My prayer for you, Kyle, is that God's Holy Spirit will be your comfort and source of strength as you face each situation. This whole theme of spiritual warfare will be another part of your training. I can refer you to a book now, though. It's very basic, but thorough, on the foundations of spiritual warfare. It is titled, *PREPARE FOR BATTLE: Basic Training in Spiritual Warfare.*[20]

"But let's look at this fabulous challenge that is be-fore you from another perspective, can we?"

Kyle nodded agreement as he inched his chair clos-er to his side of the desk.

Pastor Carl continued, "Jesus was a Master at using everyday examples to illustrate His point. The figurative language of the Bible is wonderfully varied and creative. It has us referred to as everything from 'sheep of His

19 Read Jeremiah 12:1-5   20 *Prepare For Battle*, Neal Pirolo, ERI, 1997.

pasture' to 'soldiers of the Cross' to being 'the Body of Christ' to being 'the children of God' to being the 'lively stones' in the building of God."

Kyle nodded. "Yes, my personal study of the Bible as literature clearly establishes it as the finest collections of literary genius this world has known."

The pastor looked at the many books lining the shelves. "That it is; that it is," he said. "But unless we keep our figures of speech separated we can have Noah's ark floating on the sea of God's forgetfulness!"

Kyle's face remained stoic at the punchline. The pastor straightened at Kyle's seriousness. He, too, had been that way when he was Kyle's age.

He continued, "What I am saying is this. There are two extremely vital analogies Jesus uses to communicate two totally different aspects of our Christian life. He did not confuse them. But a lot of people do. They are the illustrations of the 'cross' and the 'yoke'. The cross is an instrument of death. There is absolutely nothing you do on a cross but die! It was one of the cruelest forms of capital punishment yet devised. Jesus was continually telling His disciples (and us) to take up our cross and follow Him.[21] Not to be literally nailed to a cross, as they do in some cultures. But to daily pick up our cross (figuratively, in our minds and hearts), carry it along the Via de la Rosa and up to Calvary. And there, to reckon (put to His account) the penalty of our sins. Sometimes that cross gets too heavy for us to bear alone. Thus, as with Jesus, we may need to find our 'Simon of Cyrene' to help us struggle up the hill to lay our burden of sin down at the foot of the cross. It is beautiful picture language.

"But (and follow me closely here, Kyle), early on Sunday morning—the first day of the week—before the

21 Read Matthew 16:24

break of dawn, He arose triumphantly over sin and death and hell and the grave! He stretched and said, 'Hmm, I wonder where the gardener is? There you are. Please, let Me borrow your shovel.' Jesus trudges up the hill. Digs the cross out of the ground. Throws it over His shoulder and says, 'I've got forty more days to work the works of the One who sent Me. Oh, this cross is so heavy, but it is just My cross to bear!'"

Kyle's eyes had grown wide.

Before Kyle could speak his objection, Pastor Carl continued. "Does that sound sacrilegious, Kyle? Of course He didn't do or say that. He said to Mary, 'Tell the disciples (and Peter) that I am going ahead to Galilee. I'll meet them there.'[22] Thus, neither should we ever go back to that hill to retrieve the guilt of the sins for which we have received forgiveness. 'Whom He has set free, is free indeed!'[23]

"And here is where we sometimes mix our metaphors. We find ourselves in some very difficult work for the Lord—it is heavy alright—but it is wrong to then say, 'Well, I guess this is just my cross to bear!'"

Kyle was finally nodding in understanding.

"On the other hand, there is a beautiful lesson to learn as Jesus uses another analogy to describe our work for the Kingdom. Maybe He was standing near a field which was being plowed by a team of oxen. Or, perhaps He was outside a craftsman's shop as he was fitting the yoke to a farmer's oxen. Listen: 'Come unto Me, all you who labor and are heavy laden, and I will give you rest. Take My yoke upon you, and learn of Me; for I am meek and lowly in heart; and you will find rest for your souls. For My yoke is easy, and My burden is light.'[24]

"Kyle, did you hear those strong, comforting words?

22 Read Matthew 27:1-28, 10; John 19:1-20:18   23 Read John 8:36
24 Read Matthew 11:28-30

"Yes, this is really something." He realized Pastor Carl's understanding of Scripture had come from years of study and experience.

Pastor Carl continued, appreciating Kyle's intent to learn. "Let's keep these two vital metaphors forever separate: The cross is an instrument of death; the yoke is an instrument of labor. There are many people in the fields working so hard for the Lord. They are under the heavy weights of burdens that Christ never put on them, nor does He want them to be put under. Also, because they are so burdened down, their testimony does not exalt the King of Kings. He is calling them: 'Come to Me. You've got a wrong perspective on the work I have called you to do. You who are so heavy laden with the cares of ministry needs that are not yours, you who act almost like you need to carry the burden of the sins of the world—almost as if their salvation depended on you—you, come to Me. You have the wrong yoke on your shoulders. Put My yoke on. Learn from Me.'"

"Yes," Kyle said firmly. "Yes."

"To understand the full beauty of this metaphor, we need to know something about how they made yokes of labor in those days. They didn't stamp them out from some pre-formed mold. They individually crafted them to fit the shoulders of the specific ox.

"And in this analogy Jesus goes a step further. It is a double yoke that He is describing. When they teamed up a pair of oxen, they always put a mature ox with one who needed to learn. They crafted those yokes so the mature ox was doing the pulling and the other one was doing the learning. Are you catching this lesson, Kyle?"

"Yes. Yes! Jesus said He would never leave us nor forsake us.[25] He is in that yoke of labor with us. He is certainly the mature One; He is doing the pulling. And

25 Read Matthew 28:20b

we are learning His way of ministry."

"That is correct. So when we have His yoke of labor on our shoulders (not a cross; that analogy is for another aspect of our Christian walk), we agree with Him when He says, 'My yoke is easy and My burden is light.'

"Now, might you find yourself in some 'get down and get dirty' work on the mission field? Certainly! It may fully challenge your skills and endurance. But no matter how difficult or impossible it may seem to others, if it is His assignment for you—if it is His yoke of labor—to you it will seem easy and light. Will your physical, emotional, mental, and spiritual stamina be stretched to the limit? Possibly. Yes, no doubt! But deep down in your spirit you will know it is right."

The pastor took a moment to think, then looked up to Kyle. "On the other hand—."

"There you go again, with that 'other hand' business!"

"There is always the 'other hand.' Yokes that are not of His making are sometimes placed on our shoulders—either by us, our supervisor, the nationals or the expectation of the people back home. Oh, my! How those yokes can chafe."

Kyle watched as the pastor reached up and rubbed his neck. "Be very careful, Kyle. When you lie down at night and feel the stinging on your neck and the bruises on your collar bone, do a little evaluating. Am I wearing His yoke of labor or is this one of my own making? Best not to ever put it on, but once you discover it is not of His making, do everything you can to get it off."

"It sounds like the voice of experience," Kyle said cautiously. "Pastor Carl, are you talking about yourself?"

"Unfortunately, yes." He looked at the papers and

files all around him and sighed. "Oh, my—the yokes I have worn that I was never meant to wear! And I usually did it voluntarily!

"When we were in Spain, I took on a second yoke. Yes, I tried to wear two yokes at the same time. I was young. I was zealous. I could do it—not a problem! You should see the picture of that yoke chaffing. Remind me, I'll show it to you sometime, if you like."

"I can feel those scars on your 'emotional' neck. Do they serve as a reminder to be more careful in determining His yokes of labor?"

The pastor sighed again. "I would like to say yes. But I still sometimes find myself with a burden I was not meant to carry. And it really looks ridiculous to be wearing two yokes at the same time!"

At that thought Kyle finally cracked a smile.

"I have just one more concept to share," the pastor said. "Then I think we will have had enough for today. You have heard me use a phrase several times in our discussions. I repeat it often. I believe with all my heart that this is one of the most basic, practical lessons to help you in all of your efforts as a missionary—during your preparation, while you are on the field, and when you return home. It is an attitude that will carry you through when other workers are becoming discouraged. It will sustain you when—."

"Come on, Pastor Carl! What is it?"

The pastor smiled, pleased at Kyle's anticipation.

"It is this attitude: It is a *privilege* to be about our Father's business! I tell you, so many people have a warped attitude about missions and missionaries. It seems they are put into a separate category; they are put into a group destined for poverty-stricken misery, to be pitied! You hear it in subtle tones; you hear it in

blatant lies. You hear it in churches. It is even per-
petuated in mission agency circles.

"Let me tell you what happened to my family many
years ago, just before we went to Spain. We had made a
short one-year commitment to the mission field. My
wife's father was pastoring a church at the time. Our
kids were their only grandchildren, so on a Sunday just
before leaving, we went to visit and bid one more farewell.

"Well, the assistant pastor spotted us in the congregation. He did not know us, except that we were the
children of his boss. He didn't really know anything
about our circumstances. He called us up to the platform. There we stood, faces smiling, one son teasing the
other, all of us unsure of what was going to happen
next. But he grabbed the microphone off the pulpit and
began pacing back and forth across the stage. He began
painting this awful story about 'Look at this poor missionary family. They have given up everything to serve
the Lord in some foreign land.' Vibrato edged his plain-
tive voice. It got worse. At one point, he pulled out his
handkerchief to daub at a fake tear!"

"Unbelievable," Kyle said.

"I wanted so badly to take that mike from his hand
and shout, 'It is a *privilege!*' I refrained, however. It
would have just embarrassed everyone. But you see
what I mean? It is slowly changing, but the Church, by
and large, still has that attitude toward missionaries.
There are many reasons why that could be, but that's
another subject.

"Let's conclude with a beautiful Bible story that
should solidify the correct attitude in our hearts. It is a
familiar story. The Children of Israel are in captivity—
again! A young lady, whose parents may have been

killed or died in the trek from Jerusalem to Shushan, is being raised by her cousin, Mordecai. Well, in the third year of his reign, King Ahasuerus threw a big party. I mean, BIG! It went on for 180 days before all of his nobles and princes arrived. He then threw a great feast, which lasted seven more days.

On that last day when they were mostly drunk, he called for his wife, Vashti, to come in and show off her beauty to his nobles. She refused! She was banished. The king got lonely. His counselors suggested a Miss Universe contest. Esther won. Some time went by. Haman came up with his evil plot to rid the kingdom of all Jews. Cousin Mort heard about the plan. He sent a message to Esther to go into the king and tell him what's up. She sent a message back to Mordecai: 'Everybody knows that if anyone goes into the king's court without his extending his golden scepter, they die! And he has not called for me in over thirty days.'

"Oh, how I like what Cousin Mort answered her: 'Esther, don't think that just because you are the queen that you will escape this evil plot. But if you don't tell him, I assure you that salvation will arise from another place. Esther, God will save His people.' Esther—Kyle— He is a sovereign God that we serve."

"I know what happened next. He asked her a question."

"Yes, he asked her a question that has reverberated down through the corridors of time. If you listen carefully, you will hear it today: 'Esther, who knows but that for such an hour as this, you have been called to the kingdom?'"[28]

The pastor looked deep into Kyle's eyes. "What a beautiful story of God's sovereign plan being fulfilled through His people. And I believe with all of my heart

28 Read the Book of Esther

that each of us—you, me, even Melanie—has been called to the Kingdom of God for an hour such as today. My prayer for you is that as you continue in your preparation for cross-cultural ministry, God will more and more strongly build into the fabric of your being the attitude, 'It is a privilege to be about our Father's business.' Amen."

Kyle sat in silence a moment, digesting all that had been said. The pastor waited patiently for a response. When a response was not forthcoming, the pastor spoke first.

"I am exhausted! I get so passionate about that attitude; it feels like I have just preached a sermon!"

"Maybe you just did." Kyle said. "You've shared so much. There is so much to absorb, so much to make real and practical in my life. Could we get together again to summarize these lessons? And when do I get started in some level of ministry? I want to move forward in this commitment. By the way, you've never asked me how my grades came out."

"I apologize. How unthoughtful of me. Kyle, how did you do on those finals?"

"I don't know. The computers went down a couple of weeks ago. The grades of the whole college are lost somewhere in cyberspace! But, thanks for asking."

Pastor Carl's eyes narrowed as he grinned. "Why, you...!" He chuckled. "But doesn't that cause you some concern?"

"No. Why should it? God is sovereign. It will all work out!"

SUMMARY OF ISSUES

Kyle probably had the most difficult time in making his commitment. The challenges he faced went far beyond the one page of notes that his pastor started with. May this review of the challenges in missions assure you that you have considered the seriousness, yet privilege of becoming a missionary.

- It is good—it is vital—that a church has a clear policy leading to ministry involvement.
- Missionaries on the field benefit greatly by an occasional visit from home.
- The Perspective on the World Christian Movement is one of the finest foundations to the understanding of missions.
- There is tremendous security when our considerations have their foundation in Scripture.
- A sovereign God is the starting point of all missions endeavor.
- We must see the events of our daily living tying into God's sovereignty. "God is sovereign in my life today," has to be a reality.
- We must clearly separate our "surmisings" about the stories in the Bible with what is actually written so that we never change the meaning of God's Word.
- God chose us to actively participate in His wild and sovereign will.
- There are tremendous needs in our sin-sick world.
- The church at large is not doing much to reach out to all the peoples of the world.
- God has, before time began, determined the good deeds He wants us to walk in.
- We have the high calling to be ambassadors for Christ, representing Him to those ensnared in the kingdom of darkness.
- We are salt and light to the nations.

- Paul allowed himself to be made all things to all men so that by all means he might win some to Christ. This should be our model.
- The "all things" that we may suffer will be comparatively light next to the eternal weight of His glorious reward.
- Ministering to internationals who live among us is a great ministry in itself. But it is also very good preparation for distant cross-cultural outreach ministry.
- Interpersonal relationships—including those dealing with our sexuality (more than sex) and singleness on the field—are the most critical issue in missions today.
- We should not look down on what looks like meager activity. It is probably laying a foundation for the greater challenges God has for us. "Foot-man" battles assure us that "horseman" battles are ahead.
- The cross is an instrument of death; the yoke is an instrument of labor. Both are vital in the life of a Christian. But they must remain separate in our understanding. The cross deals with us recognizing ourselves dead to self and alive unto God. The yoke deals with our work for the Lord. When it is a yoke of His choosing, no matter how challenging and difficult the work may be, it will seem to us to be easy and light.
- It is a privilege to be about our Father's business. Like Esther, we have been called to the Kingdom for an hour such as this.

Suggestion: You might want to read back through the chapter and find the context to which each of these summary statements refers. Some times summary statements seem so trite. They are true, of course. But we can too easily pass over them lightly. I would encourage you to deliberately take the time with each one to see if it is true in your life—if you are maturing in this area. You might even find value in reviewing these summary statements with one or more of your friends who have committed to be a part of your support team.

PERSONAL NOTES:

5

COUNTING THE COST

The phone rang four times before Kyle picked it up. Pastor Carl tapped the end of his pencil against his desk as we waited, causing a cascade of papers to fall to the floor.

"Hello?"

"Hello! Kyle? Pastor Carl here. Hey, how are you doing?" There was a slight grunt in his voice as he was trying to pick up those papers.

"Better. Melanie had a date with one of my friends. He said she acted so cool and distant that he had to remind himself that she was really there. I think she's really hurting. I'm praying for her, but I think it's over between us."

"That sounds like a pretty conclusive decision. Only God will change her heart, if it is His will to do so. But I asked how *you* are doing?"

"It's hard—really hard." There was a long pause.

"Are you still there?" Pastor Carl knew that he was, but it gave them both time to think about what to say next.

"She's my best friend," Kyle said, his voice cracking.

There was another long pause. The pastor assumed

it was for Kyle to gain control of his voice and consider the choice he had made.

Kyle repeated the pastor's words. "I know it will have to be God who changes her heart." *Lord, help me believe that too,* Kyle prayed. Another pause. "Me?" his voice brightened, "I think I'm ready to go on."

"I hear a real man talking, Kyle. I have been praying for you—both of you. Listen—remember when I said that I would talk with the some other pastors about hosting a Perspectives course in Middletown? That might happen next year. But in talking with them, I found three pastors who had recently met with three different people in their youth groups who were sensing the same desire as you. Strangely, they each said exactly the same thing you did: *'I think God wants me to be a missionary!'*

"Well, the other pastors and I got together for a breakfast at Denny's. We realized that each of you was dealing with a different issue. I suggested that all eight of us get together and summarize the counsel that came out of each of our individual meetings. And then the four of us put our heads together and came up with some other thoughts we would like to share. Sound like a good idea?"

"I need all the help I can get! I think that would be a great idea. Just to relate with others who are going through the steps to the field would be good. When? Where?"

"Well, the time and place is yet to be determined. Everybody's schedule is so packed. You would think with school finally out, there would be more time! But we can sure fill our days and hours. We definitely want to make sure that all can attend. So I'll let you know."

"Great! You know my schedule, so I'm open."

A SCHEDULED TIME • MIDDLETOWN, USA

There were many introductions as each of the pastors and young people arrived. They were meeting in the conference room just down the hall from Pastor Carl's missions office. Kyle and Pastor Carl were there first. Helen had come with her pastor, Dan Harris.

Jason Thomas sauntered in, followed by Pastor Steve. Jason realized, *I like being first. Oh, that's probably not a good trait!* was his afterthought. But—he's Jason. "Hey, I'm Jason. This is my youth pastor, Pastor Steve," Jason announced to the assembly, while looking at Helen. She had immediately caught his attention.

"Oh, what is your name?" Helen asked, clearly taken back by Jason's charming up-frontness and friendly air.

"Jason Thomas. Just call me, Jason." He smiled wide. He liked the fact that he so easily befuddled girls.

Pastor Jim made his appearance next. "Where's Kevin?" he asked, a bit embarrassed thinking he was the last one to show.

"Who's Kevin?" several chimed in.

"Oh, yes, that's right. You don't even know who I am, do you? My name is Pastor Jim. Kevin is from our church. Oh, there you are, Kevin. I was just going to say some nice things about you."

"I should have waited outside and listened," Kevin said with a wink. "Don't let me stop you."

Pastor Jim chuckled.

"Actually, I was here a while ago," Kevin said, "but I got lost down the wrong corridor. I turned left instead of right at the world map in the foyer. Some custodians were cleaning down that way. They redirected me to this room. Sorry for being a bit late."

"This is wonderful!" Pastor Carl's enthusiasm

couldn't be contained. He had been praying for a break-through in the Middletown churches to lift up their eyes to see that the field is the world. "It looks like everyone is here. So let's get started with prayer. 'Father, what a mighty God you are. And how great that you have brought us together for this evening of sharing. We want to do Your will. Thank you, Jesus.'"

(Each person who had said, "I think God wants me to be a missionary," shared a little bit about themselves and a summary of the counsel that they had received individually. Those summaries, in the Invitation and at the end of each chapter, are for you, the reader, to review.)

"All right. All right!" Pastor Carl was even more excited now that he had heard from each one. "From the sounds of your enthusiastic sharing, you are each still on course to take the next steps to the field. Now, each of us pastors is going to share a couple more thoughts that we have loosely tied together under the heading, 'Counting the Cost.' Pastor Jim, why don't you go first?"

This newly formed group of eight sat comfortably around the conference table. Pastor Jim adjusted his chair so that he could see each one clearly. He appeared calm as he hesitated before the group. Then a smile broke across his face, reflecting the satisfaction in his heart. His deep, penetrating blue eyes looked at each one of the youth, before he shouted out, "Hallelujah! Glory to God!" It was as if a volcano of praise was being released. He continued, "I am thrilled to see the four of you moving forward. And equally excited about a new cooperation that seems to be developing within our churches." He immediately launched into the notes he had written.

"The first issue in counting the cost of cross-cultural ministry is what I call 'the *pew*,' itself. Now, don't get me wrong. I like comfortable pews as much as the next guy. Through the years I have sat on a great variety. And, I am sure, that every building committee spends hours with many sales people listening to the distinctive features of this or that one. I have even seen 'sample pews' loaned to churches so that they could try them out for a few weeks. We want our people comfortable when they come to our church. And, as they sink down into the plush softness of our pew, we've got 'em!"

"Man, does church leadership really think that way?" Jason asked. Being the least familiar with the ways of church life, he found talk of such seemingly simple things as pews fascinating.

"Jason, we're talking about a lot more than just the padded benches people sit on," Pastor Jim said kindly. "The pew is also the refrigerated drinking fountain and the rheostat-controlled chancel lighting and the motor-driven recessed movie screen and the zone-controlled air conditioning and the stained glass windows and the—."

"Okay, I've got the picture. It's the beautiful buildings for the beautiful people that churches are trying to attract."

Helen glanced nervously at Pastor Dan, because their church had all of those nice things—and more! But his wink and wide genuine smile assured her that they had a right attitude toward those "nice" things.

"Yes, and more," Pastor Jim continued. "It is also the activities we provide to keep the people busy, the right relationships with the right people; recognition in the community. A 'city father' or two in the congregation helps. All of the above, and more!"

"Pastor Jim, let me interject, if I may?" asked Pastor

Carl. "I just remembered something."

"Sure, what can you add to this picture?" responded Pastor Jim, always cordial even when he was being interrupted.

"Actually, all of your talk about the pew reminded me of one trip I took to Peru. I think they were the most unique pews I have ever sat on. They were in the village church of the Ticuna Indians. While our Wycliffe Bible translator was in the States, God chose to send a Holy Spirit outpouring on this group of people. The church building had to be lengthened to twice its size. Each family helped by building the additional pews needed.

"Because those believers were using scrap lumber from the saw mill, each pew was built to the dimensions of the wood available. All different sizes and shapes, some pews provided end-to-end teeter-totter action, while others offered a reclining position—flat on your back, if you were not careful!"

Jason, who had been leaning back so that the front legs of his chair were slightly lifted, quickly set the chair back on the floor at the thought of tipping backwards.

"But what was the care of that?" Pastor Carl continued. "The translator was back and had just brought some more of the Word in their language. The pews were for function, only!"[1]

"Well, I wish that was the kind of pew I'm talking about," Pastor Jim continued. "But what I'm trying to say about the American pew is probably best summed up in a book written by J.I. Packer, *Hot Tub Religion*.[2] In the preface he makes this statement: 'There is only one thing left to make the church in America totally hedonistic: Take out the pews and replace them with hot tubs!'

1 If you would like to be challenged by what God did with this people, secure the book, *God's City in the Jungle* by Sanna Barlow.   2 *Hot Tub Religion*, J.I. Packer, Tyndale House, 1987.

"Ouch," cried two of the pastors. "That is a pretty hard estimation," the other defended.

Pastor Jim gave a nod, but continued without further comment. "In warfare terminology—missions is a battle for lost souls, as Kyle alluded to in his summary—we want to replace the word 'pew' with 'fox hole'! Trenches were dug for the regrouping of troops, for receiving further strategy from the Commander-in-Chief, for eating some C rations or for catching a bit of rest. And then they got out of the 'pew' and back onto the battlefield.

"Counting the cost of going to the mission field, then, deals initially with the nature of pews."

Jason was still surprised. *Churches actually try out sample pews before they buy them! You've got to be kidding!* he thought.

"It's interesting," Pastor Jim said, "that one denomination that came into being primarily motivated to be a missions-minded Body, required that all of their buildings be nothing but a Quonset hut. Over the years, they were allowed to put up a brick façade across the front to hide the 'ugliness' of the arch of corrugated steel. And now, that denomination's buildings are as competitively modern as the next. 'Our zeal for missions has proportionately diminished,' one of their leaders recently told me.

"Counting the cost of following in the footsteps of Jesus is not a 21st Century concern only. When He walked this earth, people struggled with the cost."

The other pastors nodded knowingly.

"'When the time had come that He should be received up, He steadfastly set His face to go to Jerusalem', Luke records in Chapter 9. On the way, a certain scribe expressed his desire to follow Jesus. We don't know if he did or not—it doesn't say. But we do have the statement of Jesus: Count the cost! 'Foxes have holes and birds of the air have nests; but the Son of Man has no where to lay His head.'[3]

"Possessions—the things of this world—must also be counted as a part of the cost to following Jesus.

"One day I was presenting this lesson to a group of students preparing for a cross-cultural ministry trip. Just as a point of illustration (I had no idea if this girl had a stereo or not), I looked at Julie and said, 'Julie, when you go home today and look around your room for what the Lord wants you to keep, sell or give away, look closely at your stereo and say, 'Lord, do you really want me to keep this or sell it?'

"She went home. That day, while she was at our meeting, someone had ripped off her stereo!"

"Man, that's cold," Jason said.

Pastor Jim looked at Jason. "God doesn't always speak that dramatically. But for her (and her team members), in that situation, the answer was clear."

Not knowing if she had one or not, Jason said, "Hey, Helen! There goes your DVD player." He chuckled with amusement.

"Jason, your humor is to be commended. But I'm not suggesting that you go with just the clothes on your back. A CD player with some good Christian inspirational music would probably be good to take along. But, having said that, do not plan on taking a whole footlocker full of 'things.'

"Some men—I would mention one, Viv Gregg—have gone to extreme lengths to understand counting the cost of possessions. He had been a part of a large collegiate mission agency. One day as he was walking down a street in Manila, a beggar lady grabbed hold of

3 Read Luke 9:57-58

his leg and wouldn't let go! 'What are you going to do to help us?' she cried out. Though he was able to finally wrest himself free from her physical grip, he could not free his mind from her probing question.

"To make a long story short, to build a strong compassion in his heart for the lost of her kind, he stripped himself of everything but the clothes on his back, walked into the poorest barrio in Manila and lived among the people—for five years! He almost died a couple of times. He could have walked out and gotten the medical treatment he needed. But, he reasoned, they can't do that, so how can I? You can read about his ministry in a book called, *Servants Among the Poor.*[4] It'll challenge you to a perspective not too well thought of in affluent America. But a perspective that might help you in choosing what possessions you will leave behind.

"As I said," Pastor Jim added, looking at Jason once more. "God doesn't always speak that dramatically. But as you begin to assess your possessions, God's peace will guide you. You'll know."

Why does he keep looking at me? Jason wondered, defensively. All he could think about was that his only possession was an old beat-up ten-speed bike. *Possessions mean nothing to me,* he assured himself.

Helen smiled at the thought of God's peace being her guide. She had a deep love of the Lord, and there was no one she trusted more. *But I do have a lot of possessions,* she realized.

"Scripture is almost silent regarding Jesus' possessions. We do surmise that His family was poor. At His circumcision the lowliest of offerings was presented.[5] The gifts of the wise men were probably spent during their two-year stay in Egypt. At His crucifixion, His only

4 *Servants Among the Poor,* Viv Gregg, Servant Partners.   5 Read Luke 2:21-24

concern was for the care of His mother. He didn't say, 'Okay, Matthew, you inherit My library of scrolls' Or, 'Peter, that new speed boat I just bought. You can have it for your recreational time.'" Pastor Jim paused. "That almost sounds sacrilegious."

"Almost?" blurted Kevin. "It is sacrilegious! How can you talk that way?" he said, still not sure that "surmisings" are appropriate when talking about the Bible.

"Hold on, Kevin. Hold on. I can appreciate your concern. That's exactly why I said that. When we think those things about our Lord, it just doesn't sound right. Yet, what have we as affluent Americans stored up for ourselves? Even needing row upon row of 'self-storage' units to keep what we can't store in our homes.

"'Oh, but He was different,' some people would say."

Kevin nodded his head in agreement. Jesus was different. And Kevin wanted everyone to remember that.

Pastor Jim continued. "Then, I guess we're to be different, also. For, it is written, 'As the Father sent Me, so send I you.'[6]

"Let me give another example: A young couple was planning their wedding. Following their marriage and pre-field training, they were going to spend their 'honeymoon' year on a kibbutz in Israel. Enclosed with their wedding invitations was this note: 'Because we are not setting up a home here following our wedding, but rather spending our first year on a kibbutz in Israel, please do not give us any gifts. If you care to help with our airfare, that would be great.'

"Kevin, does that help to give you a broader perspective?"

Kevin nodded in agreement, but knew he would need to take some time to sort this out. His parents didn't need to rent a storage unit. They had two metal

6 Read John 20:21

sheds next to their house. He owned that old Toyota, not because his family couldn't afford a new car for him, but because he liked it. It was like his 'buddy'. He was also remembering the fun his extended family enjoyed on the outings in their cabin cruiser at the lake!

"I'm sorry to end on such a hard note, but I would ask you to take these thoughts into your closet of prayer and let the Lord deal with you. He will no doubt be gentler than I was. We do need to realize that a part of counting the cost of discipleship is the comfort of the pew and our personal material possessions. I believe Pastor Dan asked to follow me. Pastor Dan?"

Everyone took an uneasy shift in their chairs as Pastor Jim closed his folder of notes. All except Jason. He beamed with "pride" that all he owned was an old beat-up ten-speed bike. Then, a pang of conviction reminded him that pride is sin! His countenance dropped. Helen took note of that, wondering what thoughts had just coursed through his brain.

Trying to lighten the mood (and maybe being a bit defensive), Pastor Dan (who, remembering his own office—indeed, the whole church—was full of international memorabilia) admitted, "In a society blinded by materialism, counting the cost of our possessions is a difficult exercise. But we do need to be very careful that we recognize that God deals with us individually.

"I remember my initial shock when a friend of mine testified of God's goodness in helping him find a one million dollar house for just under $600,000. (This was when the average house was about $80,000!) My pulse began to slow down when I realized that he worked with the up-and-outers of Hollywood, where a million dollar house at that time would have been quite average.

"Care must also be given when we consider one

ministry or another. A missionary family that is living in the frozen tundra of Central Siberia would laugh at the idea of needing a boat. On the other hand, Operation Mobilization pulls one of their ships into the 'service station' and has $500,000 worth of maintenance and repair done on it. And, 'Oh, by the way, top off the fuel tanks, would you, please? Yes, we also have the $100,000 for the fuel bill!'

"But, on the other hand, I do have to agree with Pastor Jim. This is a really tough issue. The way most missionaries deal with their possessions is to take them with them. Let me read you a story of one missionary's experience."

Pastor Dan took a mission magazine out of his brief case and opened to a page well-worn from many readings. He cleared his throat and began to read.

"18 BARRELS AND TWO BIG CRATES
by Roger S. Greenaway

"The most embarrassing moment in my missionary career occurred near the beginning, 33 years ago, when our baggage arrived in Colombo, Sri Lanka. Its arrival had been delayed for four months due to a dockworkers' strike that paralyzed the port. When finally the long-awaited baggage came to the door, it gave us mixed emotions.

My wife and I and our infant daughter had arrived on the field in early May. We moved into a house the national church had rented for us, and we purchased everything we needed in Colombo. Our furniture was made by local carpenters. The only imported items we purchased were fans, a small stove, a refrigerator, and a water filter. Besides that we had only the contents of our four suitcases.

We were getting along fine, when word came that our baggage had finally been unloaded from the ship. As soon as it was cleared by customs it was loaded onto five bullock carts and delivered to our home. How well I remember the sight of the bullocks trudging slowly up the road. The combined load consisted of no less than 18 barrels and two big crates.

On the one hand we were excited, for it was like 'Christmas in August,' with bullocks instead of reindeer bringing wonderful things from the North. But on the other hand there was something terribly disturbing about it. We kept saying to ourselves, 'We don't need all of this stuff. Why did we buy it in the first place?'

Our neighbors turned out in force to see what the Americans were getting. As we opened the barrels and crates by the side of the house, our neighbors stared in wonderment. How rich and important this young couple must be to afford five cartloads of marvelous things!

For four months my wife and I had been building relationships and seeking to identify with the community. Our blonde baby daughter provided a natural opener for conversations and a jump start for new relationships. Neighbors could see that we were not altogether different from other young parents trying to raise a child, solve everyday problems, and meet basic needs.

But then, suddenly, we were discovered to be what some probably suspected all along—filthy rich Americans who could fill their home with every conceivable comfort and adornment. A thousand sermons could not undo the damage done that day!"

"Whoa! That's wild," Jason blurted out.

"What a shame," Helen said. "That's terrible."

Kyle more thoughtfully asked, "Do missionaries still do that?"

"Unfortunately, many do. But, wait a minute," Pastor Dan said, not wanting to get bogged down on one issue, no matter how important it may be. "I have strayed from my assigned topics. Let me look at my notes. Yes, following up on the story that Pastor Jim read in Luke 9, Jesus and His disciples took a few more steps and another man shouted, 'Lord, I will follow You, but first let me say "good-bye" to my family.'[7]

"It is amazing how self-sufficient each member of a 'nuclear' family can be, until one decides to go to the mission field. 'You're needed here.' 'What if grandma gets sick?' 'What about our family reunions? You haven't missed a one.' I kid you not; I have even heard some express grave concern about what will happen to the pets. 'Your dog has been your constant companion since you were a child. You aren't going to leave him behind, are you?'

"I'm not saying it is easy. To say good-bye to family when you are off for a weekend at a friend's house—or even a three week ministry trip—is no big deal. But to say good-bye when you are going for a two-year commitment half way around the world is something else. Jason, does that glint in your eyes suggest that you think it will be easy?"

"Maybe," Jason said flippantly. He was glad for the attention, and he was sure that leaving home for two

7 Read Luke 9:61

years would be no big deal. *Just a bunch of three-week trips, back-to-back,* he thought.

"Time will tell. Time will tell," the pastor continued. "I encourage you to remember these words as that time approaches. Some people who have enjoyed a successful short term trip think that a one- or two-year commitment is simply a succession of short term trips put back-to-back. This is not so."

Whoops, Jason thought, *that's what I just said. Maybe I had better listen up. These guys seem to know what they are talking about.*

Kevin was seriously processing everything being said—even Jason's candid remark. To this concept of saying good-bye for two years, he reasoned, *I've lived on campus for four years. But I have come home at least three weekends out of five. This will be very different.*

Kyle's heart ached at the thought of being away from Melanie. He was having a hard time concentrating on anything else. Oh, yes, he could say that it was over, but...was it?

Pastor Dan continued, "Jesus had left home. He was about His Father's business doing some pretty radical things. His half-brothers had convinced their mother that they had better go down to fetch the 'eldest Son' home. When notified that His family was there to talk with Him, He questioned, 'Who is My mother? And who are My brothers?' He answered His own questions: 'Whoever does the will of My Father.'[8]

"Jo Shetler, who left her family for a 20-year commitment to translate the New Testament into the Balangao language, found Jesus' statement to be true: 'And anyone who has forsaken houses, or brothers or sisters, or father or mother or children, or lands for My sake, shall receive a hundredfold in this present time,

8 Read Matthew 12:46-60

and in the world to come, life everlasting.'[9, 10]

"These sayings of Jesus are sometimes hard to understand and accept. But, without doubt, we know that when our perspective does not line up with God's perspective, it is ours that is out of focus. May God help us to count that cost, also.

"Many years into his ministry, Paul, the Apostle, found himself in a position to encourage his workers (specifically, Timothy) to count the cost: 'No man that goes to war entangles himself with the (business) affairs of this life.'[11]

"Timothy was from a family of mixed heritage. His mother and grandmother were both Hebrew believers. His father was a Greek. There were few Greeks in the city of Lystra. Most were merchants. I am sure there had been serious discussions about Timothy's future career. In those days, most sons followed in their father's business footsteps. The life of a merchant might have been his lot, had not an itinerant evangelist named Paul come along.

"When Timothy got this Letter of encouragement from Paul, he had been working with him for some years. Might there have been some concerns within him, or in his family about the family's business matters that prompted Paul's statement?"

It was a rhetorical question, and the group awaited the answer in silence. Instead, Pastor Dan gave another example from Scripture.

"Mrs. Zebedee had come to realize that her sons were not going to follow in their father's footsteps. No 'Zebedee & Sons' over their fish market! Was it her ambition for prestige for her sons in their 'chosen field of endeavor' that prompted her plot to ask Jesus for the seats of honor?[12]

9 Read Matthew 19:29   10 To learn more about this exciting venture, contact Wycliffe Bible Translators for the video, *From Pop Beads to Pearls,* or schedule through them a dinner theater production called, "And the Word Came With Power."   11 Read II Timothy 2:4a
12 Read Matthew 20:20-23

Helen smiled her appreciation that her pastor was able to make such valid 21st Century application from Biblical examples.

Digressing from Scripture, the speaker now decided to bring together into the life of one hypothetical college graduate, stories of many young people he had had to deal with as they were preparing to go to the field.

"A prominent student graduates *summa cum laude* in engineering. At the party his family has thrown in his honor, instead of declaring which of the three job offers he will accept, he stands to announce that he will now begin his preparation for a life of service on the mission field. He had been grappling with this change in life plans for some months. His family was aware of it, but they were sure he would make the wise decision, following their counsel to stay at home. Of course, they each had a different idea about which job he should take.

"After the initial gasps—silence. Mother begins weeping softly. Dad's face is getting redder and redder. Little sister breaks the silence with, 'You're kidding! How do you expect to find a wife out there at the end of the world?'"

They all chuckled. All except Kyle, that is. He remained serious, nodding his head. Again, that aching pang hit deep in his gut.

The story continues: "Mother, through three timely sobs, says, 'Son, how can you do this to your very own mother?' Dad simultaneously stands to his feet and pounds the table with his clenched fist. 'No son of mine is going to waste his education in some primitive Third World country! Your skills are needed here in America! You need to make something of yourself! You...you owe it to yourself!' But Dad hesitated on that last reason, realizing it was a weak argument. In fact weren't all of their statements lacking in good judgement?

"Silence again. A long silence.

"Aunt Sarah brightens. Attempting to console her brother and sister-in-law, she addresses them. 'Now, Wilber, maybe you should let him go on a short trip. Let him get this crazy idea out of his system. He'll see the importance of settling down.' She casts a condescending look at her nephew.

"And to a greater or lesser degree of intensity, this scene is repeated in the lives of many who would disentangle themselves from the business affairs of this world to attend to the affairs of the Kingdom of God."

Kevin and Kyle who had just graduated from college had a very clear understanding of this last illustration. Kyle's mother had joined Melanie in the fight to keep him home. It was not a verbal battle, but more the 'silent treatment' whenever he talked about his developing plans. The two high school grads registered this thought, but it did not hold the same significance for them. They would be returning to college after this missions venture.

"And these are the comments of his friends and family," Pastor Dan said, continuing with his illustration. "What of his professors and career recruiters? The representatives of the three companies? Unprintable expletives! But the cost must be counted.

"This is not to say that God cannot use the honor graduates to involve themselves in the business affairs at home. Rather, yes, let them also, as God leads them, become wise in business leadership. Let them learn how to handle the riches of this world, so that God can entrust to them eternal affairs, and even let them become the financial support to those others whom God directs to go. Yes, serving as a sender is equally important to those who go.

"But when He says, 'Follow Me,' we must immediately 'drop our nets' and follow Him. The work of the Kingdom is an all-consuming spiritual, mental, emotional, and physical business. Full concentration must be given to it. Paul gave Timothy (and us) the reason: 'That he may please the One who has called him to be a soldier.'"[13]

Pastor Dan sighed heavily. He had a "thousand" stories to tell of the good and the bad reactions of families and how business affairs interrupted the working of the Kingdom. "It is true," he continued, "that we can 'Limit the Holy One of Israel' by our unbelief.[14] Or, as Paul indicated that we can 'quench the Holy Spirit.'"[15] Again, he breathed heavily, as if releasing a deep heartache. When he realized that they were all looking at him for what he would say next, he apologized, "I'm sorry. Pastor Steve, I believe you get to carry on from here."

Pastor Steve uncrossed his legs, stood, and stretched his long arms to the ceiling. "I think it would be good for us to take a short break before I continue. What do you think?"

The four young people, still awkward with their unfamiliarity toward one another, agreed a break would be good.

Pastor Carl asked Kyle to follow him. "There are restrooms down the hall," he said, over his shoulder. "Just past the world map. I think Kevin probably knows the way. Kyle and I are going to get some drinks and cookies from the staff room. We'll be right back."

"Just water for me, please," Helen said, still sitting with poise in her chair.

"I need something stronger than that," Jason said.

13 Read II Timothy 2:4b   14 Read Psalm 78:41   15 Read I Thessalonians 5:19

Helen exhaled sharply, but quiet enough that Jason didn't hear her. She was going to have a difficult time liking Jason.

A short break, drinks and cookies, a good stretch of their legs and they were ready for Pastor Steve.

"I'm simply thrilled with the attention you all are giving to these issues. I have been watching each of you and feel confident that God is building a deep, realistic, and sane perspective in each of you. And that includes even you, Jason."

"Hey," Jason said with mock indignation.

Pastor Steve raised his bushy brows and smiled. "I'm sure these words will come to your mind as you take the next steps. My topic is not any easier to talk about. I need to talk about death. Two kinds of death. Recent terrorist acts blatantly directed at Americans point to this aspect of counting the cost, and the first kind of death—actual physical death.

"Further, statistics now say that more Christians were martyred for their faith in the 20th Century than in the previous nineteen put together. And the way things are going in this millennium, I don't expect that things are going to get any better."

The youths shifted nervously in their seats.

"Now, those aren't just deaths of missionaries, but it does include many. A young mother was walking up to the front door of a medical clinic in Lebanon. She and her husband and two children were ministering there. Her joy was to help young single mothers keep their babies, instead of having an abortion. As she put her hand on the knob, a man came out of the bushes and put five bullets in her head. When arrested, he said, 'Allah told me to do that.'"

Helen gasped. No one but she and her pastor knew

that she was going to a Muslim-dominated country. The cost to be counted was suddenly becoming very real.

"Christianity is becoming more and more un-popular," Pastor Steve continued. He did not think it was necessary to comment further. Helen's gasp put the appropriate punctuation mark on his words. "When we carry an all-inclusive (whosoever will may come) but an equally all-exclusive (there is only one way to a God of mercy and grace) Gospel Message, a world that says it's becoming more tolerant (pluralistic, is the word they use) becomes quite intolerant of intolerance!"

Kevin was repeating that thought several times in his head to fully grasp it: *"Tolerant, but intolerant of intolerance."*

"I realize that's not logical, but as our world is more and more becoming a global village, moral standards are becoming more and more relativistic. Situation ethics is the rule of the day. Now, don't get me wrong. As we relate with people of other world views, we don't just come in and blast them out of the water. We do want to respect them as equally intelligent people for whom Christ died; however, we cannot accept their position. But this is getting into an altogether separate issue. We better get back to the point. We must anchor our truth in the Truth of God's Word. Okay, back to the subject. There is a second death we must consider.

"Paul, the Apostle, a missionary to the Gentiles was reflecting upon his ministry in a meeting with the elders of Ephesus. He said, 'But even the sacrifice of my life I count as nothing....' Also, 'I run the risk of dying every single day....' Again, at another time, 'For we, in the midst of life, are daily surrendering ourselves to death for the sake of Jesus....'[16]

"Yet, that great missionary statesman, 'always fac-

16 Read Acts 20:24; Acts 21:13

ing death for the Gospel's sake'[17] saw another perspective on death. Death—"

Jason jumped out of his chair. "Hey man, this is
enough about that subject! I'm not ready to die! You
never talked with us about this stuff in youth meetings.
What's with this?" Just as quickly, Jason sat down and
buried his head in his arms, his face turning red with
embarrassment.

There was a long silence, which was broken when
Pastor Steve continued. "Jason, I know that you're embarrassed by that outburst. And you probably only said
out loud what some of the others are thinking. I realize
this is serious stuff. But it's better to grapple with these
issues before you get on the field than after you're out
there facing all of the enemy's attacks. Remember when
we talked about motivation?" Pastor Steve was talking
softly, gently, now. "Unfortunately, many go to the field
motivated by 'Try it! You might like it!' Remember,
those were your words when you first came to me. You
didn't want that to be your reason for going to the
field."

Jason raised his head, wiping his eyes with his
sleeve. The other students were surprised at his open
display of emotion. "I'm sorry for making a scene. I
want to serve the Lord. With all that I am. But this is
just a lot of stuff to digest all at once."

"No problem," Pastor Steve said, as Kyle reached
over and gave Jason's back a pat and rub of comfort.
Jason was glad for the camaraderie. This interaction
even softened Helen's thoughts toward Jason, though
she could not bring herself to verbalize them.

"As I was saying," Pastor Steve continued, "there's a
second perspective to this issue of death: 'Death to self.'
As Paul progressed through the logic of Romans, he

17 Read II Corinthians 4:10-12

gave us eleven chapters of God's wonderful gracious Plan. When he got to Chapter Twelve, he made a transition. He's now talking about our response to God—a life of service, and he says, 'Present your bodies as a living sacrifice....'[18] Not like so many of this world's singing groups that continually talk about death. Rather, again, Paul's words: I am crucified with Christ; nevertheless, I live. Yet, it is not I, but Christ who is alive in me....'[19]

"A recently returned missionary said it this way." He read from a hand-written letter: "'It was not easy leaving America—your family, your job, friends, all your securities. It's kinda' like dying—dying to yourself—to your American way of doing things. But it was worth it. We had an incredibly enriching two years of ministry in China.'

"It might even seem easier to be a martyr for Christ than a living sacrifice. Death to self is not some 'Are we having fun, yet?' concept. It is a total commitment to lay aside all personal ambitions, plans and goals, and to be resurrected into a new life of His purposes—those 'good deeds that He beforehand planned for you to walk in.'"[20]

Now it was Helen who was getting emotional at Pastor Steve's words. Even Kyle lowered his head as he considered the recent events in his own life and how he had to lay aside so much for what he knew was God's plan for his life.

Kevin had not yet faced this issue. Everyone from his family, his friends at college and the leadership at his church have been so supportive that this issue of 'death to self' didn't seem real. He made a mental note: *I better take a closer look at those Scriptures.*

Jason had calmed himself a bit, but this was still

18 Read Romans 12:1   19 Read Galatians 2:20   20 Read Ephesians 2:10

hard going. *I don't want to die.* He was sure of that. Under the table, he struck his fist into his cupped hand. His attention was brought back to the present as his pastor continued.

"Many years ago five young men were martyred in their attempt to make contact with a South American Amazon people group. Much has been written about them and the ministry as it was carried on by others, and about the untold thousands who were challenged into ministry as their story was told. A statement of one of the men, Jim Elliot, made famous after his death is this:

'He is no fool who gives up what he cannot keep
to gain what he cannot lose.'[21]

"And you will find this true as you follow in the footsteps of Jesus. Pastor Carl, will you conclude this evening's discussion?"

The group of four was now stilled and silenced by all that they had heard. Could there be more of this counting the cost? This was going to be closet work, for sure.

"Well, when we sat at that Denny's breakfast, I don't think any of us realized how involved this would get. But, as I have been a missions pastor for some years now, I can only say that you young people are fortunate to be hearing about these considerations now. A lot of my time is spent trying to help returned missionaries cope with what they faced on the field because they had not, as Pastor Steve said, 'wrestled' with these issues before leaving. Unfortunately, it is only recently that I have been trying to do a better job of it at this church."

The night was growing long, but he plunged into his two assigned topics. "Yes, the alternative of following in the footsteps of Jesus must also be counted. My father died when I was eight years old. My mother never re-

---

21 Read the amazing story of this mission in the classic, *Through Gates of Splendor,* by Elizabeth Elliot.

married. Our church went through a new pastor at least every year. In my growing up years, I looked to a cousin (then, already a successful businessman) for my male role model.

"And he modeled well. Working up through the ranks, he became a bank president. He was the head of a well-disciplined, happy family; he was a solid, active church member; he lived a conservative lifestyle.

"He retired. Within months, a fatal disease had him facing death. I was told that in his dying hour, he screamed and cried out, 'I don't want to see God. I can't face my Maker!' And then, to his wife and family, he poured out his heart: God had called him in his young life to be a minister. Sharing that calling with no one, he had lived out his 'exemplary' life. But, now, facing the reality of eternity, he was fearful of his wrong choice."

Kyle was nodding fiercely now. His decision solidified. He knew this was God's will for him. His church leadership had confirmed it. There was no alternative. He must follow the Lord's calling.

"I don't want to get too theological here. I do believe God received him into his heavenly home. But think of the agony he suffered all alone in those years of realizing he had denied God's call on his life.

"Does anyone remember the story of Jonah? Of course you do. He tried running from God's call on his life and he ended up in the belly of a great fish. 'You can run, but you can't hide,' goes the saying."

The seriousness of this evening had them all in deep concentration. Even Jason had no quip about Jonah's experience.

"One final topic: 'There are many adversaries!' Paul said, 'But I will stay in Ephesus until Pentecost, for a great and effectual door is opened to me, and with many adversaries.'22

"Paul had come to expect that in his aggressive, front-line, evangelistic ministry to reach the unreached, for every great and effectual door that Christ was holding open for him, there would be many adversaries.

"To the elders of Ephesus, he said, 'Behold, I go bound in the Spirit to Jerusalem, not knowing the things that may befall me there: Except that the Holy Spirit witnesses in every city, saying that bonds and affliction await me.'"23

Pastor Carl took another moment to look at each one of them. "My dear friends—missionaries-in-training—how ready are we to walk through His open doors, knowing that the enemy has adversaries behind each one, waiting to trip us up?

"Unfortunately, time and again, I have seen the following happen. A person takes that first bold step out of the pew into the battlefield saying, 'I think God wants me to be a missionary.' They're zealous. They jump the hurdles of the critics; they 'un-encumber' themselves for battle; they face the issues of physical death and present themselves as living sacrifices. They do not think of themselves more highly than they ought, but they have a sane estimate of themselves in the light of the faith the Lord has given them.24 They sort through their earthly possessions and think no ill of the greed shown by those who gladly take their possessions as 'gifts.' And then—!

"Everything goes wrong. There are differing opinions on what service they can offer on the field. Some question their readiness. One says more training is needed; another says that none was needed in the first place. People who were once supportive now say that they

22 Read I Corinthians 16:9   23 Read Acts 20:22-23   24 Read Romans 12:3

have 'heard from the Lord' otherwise.

"A dull ache clouds their thinking; a confusing frustration plagues their emotions. 'Lord, where is the assurance we once sensed?' And often, too often, not recognizing this as one of those 'many adversaries,' they settle back into the pew, and say, 'This is sure comfortable. I must have just made a mistake about all of this. I am sure glad God closed the door on that idea.'"

Kyle, finding himself relaxed in his chair sat up straight. "'Comfortable,' indeed! he blurted out. "More likely, an attack of the enemy to keep the soldiers off of the line of battle." He had already begun reading that book on spiritual warfare.

Kyle's pastor smiled in appreciation that Kyle was taking these issues so seriously, sure that he would do well on the field.

Pastor Carl had so much more to say, particularly about the "revolving door" of God's will, but he knew he needed to bring the evening to a close. "Dear young people," he concluded, "I realize we have thrown a lot of heavy thoughts at you this evening. So much to consider. I understand that you have begun developing your support teams. You have people who have made a commitment to pray with you through these steps of preparation. I would encourage you to take these eight thoughts to your prayer team:

- The comfort of the pew;
- Material possessions;
- Family cares;
- Business affairs;
- Threat of physical death;
- Death to self;
- The alternative of doing His will; and
- The many adversaries.

"Discuss them, honestly admitting areas of struggle in your lives. Remember Jason suggesting that leaving for two years would probably not be a big deal? Not all of these issues will necessarily be problems in your life, but those that are need to be dealt with long before you say, 'Good-bye.' And one of the best places to deal with these issues is in that circle of prayer with your developing support team. Being 'real' with them now, while you are preparing to go, lays a foundation of sustaining prayer while you are gone."

Helen had already met with several who were considering making a commitment to support her in prayer. Sharing her needs in reference to these eight issues—and she realized she had some—would certainly put her friends' commitments to the test. *Do they really understand the importance of their prayer for her?* she would ask them.

"That passage in Luke referred to earlier ends with these words: 'For no man, having put his hands to the plough, and looking back, is fit for the Kingdom.'[25] The cost of commitment is best considered before you go.

"If Jesus had come to our generation, He probably would have said, 'For, no person having put his hands on the steering wheel and looking back....' You all know what happens when you turn your head to look at your friends in the back seat. Watch out, oncoming traffic! And that is what happened when a farmer began plowing a furrow, if he failed to keep his eye on a stationary point on the opposite end of the field. In other words, if he kept looking back to see how far he had come, he would cut a very crooked furrow.

"We are instructed to keep our eyes fixed on Jesus, the source and goal of our faith.[26] Once we have made a clear commitment and sense that that commitment has

25 Read Luke 9:62   26 Read Hebrews 12:2

been confirmed as a true call from our Lord, there is no looking back."

He fully had their attention, each one, as they sat in silence, eyes fixed on him.

"Well, this has been good," he said with a smile. "I can see from your faces, though, that it has been a full night. And, as I was sitting here, I realized that it would have been good to have invited your support teams to join you. It would have been good for them to hear some of the challenges that you might have to face. For, all of those who become very active on your team will face the adversaries, also. If the enemy can weaken your team—at any point—he will have weakened the whole.

"Let's pray: Father, we thank You for revealing Yourself to us through Jesus, and drawing us unto Yourself by Your Holy Spirit. Creator of the Universe, thank You for allowing us such intimate relationship with You that we can call You, Father. Thank You for the privilege to be about Your Kingdom business. Please continue to direct us as leaders, and these four young people who sense Your call on their lives to be missionaries— ambassadors of the Good News of Your Kingdom to those trapped in the kingdom of darkness. We pray for the commitment of those who are forming around them as their support teams. May they learn that their discipline of commitment is as vital as that of these who go. We love You, Lord. Thank You, Jesus. Amen.

"Well, let's go home and get some sleep. Hey, what do you think of the idea of getting together again? This time with your support team members?"

Kevin held a hand on either side of his head to quell a supposed headache. "Yeah, but not tomorrow! It will take me a while to download just what I heard tonight."

"Sure!" Helen agreed, "I think it's a wonderful idea."

"I'm cool with it," said Jason enthusiastically.

"How about you, Kyle?" the other three asked.

Kyle looked at Pastor Carl. "I'm not sure. Melanie has been on my mind all evening. Things are getting tough! This involves more than I thought it would. I feel really bad. I feel like a wimp! Am I even cut out for this?"

"Oh! I'm so sorry, Kyle," confessed Pastor Jim. "I did notice a couple of times that you seemed quite distracted. We should have stopped at that time to deal with it. Pastor Carl, what do you suggest?"

"Kyle, I will be happy to meet with you again. However, I believe this is the time for you to start transferring your relationship to your support team. There is nothing that builds teammanship like having to work through an issue together."

"Yes, it will be the first—the only—prayer request I bring to my prayer group."

"Good night, Kyle. We will be praying also. And when you need a listening ear, I will be there for you," his pastor said.

Kevin, not wanting the evening to end this way and having been emboldened by the firm commitment God was giving him through a supernatural peace, asked if he could pray for Kyle right now.

Students and pastors gathered around Kyle. Several placed their hand on his shoulder or back. And Kevin prayed.

PERSONAL NOTES:

6

SERVANT-LEADER

Some time has passed. Team building has been developing as each missionary-in-training has met with those who have caught the vision of their friend's mission. Some have committed to the team. At each meeting, others have attended to better understand what would be their part, if they did sense God leading them to commit to such a vision.

"Hello, Kyle. It's very good to hear your voice," Pastor Carl said brightly. Kyle and his pastor had met several times since the last group meeting. The pastor knew that Kyle was dealing with a very serious issue. He also knew that Kyle was still wavering on his decision to become a missionary. But the pastor's constant prayer for Kyle and Melanie was simply that the Lord's will would be done—in both of their lives.

But today when Pastor Carl called him, the tone was different. Today there was great excitement in Kyle's voice. "Pastor Carl, I'm in! What you said about the alternative to doing God's will has been echoing in my ears. Not with any condemnation. Just a strong conviction. As I shared with my prayer group, it became clear that this is it. I have to keep focused. I have to leave Melanie in God's hands."

"Wow, Kyle, that is great to hear. Tough, I'm sure, but great. You will find that it is the problems that come our way that will strengthen us and give us a more clear resolve. I am so happy to see your team building strong relationships.

"Listen, the reason I called is because I recently spoke with Pastor Dan. He said that they are having a special speaker at their church. Their guest has been a missionary for many years now. He thought it would be constructive if we all joined them for this meeting. Pastor Dan is calling the others."

Like a horse chomping at the bit to start a race, there was no hesitation in Kyle's answer. "Great! When is it?"

"Well, that may be a problem for you, Kyle. It's next Wednesday. And I know that you work evenings."

"I'll just take off work. This is important. Anyway, my boss has an idea that something is going on. This will be the opportune time to tell him."

"Very well then. I will be praying for an understanding spirit."

"Thanks, Pastor Carl. I'll be there, one way or another."

AT WORK THAT EVENING

Upon hearing the news, Kyle's boss exploded. "You what?! I knew you were a good guy. You've done a great job here. But, what in the world?"

Kyle had seen the man's temper flare before, but it had never been directed at him. And Kyle knew where lay the root of his boss's problem. Without the Lord in one's heart, trying to make a business go is not easy. What *is* easy is to cut corners and deceive customers. That was the part that made it hard for Kyle to work there. But he stayed because he also saw that his influence had had a positive effect on his boss a number of times. Today, however, Kyle was actually feeling sorry for him.

His boss continued his bellow. "I can't believe you would throw away the opportunity I'm giving you at this job to advance, right to the top! In fact...," the man paused just for a second, breathed in deep, and tried to smile through a red face, "...if you tell me this is a joke, I'll give you that promised promotion—with a healthy pay increase—right now."

Following Pastor Carl's example, Kyle's voice was calm and even. "Sir, I couldn't be more appreciative than I am for the great opportunity this employment offers. You even flexed my schedule for me to participate in those school activities. But—."

"No, let me be the one to say, 'But'!" The blood vessels in his neck bulged; his face was red as a beet; his hands—indeed, his entire body—shook with agitation. "This is crazy! This is different than me just altering your schedule for school. What do you think you can do out there? This whole world is in such a mess. What can you possible do to fix it? Just let it go to hell!"

Even with his boss's heightened agitation, Kyle still remained calm. "Sir, that's exactly why I believe God wants me to be a missionary. So many people in the world are going to hell. And He has commanded that as we are going throughout the whole world we are to broadcast the Good News of His love and salvation from hell." He was surprised at how he was able to maintain his patient conviction. *It must be the prayers of my team—and Pastor Carl—that are giving me such assurance in this situation,* he thought.

"Oh, Kyle," his boss said, shaking his head. "Have

you gone crazy?" He paused. Kyle was so calm, so assured. And Kyle could guess by the myriad of expressions on the man's face what was going through his mind: I'm the one out of control. No! I've circled the world in my thoughts a thousand times. It's just a hopeless mess out there. I've got my business to run—my life to live. But how do I save this good worker?

After a moment, Kyle's boss continued, his voice more even now. "I have a mind to fire you right now. My only reservation is my hope that this will pass as a bad dream—that you'll come to your senses and move on into a career." Then he brightened. "In fact, go ahead to your meeting. I'll get someone to cover for you. Further, I won't even dock your pay. Go with my blessing," he said, as he extended his arms in encouragement. "But, be aware, my intention in letting you go is so you can see the folly of such a move. You'll be back, I'm sure!"

"Thank you, sir. I appreciate the opportunity." Kyle was always respectful of his boss. He had given Kyle some good breaks for school. With the parting words of his boss, Kyle also realized that he was not just being given a break for a school activity. This was two years of living in another culture. His excitement was clearly tinged with apprehension.

WEDNESDAY EVENING
"Whoa! What a beau-ti-ful church!" Jason exclaimed as he looked around the sanctuary.

The only other person there that he knew was Helen, so she assumed his comment was directed at her. "You mean church *buildings*, Jason. The Church is the people," Helen told him quickly. There was something about Jason that didn't sit right with Helen. But she resolved to watch her tongue around him.

"Yeah, but Helen, look at the beautiful paneling, and those brass pipes and horns on that organ! My uncle sells pipe organs, you know. That system must have cost a mint—at least several hundred grand!"

"Four hundred ninety-four thousand, five hundred dollars, to be exact," Helen answered.

Jason stared at her unblinking. "Helen, now how did you know that?"

"I play the organ. They came to me for my input before purchasing this one."

Jason looked back at the organ, one eye squinted. "My uncle would have given you a better deal." The conversation didn't seem to be going the way he wanted it to. But then, which way did he want it to go?

"It *was* your uncle who sold us this system." Helen glanced up at the ceiling. Lord, save me from this obnoxious conversation.

Although embarrassed, Jason didn't know enough to quit when he was ahead. "Couldn't that money have been used for something else? Like feeding the poor in Africa?" *There,* thought Jason. *She'll see I have some good sense with that one.*

"Jason, a beautiful church building and all that goes with it, including this pipe organ—which I get to play once in a while, by the way—is not bad. Our church leadership teaches and practices that for every dollar that we spend at home, we send one dollar into international ministry."

"Then they're going to pay your way to the field?" Jason was excited at that thought. He was beginning to realize the financial ramifications of his own venture.

She was terse in her reply. "Yes." *If I just say the bare minimum,* thought Helen, *maybe he will stop his incessant running on.*

"Then you don't need a support team. They're going to give you all the money you need." Oops! Jason knew he had just displayed his ignorance about support teams.

Helen tucked a strand of hair that had fallen loose behind her ear. "Oh, Jason! Haven't you listened to those tapes yet? The 'Building Your Support Team' tapes? You probably haven't read the book, *Serving As Senders*, yet, either. Aren't you even serious about this?"

Jason's tone turned defensive. "I've started the book."

"What? Page one? No. You haven't even gotten that far. The opening story is quite dramatic. You would have at least gotten through page three."

"Alright, already! I'll do it," he said. *If you get off my back!* he thought. Finally getting smart, he quickly changed the subject. "Hey, quite a crowd—and on a Wednesday night. Whoa, isn't that Melanie sitting over there, Kyle's gal—um...ex-gal? I wonder if she's here just to spite him."

"Maybe she's here because she wants to be open to hear God speak to her. Why don't we pray for her?" Helen was still trying to maintain some sort of Christian decorum, but she found it difficult in the presence of Jason. But before they could pray, Kyle walked up.

"Hey, Kyle. You see Melanie over there?" Jason was anxious to know her real reason for being here.

"Yes, I invited her. I'm going over to ask her to sit with us."

Jason's eyes went wide. Helen, surprised herself, smiled kindly. "How'd it go with your boss?" she asked.

"You wouldn't believe it. Well, maybe you would," Kyle said. "It was almost a duplicate of what Pastor Dan said about counting the cost. Would you believe I'm here tonight because he's attempting to bribe me? He said he wouldn't dock my pay. But from the sound of his voice, I could tell he wasn't sincere. Jason, any of your support team here with you?"

"No, he hasn't even read the book yet," Helen said, her smile now faded.

"Hey, that doesn't mean I haven't talked with some friends about it," Jason said, still on the defensive. "And I see that several of them are here," he added, pointedly.

What is wrong with me, Helen thought. *How can those hurtful words come so easily to me? That's not like me.* Perhaps it was caused by the new tensions that they could expect in the warfare of getting out of the "pew".

"I'm sorry, Jason. I guess that wasn't very encouraging of me."

"Hey, that's okay. You know, we're all going through our own stuff here. Anyone seen Kevin?"

"Yes," Kyle said, nodding to another section of the church. "He's over there with a whole bunch of his team. Pray for me while I go over and talk with Melanie." Kyle strode away.

"Better hurry," Helen called after him. "I think the service is about ready to begin." She turned to Jason. There must be a way to make up for her shortness. "That's our senior pastor, Joe Snowdown. Would you believe he's so involved with our missionaries that every few years he goes to the field to encourage them? If he can't go, he makes sure that one of the elders goes."

"That's some dedication," Jason said.

Kyle drew upon all the tenderness and respect he felt for Melanie as he approached her. Their relationship had been completely God-honoring. He had no regrets as they had grown to love and appreciate one another. They had come to depend on each other's counsel and strength in the tough times. As much as he wanted to embrace her now, he knew it would be best not to. Instead, he touched her arm gently. "Hi, Mel. I'm glad you came."

Her response was soft. "Hi, Kyle." The bright lights of the church glistened in her eyes. Kyle wondered, *Are those tears, or is it simply the sparkle in her eyes that I have come to appreciate. Her greeting was so abrupt. Had I made the right decision in inviting her? Maybe I shouldn't have asked her. Will this be too much for her?*

Melanie was first to break the awkward silence. "I see that your boss let you off for this evening. How did that happen?"

Just as Kyle was about to tell her, Reverend Snowdown approached the pulpit. They quickly sat down where they were, much to the chagrin of Jason, who had been watching them the whole time from the back. He was hoping they would have taken a seat closer. He didn't want to miss a thing.

Much to Helen's relief, Jason motioned for his friends to join him. Helen's own budding support team had surrounded her now, and she was relieved that Jason wouldn't be joining them. *That's not very kind,* she realized. *Why am I still acting this way. He's an ok guy.*

Pastor Joe smiled broadly as he looked out over the assembly. After a greeting, a chorus, and a brief prayer, he was ready to introduce his friend. He and the speaker had met on one of Pastor Joe's visits to the field. Impressed with this missionary's strategy of Biblical church-planting, they had soon bonded, developing a deep friendship. He beckoned the speaker to stand with him at the pulpit. *They were about the same height,* Helen noticed.

"What a privilege it is to introduce you to a good friend of mine. He has served the Lord faithfully on the field for many years. This evening he would like to share what he believes to be a fundamental factor in ministry. He says it is valid whether we go or stay. It is a way of—" he stopped himself. "Well, I'd better stop here and let him talk. Please give a warm welcome to Missionary Ben Wagner."

"Thank you, Pastor Joe. I do regard it a privilege to be with you this evening. What a great God we serve. Let's pray. Father, out of Your great goodness, You allow us to be a part of what You are doing in Your world. We look forward to the day when it will be fully redeemed back to Your Son. In the meantime, we do the work You have called us to do. May You find faith on the earth when You return. And now, Lord, please give me the facility of thought and speech to accurately communicate this concept that You are making real to me. May Your name be honored and glorified. Amen."

Pastor Joe stepped down and Wagner looked out over the audience. "As your pastor said, this principle of life is true whether you are a missionary or not. But I'll be sharing it in the context of missionary living."

Wagner launched into a lesson he was learning by experience, one that he obviously held in great respect. "The list is long describing the characteristics one is to possess to successfully become culturally adaptive. Another page or two would be needed to tally off the qualities of one who is to become an able communicator of the Gospel and teachings of Christ to those of differing cultural distinctives. And every consideration of training has value.

"In a world that has grown complex in social, political, economic and religious ramifications, every effort made by church leaders to sense God's call on the lives of those from their churches who wish to minister cross-culturally is valid. The fields of the world are strewn with laborers who don't know the difference between a sickle and a pruning hook. Or, to change the metaphor, they cannot distinguish the decisive points of battle.

"Notwithstanding, there is one characteristic, one quality, one approach, one lifestyle, if you will, that stands above all others in demand for the successful cross-cultural worker—or any Christian. As I have already said, this characteristic is vital for all who believe."

The audience was still as they listened carefully to the words being spoken. It was obvious this would not be a light subject to consider.

"Without equivocation, this evening I will emphasize this lifestyle quality: That of 'Servant-Leader'. Sermons abound on the subject; articles dance around the subject; a lot of lip service is given to the subject. Yet, it remains one of the most challenging 'unknowns' in practical attainment. It is the elusive element of dynamic Christian leadership. Everybody needs it! Who has it?

"For one thing, the idea itself appears contradictory. How can one be both servant (one who obeys and carries out the wishes of another) and a leader (one who provides direction and gives orders to another) at the same time? It's not like my little granddaughter, Naomi, who plays 'hostess and guest for tea' with her friend. 'Today,' she says, 'I'll be the hostess and you be the guest. Tomorrow you will be the hostess and I will be the guest.' We are saying that both of these characteristics must be active in the same person at the same time. It is at best a paradox.

"To further confuse the issue, servant-leaders don't wear badges to identify themselves. Or brandish gold-embossed business cards labeled: Servant-Leader. Nor is 'it' a cloak or glove to put on as they reach out to help someone. It must permeate all of life. No one can be a servant-leader at church and not at home. No one can be a servant-leader in the community and not in the workplace. It's not a role to play; it's a way of life to live."

Jason looked over at some of his guests, wondering if this was going to be too heavy for them. He had sat through the last session by the four pastors, and had had time to "digest" all that was said. But this guy was intense.

Helen was beaming. She could see why her pastor had become strong friends with this man. There was a sincerity and intensity in his voice. Certainly stemming from the "leader" part of the quality that he spoke of.

Kyle was hoping that because the speaker had said this is for all, not just missionaries, that Melanie would be able to enjoy the message. When he glanced sideways at her, she was listening intently, fully captivated by the man who gripped the podium and seemed to look at each one of them at the same time.

Kevin had heard Ben Wagner at a college chapel earlier that year. He knew he was good. He lived the words he spoke. He was the kind of man Kevin aspired to be.

The speaker continued. "Well, lest this talk join the accumulated words paying only homage to the subject, let us move on. How is this elusive element of life found? What is the key to attaining it? We want to look to Jesus, for only in Him will we find the perfection of the Father, to whom we have all been called.

"Though Luke spoke of the strife that was going on among the disciples at the Last Supper as to who should be accounted the greatest, it was left to John to record this act through which Jesus teaches this principle of servant-leader.

"In John 13:4, we read: 'He (Jesus) arose from the table, took off His robe and wrapped the servant's towel around His waist. Then He poured water into the basin and began to wash the disciples' feet, and dry them with the towel.'

"This is definitely the action of a servant. Why Peter and John didn't make provision for this servant in their preparation of the Passover is not known, but Jesus used the occasion to their (and our) benefit.

"Let's join Jesus and His disciples in that Upper Room. They are reclining on benches around the table, each leaning against the shoulder of the one next to him. John has had to adjust his position since he had been reclining against Jesus. In so doing, he looks at Peter. He motions to Peter, suggesting that he should take the basin of water. With a vigorous shaking of his head, Peter mouths the words, 'John, you wanted to sit at Jesus' right hand.' To which Jesus had said, 'If you want to be great in God's Kingdom, learn to be the servant of all.' You take the basin, John.' Probably for their own reasons of pride, they both left the task to Jesus.

"The room must have been hushed with silence. *Our Master shouldn't be doing this,* they each might have thought. The one who washes the feet of guests at a dinner feast is the lowliest of all household servants.

"I don't know who Jesus came to first. Maybe Matthew. As Jesus unloosed his sandals, we might have heard Him say, 'Matthew, do you remember where I found you?' 'Yes, Lord. I was collecting taxes from our people for Rome. You simply said, "Follow Me." I am so glad I did.' Jesus replies, 'So am I.'

"Who do you think might have been next? Maybe Thomas. Or James. Or maybe, Judas! Yes, Judas was at the foot washing. Can you even imagine Jesus washing Judas' feet, knowing of his eminent betrayal? As Judas swings his feet down off the bench, Jesus hears the jangling of the thirty pieces of silver. What could Jesus have possibly said to him?

"I realize that Scripture does not tell us all of that, but we do read His conversation with Peter. Jesus places the basin of water at Peter's feet. He kneels down, waiting for Peter to swing his legs around. Thoughts of frustration must have been coursing through Peter's mind, for he again says the ridiculous: 'Lord, are You going to wash my feet?' ('It's only obvious,' Judas might have chided, as he pulled his washed feet back onto the bench.)

"'You don't realize now what I am doing,' Jesus replied, 'but later you will understand.'

"Then Peter said to Him, 'You must never wash my feet!'

"Jesus' gentle but firm voice encourages Peter: 'Unless you let Me wash your feet, Peter, you cannot have fellowship with Me.'

"'Then,' returned Peter, 'please—not just my feet, but my hands and face, as well!'

"'Oh, Peter,' Jesus chuckled. 'The man who has bathed only needs to have his feet washed.'

"In this brief interchange of words, Jesus definitely demonstrated the lifestyle of a servant. But He also clearly showed His position as leader. Had He only been a servant, what would He have done when Peter said, 'You will never wash my feet?' He would have passed him by, for a servant does only what he is told to do. Or, when Peter said, 'Wash all of me,' what would a servant have done?"

"Given him a bath," Jason blurted out. He was so deep into the speaker's story that the words just came without his thinking. Embarrassed, he looked at his friends to see their reaction. They just smiled and shook their heads. They knew Jason well enough to know that his thinking-aloud comments were normal.

"Yes, given him a bath." Wagner continued. "That's what servants do. But Servant-Jesus was in charge of the situation. He was also the Leader-Jesus. So gentle, yet firm in His dealing with Peter: 'Peter, it has to be this way. No, no, I don't need to give you a bath. Just your feet. You have to choose, of course.' Jesus knew what needed to be done, and then He did it. I believe this is a fair definition of Servant-Leader: To be able to see things from God's perspective, then minister unto people from that perspective."

Wagner looked over the audience to see if they were following him. From Jason's comment, he knew at least one was caught up in the story. And from the subdued audience, it was clear that all the people were with him.

"There are many other acts of Jesus that demonstrate His lifestyle of Servant-Leader. I have chosen this one, however, because I believe with all my heart that the key to His ability to take this position—and the key to our being able to learn to become a Servant-Leader—is found in the verse preceding where I began.

"Yes, I didn't start that story where it really begins. Let's go back and look at what John wrote about Jesus in verse three of John 13." His voice grew intense and the volume increased as he punctuated each phrase: "And Jesus, knowing that the Father had put all things into His hands, and (knowing) that He had come from the Father and (knowing that He) was going to the Father, took off His outer garments, put on the servant's towel, poured water in the basin and began washing the disciples' feet and drying them with the towel.' I say it again; I am convinced that the key to the development of this lifestyle in our lives is found in those simple statements John wrote about Jesus.

"All of the mysteries of life, all of the philosophical pursuits, all of the experimental fancies of man can be traced back to an attempt to answer one of the three questions of life that Jesus answered, so simply."

The intensity of this man's voice captivated the attention of everyone. His mannerisms were adding to the forcefulness of the moment. He continued. "The questions are: Where did I come from? Why am I here? Where am I going?"

He gripped the pulpit. He rose on his tip toes. While elevating his body and his voice, he spoke this summary statement with the skill of a practiced orator: "To the degree that we are free from the struggles that encumber and entangle us in our pursuit of the answers to these three questions of life and can simply say with Jesus, 'I came from the Father, I am doing the Father's will, and I am going to the Father, we are free of ourselves to be servant-leaders. Free to see things from God's perspective and free to minister unto people from that perspective."

He stood back down to his normal height. His shoulders shrugged as if exhausted from the forcefulness of his words. He continued, "Let's take a closer look at these three questions:

WHERE DID I COME FROM?

"Fascinated as I am by the archaeological discoveries of man, I have fortunately never had to struggle with the Creation/evolution 'question'. And with the evolutionary camp in such disarray, I'm almost embarrassed for them for the new postulates they are advancing to shore up their crumbling laboratories.

"But to those who have been schooled in a system that taught these human theories as fact, I can understand a slight nagging concern that the seekers just might find the right tooth, or toenail—or something—to 'prove' their position correct.

"Jesus affirmed, 'I came from the Father.'

"But the issue of 'Where did I come from?' encompasses a host of other inquiries. Roots, for example. My father-in-law, once on this pursuit, decided to find out 'where he came from.' He only went back as far as his mother's cousin. When he discovered her to be the infamous 'Bonnie Parker,' he wasn't so interested in his roots, anymore!

"The roots of Jesus' earthly father are twice delineated, including some rather unsavory rascals. Yet, He simply said, 'I came from the Father.'

"If our heritage is not suspect, it might be our position in the family. The 'baby of the family' has his struggles; the oldest has to pave the way for the younger; the rest are sometimes 'lost' somewhere in the middle. Can you even imagine Joseph and Mary's difficulty in raising the rest of their family after having Jesus? It's no wonder to me that his brothers initially rejected 'Mr. Goody-Good.'

"This is the way it happened in my family: My mom and dad had three boys, each a year or so apart. Two and a half years later, another baby was on the way.

Daddy wanted a girl. Oh, how Daddy wanted a girl! But they got me, instead."

A ripple of laughter played across the audience. But upon seeing the intensity in the speaker's face, they were soon still again.

Wagner continued. "Two and a half years later, Daddy got his girl! Another year and a half: Twins! 'Yes, two of them, boys!' he came home shouting. So, where did that leave me? I had three older brothers that I couldn't keep up with. Oh, I tried. I got nicknamed 'Tag-along.' And I had three younger sisters that I couldn't compete with. I was (at least I thought I was) a nobody, lost in the middle of seven kids.

"I tried to win my dad's approval. But I was never quite good enough. Then, when I was eight years old, he died in a plane crash. I spent my energy trying to win approval from everyone. Oh, on the outside I was sure that nobody knew about this. I probably didn't even understand all the dynamics, myself. But from my youthful perception, I was unloved and unaccepted. And now my dad was gone. I would never know the love and acceptance and approval of a father. Until, one day...."

Wagner paused, gripping the podium even tighter as his voice intensified.

"One day..." He paused again, trying to maintain his composure. He repeated, "One day—I don't know how many times I had previously read this Scripture—but, one day as I read the 139th Psalm, I was totally enveloped in God's love. Billowing waves of divine love washed over me. I was immersed in the pure love of my Creator. With each new wave came more tears—not tears of sorrow, but tears of the release of my huge burden of feeling unloved, unappreciated. The years of loneliness were absolved in the tenderness of His enfolding arms of love. I rested in the open and accepting arms of my Heavenly Father."

Wagner took a moment to dab the tears that had formed in his eyes. There were a good number of other hankies in the audience doing the same work.

"Can you imagine my inability to freely minister to others in areas of 'Where did I come from?' with such deep feelings entangling me in a web of despair? But, thanks be to God, in that area of my life, resolve had come. I, with Jesus, can now say, 'I came from the Father.' Notice that I said, 'In that area of my life.' God and I know there are other areas still being worked on. I believe we are all a 'work in progress,' to find completion only at some future time.

"Are there other issues in this question? Maybe you were a desperately wanted (thus an overprotected) baby. Or unwanted! Can you imagine growing up as an unaborted child? I shared these thoughts at a seminar once. At a break, one lady came to me in tears. She said that ever since she had trusted in Christ as Savior, all her mother will say to her is, 'I could have aborted you!' We cried together for a few moments, asking God for healing of this cruelest hurt in her life.

"Another friend, a young man, shared how he had been raised in a home of anger and hate and fear. He struggled until the age of twenty-nine with the thought that God didn't want him to be born. It seemed obvious (to him) that his father hadn't wanted him to be born. In seeking help to have victory in this area of 'where did I come from,' he was encouraged to visualize—to picture in his mind—God bringing the sperm to the egg that created him. Though he was a very artistic, visual guy, he could not allow himself to see the hands of God bringing them together in his mother's womb. He would see the precious stuff that would become him in God's hands. He could see His hands beginning to come together. But before they could unite, God's hands would drop. Again and again. Each time in bitter depression, he could not see that God wanted him to be born.

"Until, one day! That one day when victory broke through. He was quoting every Scripture he could think of about God's love for life—about His creativity. He saw the hands of God coming closer and closer together. Saturated in Scripture, his mind would not allow him to think of the previous times when the hands had come this close, only to drop at the last moment. But this time! Yes, this time he saw the tender hands of God enfolding and surrounding that sperm and egg, bringing them together, beginning the creative process of life. Yes! God was there. It was God's intention for him to be born. God does have a purpose for his life!

"There may be other issues people struggle with. Too tall; too short. Too fat; too thin. Too much smarts; not enough smarts. Too much hair; not enough hair!"

At this point, Wagner leaned forward, letting the platform lighting glare a bright reflection off of his hairless head. The laughter from the audience could not be contained. When Ben lifted his head, he was laughing with them.

He continued. "Don't even try to come up to me after the service with your favorite 'bald-head' joke. I know them all. Don't worry, though, I won't 'sic' the bears on you like Elisha did when those kids made fun of him. Yes, read about it in II Kings 2:23. Forty-two of them were mauled to death!

"Well, how did our gracious Lord resolve this issue for me? One day, my family was gathered to celebrate my birthday. By the way my boys were trying to get me to open this particular package, I knew I didn't want to. But finally all the other gifts had been opened. This one remained. I opened it slowly. To my great chagrin, there lay a comb for bald-headed men. It was two arched pieces of plastic with comb teeth at the ends, facing inward. They were joined at the top with a pivot point, allowing the double comb to expand or contract with the size of the man's head."

The auditorium was shaking with laughter. Ben Wagner had to wait a minute before he could continue.

"Oh, it was funny, all right. They had really done it this time. They were all laughing, just as you are now. And I was laughing with them—on the outside. But on the inside, I was crying, 'Why, God? Why did you make me this way?' You see, nobody knew that this was such an issue with me. We can get real good at hiding our hurts.

"But, then, as I was expanding and contracting this, the latest of cruel jokes for one who had not come to a resolve on this issue, I contracted it so the two arches crossed over themselves. The shape it took was my healing. In this position, it looked like the Ichthus fish, one of the most sacred symbols of the early Christians. In that instant I was healed! Am I still bald? Of course. Would I like a full head of hair? Of course I would. Though I'm not sure I would want as much hair as that young man has, sitting over there," he said, pointing to Jason's full head of hair.

"Jason, he's looking at your Afro!" Kevin laughed from a few rows behind him.

What to say? What to do? Jason wondered. For once he was embarrassed beyond words. Not that he was ashamed of his full head of hair. He worked hard to make it look perfect. But all attention for a moment turned on him.

Wagner, aware of his embarrassment, offered an apology.

Now Jason had words. He stood, shook his head and said, 'I like it!' Others in the audience made various comments. There was even a bit of applause as he took his seat again.

"Well, there are other issues that I'm sure each of you is thinking about. But let's go on. Let's get our eyes back on Jesus. If we momentarily sidestep the modern image-makers of Jesus, and search Scripture for a valid perspective of where He came from, we might get the following thumbnail sketch:

- Heritage—Joseph isn't Your father?
- Birthplace—A barn.
- Birth announcement—By shepherds, not too well known for their integrity in those days.
- Name—One of the most common in the land.
- Looks—No beauty in Him, that we should desire Him.
- Neighborhood—Can any good come out of Nazareth?
- Wealth—A pair of turtledoves at His circumcision; a borrowed tomb at His death.
- Status—Servant of all.
- Possessions—Not a place to lay His head.
- Goal in life—Born to die.
- Temperament—A Man of sorrows; acquainted with grief.
- Popularity—Despised and rejected of men.
- Companions—A friend of prostitutes and sinners.

Wagner looked up from his notes at an audience under his full control. They were hanging on his every word. To postulate his concluding thought, he again rose on his tip toes, gripping the pulpit for balance. Beginning softly, his voice rose to a crescendo with the final words: "Yet Jesus, to Whom we are to look for modeling the Christian lifestyle of servant-leader, reduced to nothing all the hassles of 'Where did I come from?' by simply saying, 'I came from the Father.'"

With equal firmness, he brought the application to each of his listeners: "And I say to each of us, that to the degree that we can cooperate with the Holy Spirit to find a resolve and lay to rest the laments of our past that would cause us to question, 'Where did I come from?' and simply say with Jesus, 'I came from the Father,' to that degree we are free of ourselves to see things from God's perspective and minister unto others from that perspective. Free to be 'of no reputation.'[1] Free to be poor so that 'through our poverty others may be rich in Him.'[2]

"Are you with me?" Wagner asked. There were various comments of agreement from the audience. It was obvious that the passion with which he was speaking was straining his entire being. Sweat beaded his brow, and his knuckles on the podium had grown white. He continued, "There's more!

WHY AM I HERE?

"An interview published some time ago in a news magazine quoted Sir John Eccles, Nobel Laureate in medicine and physiology, and a pioneer in brain research. He said, 'Science cannot explain, "Why am I here?"' He further stated, 'We need to discredit the belief held by many scientists that science will ultimately deliver the final truth about everything. I have spent my life working on the brain and know what a wonderful structure

1 Read Philippians 2:7   2 Read II Corinthians 8:9

it is. But we live in a world of experiences, not brain events. There are mysteries beyond science.'

"And what a breath of fresh air to hear such a perspective. Yet, with a worldview blasting us with its commercial messages: 'Do your own thing.' 'If it feels good...' 'Grab for all the gusto.' 'You only go around once,' how can we hear His still, small voice saying, 'You are My most finely crafted work of art, created in Christ Jesus to walk in those good deeds that I have beforehand determined for you to walk in.'[3] We are too easily blinded to the fact that implanted in the spiritual DNA of every living person are the words: 'Created for My pleasure.'[4]

"Dr. John Brewster's research theorized: The cultural universal, that which is the common denominator of all men of all ages, is 'striving for significance.' Being 'somebody' is why I'm here! Striving, of course, within the standards established by one's own culture, or counter-culture.

"And God does want each of us to be a unique 'somebody,' yet fitting into that corporate tapestry of His making, for His glory.

"But the world over and over again screams its virtues through commercials, music, billboards and the printed page. What are the golden apples of our culture? What beliefs and values does our society revere?

"One golden apple is a 'Work Ethic of Free Enterprise.' Yet, it is dominated by a competition that crushes and destroys.

"In a masterfully written allegory that has become a classic through the years, Trina Paulus wrote of the struggles for success through the eyes of a caterpillar. He thought the only way to 'get high' (For he knew that within him was the yearning to join the earth to the

3 Read Ephesians 2:10 (Reader, I have quoted this Scripture so many times in this writing. You should have it memorized by now!)   4 Read Revelation 4:11

sky.) was to climb the caterpillar pillar." Mr. Wagner began quoting excerpts from the book. "'From the beginning he was determined to get to the top.... He especially avoided the eyes of the other crawlers.... He disciplined himself to neither feel nor be distracted.... He didn't think he was against anyone.... He was just doing what he had to, to get to the top.... Then one day he was near his goal.... He heard a tiny whisper from the top: "There's nothing here at all!" It was answered by another, "Quiet, fool! We're where they want to be. That's what's here!"'"[5]

Ben Wagner waited for a moment for the truth of that allegory to sink in. With a low, thoughtful voice, he continued, "How many people today are trying to 'get high' by every means but by the One True God?" He knew that the people were following his thoughts.

"Bored by the paucity of creative challenge, my father-in-law and a friend decided to 'strive for significance' in a less-than-usual direction. They competed, all right—to see who could get the *lowest* scores without the teacher catching on. This competition took place for one year, their entire seventh grade. They succeeded. They both flunked! (They did make up their grades the next year.)"

Oh, my, Helen thought, reflecting on her home-school courses. *There was always a challenge. How could anyone be bored with school?*

"Howard Hughes, when he was the richest man in the world, was asked, 'How much money would make you feel significant?' His answer is classic: 'A little bit more!'

"Here is another golden apple of American culture— a reason, we say, why we are here: 'An activity orientation that has us so stretched by *doing* that we have no

5 *Hope For The Flowers*, Trina Paulus, Paulus Press, 1972.

reflective time of *being*.'

"And some more: Are we having fun yet? TGIF! Living for the weekend. Born to shop. Looking for the light at the end of the tunnel, only to realize it is a hulking locomotive bearing down on us. The worst day of fishing is better than the best day at work. When my ship comes in, I will probably be at the airport. If it feels good, do it. Shop 'til you drop. I'd rather be... and here you add whatever you would rather be doing. Like it or not, many 'live' by these and other bumper sticker philosophies.

"Here is another: 'Man is basically good,' American society says. Yet, moral and ethical decay rises to the nostrils of God as a putrid stench. Situation ethics and relativism have produced a culture of debauchery."

Ben Wagner looked across the auditorium. "I make no apologies for the straightforwardness of my language. Yet I grieve with you at a country so far removed from its godly foundations." Looking back at his notes, he continued.

"And yet another: Our mode of social relationship is so individualistic that we are often seen by each other as simply 'ships passing in the night.' We are as bundles of atoms encased each one in a translucent capsule, bobbling about in a cosmic vacuum. Possibly, once—or twice—in a lifetime, we may catch a zephyr of solar movement and come close enough to another to enjoy a brief relationship.

Jason looked down the row at his friends. *Were they catching all of this?* he wondered. *Mr. Wagner is going from one point to the next so rapidly, I am getting confused.* As quickly as Jason could think that thought, Ben Wagner was already on to his next point.

"Another: American culture believes that man is the

master of nature. Yet an itsy-bitsy spider, threatened by extinction, can stop a multi-million dollar hydro-electric project.

"What does all of this confusion say?" Wagner paused, though he didn't expect an answer. He continued, slowly, emphatically: "Somewhere along the way, we have missed the mark in our pursuit of 'Why am I here?'"

Kyle was trying to put this all into perspective through the filter of his and Melanie's difference of opinion. He dared not look at her just now. He did wonder, though, what she was thinking.

"Peter had a willing spirit. And during his training years, he did catch a glimpse of the picture: 'You are the Christ, the Son of the Living God!' he declared. Yet, three paragraphs later, his statement draws this rebuke: 'Get behind me, satan! For you are not seeing things from God's perspective, but from man's.'[6]

"We, too, can become so immersed in 'man's perspective' that we cannot (more likely, will not) seat ourselves with Christ in heavenly places and view life from His perspective. Let's sit with Him for a moment and learn from our Example, Jesus Christ.[7]

Back to Scripture again, Helen thought. *I like that.*

"I don't know just when Jesus became aware that He was the Son of God. But we do know that it was at least by the time He was twelve years old, for His explanation to His mother for His delay in the temple was, 'Didn't you know that I need to be about My Father's business?'[8] And He wasn't speaking of Joseph, else He would have been with the company returning to Nazareth."

I wonder where he spent the two nights in Jerusalem. This thought had never entered Jason's mind

6 Read Mark 8:27-33   7 Read Ephesians 2:6   8 Read Luke 2:49

before. *But, it was three days before they found Him. He had to have stayed somewhere. This is a good question to ask Pastor Steve,* Jason thought. *It'll stump him, too.* Jason smiled at his own cleverness.

"Yet, He went home and 'learned obedience.' Or, as another translation says, 'He was subject to them.'[9] So much so that eighteen years later, when He was to begin His public ministry, in another conversation with His mother, He said, 'My hour has not yet come.' She, ignoring Him, told the servants to do as He said. 'This is the beginning of miracles that Jesus did in Cana. He revealed His glory, and His disciples believed in Him.'"[10]

And I am so glad that I believe in Him, Kevin affirmed in his heart.

"From that hour to the hour of His passion, He sensed keenly the Father's timing in His life. He could say, 'I have done nothing of Myself, but only what My Father has said.'[11] Then, in one of His last prayers, He said, 'Father, I have finished the work You sent Me to do.'[12] Jesus dealt with every issue that we do, for He was 'tempted in like manner as we are.'[13] Yet, He found the resolve for each one, so that He simply 'knew that the Father had put everything into His hands.'"[14]

Though the King James English was sometimes difficult to follow, Helen really appreciated that sound of Scripture. Her church leadership and her family had chosen to stick to it, even with the proliferation of modern translations. But, she had to admit, that with the old English she did have to think and reinterpret for how we say things today.

Ben Wagner continued. "What did Jesus have available to Him that is not ours also?

"He had the Scriptures. We have a complete revelation of God's Word, the Holy Bible.[15]

9 Read Luke 2:52   10 Read John 2:4, 11   11 Read John 8:28   12 Read John 17:4
13 Read Hebrews 2:18   14 Read John 13:3   15 Read II Timothy 3:16

"He had the anointing of the Holy Spirit. We dare not leave 'Jerusalem' without it."[16]

Kyle had a clear understanding of this Truth. It was a strong point of emphasis at his church.

"He had fellowship with the Father. We, too, are admonished to 'pray without ceasing.'[17] While our life carries on, on a physical-mental-emotional level, our spirits, made alive by the power of God, can interpret and express the impressions of our conscious existence in words of praise and petition to God. And when we 'don't know how to pray as we ought, the Spirit Himself makes intercession for us.'[18] We stand boldly in His presence because we have 'a High Priest who has been touched by the feelings of our infirmities, yet without sin.'[19]

"Through the Word which is the revelation of Christ, through the anointing of the Holy Spirit which is the Power of God, and through the endless fellowship with the Father, we can cut away the layers of this world's thoughts and have the mind of Christ."[20]

Ben Wagner paused. It seemed like forever. Were there more thoughts he wanted to share regarding this question? He again gripped the pulpit. His face grew even more serious, imploring the audience to give heed to his summary statement to follow:

"To the degree that we can find resolve and lay to rest the frustrations of the present and firmly grasp His will for our lives, prepare ourselves and do according to His will,[21] to that degree, we are free of ourselves to choose to serve others. To 'work the works of the One who sent me.'[22] To 'plead the cause of the poor and needy.'[23] To 'visit orphans and widows in their distress.'[24] To 'feed the hungry; to clothe the naked; to give drink to the thirsty.'[25] As we are going throughout our

16 Read Acts 1:4   17 Read I Thessalonians 5:17   18 Read Romans 8:26
19 Read Hebrews 4:15   20 Read I Corinthians 2:16   21 Read Ephesians 5:17; Luke 12:47
22 Read John 9:41   23 Read Proverbs 31:9   24 Read James 1:27   25 Read Matthew 25:35-40

sphere of influence, 'to preach!'[26] As we are going throughout our sphere of influence, 'to teach, making disciples of all peoples.'"[27]

Kevin was sitting between two of his college friends who had already committed to be a part of his prayer support team. Their look at him let him know that they were grasping the seriousness of their commitment.

Ben Wagner, head lowered as if in prayer, paused again. It was obviously taking a massive amount of energy to deliver this passionate message. The truth of every point had been born out of personal experience. He continued:

"And now, the third question of life.

WHERE AM I GOING?

"The initial consideration (at least, my first thought) is eternal destiny. And immediately we are thrust upon an age-old doctrine of the assurance of His gift of salvation. It has denied fellowship among brothers (at the least) and has caused roots of bitterness and hatred and murder (at the most). I was raised at one extreme of this theological issue. I have met with those who have been raised at the other extreme.

"As I became an adult and began taking seriously the study of Scripture—the Whole Counsel of God—I realized my Bible would be torn to shreds if I cut out either the Scriptures that suggest one position, or the other.

"For example, which of the following should we ignore?

- Keeping yourself in the love of God....[28]
- God has given us all that pertains to life and godliness. For this very reason, you must do the utmost on your part: Add to your faith....[29]

26 Read Mark 16: 15   27 Read Matthew 28:19-20   28 Read Jude 21
29 Read II Peter 1:3-5

- Work out your own salvation with fear and trembling....[30]
- ...for it is God who is at work in you, both to will and to do His pleasure.[31]
- Nothing can separate us from the Love of God...[32]
- Whom He foreknew, them also did He predestinate....[33]
- No one can snatch them out of My hand....[34]
- Elect, according to the foreknowledge of God....[35]
- Not willing that any should perish....[36]
- For God so loved...that whosoever....[37]

"And then the writer of Hebrews (the Holy Spirit) had to add this thought:

- 'When you find men who have been enlightened, who have experienced salvation and received the Holy Spirit, who have known the wholesome nourishment of the Word of God and touched the spiritual resources of the eternal world and who then fall away...is bound sooner or later to be condemned....'[38]

"And I realize that those who have made it their goal to fight for one position or another can explain each of the above references (and others) to support their position. But when the 'sparks' stop flying, honest students of the Word will acknowledge that there remains some mystery. I heard one minister say, 'Believe like a Calvinist; live like an Armenian!'

"Rather may it be said: The whole Counsel of God on this matter is to give assurance to those who fear and strike fear in those who are so sure!"

That is sure a resolve that I had never before heard, Pastor Dan thought. *I wonder if Pastor Joe knew his friend would share such a hot issue.*

Ben Wagner continued, pressing his point. "For all of our attempts to 'explain away' Scripture on one side

30 Read Philippians 2:12   31 Read Philippians 2:13   32 Read Romans 8:35-39
33 Read Romans 8:29   34 Read John 10:28   35 Read I Peter 1:2   36 Read II Peter 3:9
37 Read John 3:16   38 Read Hebrews 6:4-6

or the other, God will not allow Himself to be squeezed between the pages of even the best-written theological book. He is best understood through the pages of His Holy Word.

"Thus, let us cry out with Paul: 'That I might know Him in the power of His resurrection and in the fellowship of His suffering so that if by any means I might attain unto the resurrection of the dead.'"[39]

Wagner sensed the uneasiness in his audience, but felt it necessary to speak from his heart. For a moment he hesitated, wondering if he should address that feeling. Rather, he continued with his concluding thought. "Within hours of His impending death, Jesus declared with full assurance, 'I go to the Father.'[40]

"But there are other issues in this question, 'Where am I going?'"

The auditorium seemed to take a united breath of ease as the speaker left this sensitive subject.

"The American culture values a sense of time that is future oriented. Yet, plagued with regret of the past, we're not allowed to enjoy the present. Suffocated by the lament—could have, should have, it might have been, if only—we wallow in a cesspool of regret. We look back on a road strewn with wrong choices, hurtful relationships, shattered dreams, frustrated plans, wasted opportunities and careless acts of disobedience.

"We do err, for we know not the Scripture: 'Anyone who is in Christ, he is a new creation; the old is gone, the new has come!'[41] And: 'I, even I, am He Who blots out your transgressions, for My own sake, and remember your sins no more.'[42] Further: 'I do not consider that I have yet 'arrived,' but I concentrate on this: Forgetting (for my sake, as God has for His own sake) what lies behind and stretching forward, I press toward

39 Read Philippians 3:10-11   40 Read John 16:16   41 Read II Corinthians 5:17
42 Read Isaiah 43:25

the mark of the high calling of God....'[43]

"But what of the future? Where am I going? What will I achieve if I accomplish what I am now working on? Halls of Fame have so proliferated that recently one was looking for a city willing to house it. They couldn't find one!

"What notable note will be written in my epitaph? Will my tombstone read, 'I have finished the work You sent me to do?'[44]

"We scheme short and long-range plans. Our Day-Timer or PDA allows us to keep minute record of all that needs to be done. Yet, godly priorities crumble as we give way to the tyranny of the urgent. James reminds us: 'Hold on a moment, you who say with such confidence, "We are going to do such and such." Say rather, "If the Lord wills...."'[45] Solomon said: 'The lot is cast in the lap, but its every decision is from the Lord.'[46]

"But what of the future? Where am I going? What about investments? F.D. Roosevelt ushered us into a secure future on earth with the Social Security Act. Long before that plan tottered and fell to its current position, insurance companies were touting life insurance policies with 'cash value.' With double digit inflation, those huge cash reserves dwindled to insignificance.

"But, Yes! Then came the assurance that you can be in control of your own future. Open the IRA of your choice. But the corporate mismanagement has left millions of investors destitute. And now—" He stopped, punctuating the pause with a pointed finger. "And now—" He thrust his finger higher into the air to indicate the failing promises of each new deal. "The disappearing ink on each new contract will leave the future as bankrupt as any other.

"But what of the future? Where am I going? At the

43 Read Philippians 3:13-14   44 Read John 17:4   45 Read James 4:13-15
46 Read Proverbs 16:33

end of every month are there more days than dollars? Buy now; pay later. And all the ramifications of credit card living cry out: *Don't worry about where you are going!*

"It should not take us by surprise that all of this borrowing on the future is in place; plastic money-makers vie for our signatures. The god of this age controls that motivational thinking. Moses recognized that there was pleasure in sin—for a season.[47]

Pastor Jim wondered where that Scripture came from. Then he realized that most of the "plastic money" spending is on the sinful pleasures of this world.

The speaker continued, "It is perfectly logical that the enemy of our souls has to make earth and its limits attractive. Can you imagine his beckoning: Lay up for yourselves treasures in hell where you can burn with me for all of eternity?"

The audience was too entranced by Wagner's sermon to even smile at his sarcasm.

"But what of the future? Where am I going?" Wagner pressed into his point by repeating those words with each new thought. He was not letting up. His entire manner of speech—right down to the intense, rigid body language—was saying, 'This is vital.'

He continued on. "Career changes; mid-life crises. One survey says 90% of Americans are working in jobs that they don't like; multiple shift jobs to increase one's 'standard of living.' How can one even remotely consider a sixteen-hour work day, an 'enhanced' lifestyle? 87% of Americans retire with less than is needed to maintain a moderate lifestyle. 67% retire below the poverty line.

"Escape through drugs, drink, sex, workaholism, mental irresponsibility, and the ultimate 'escape,' suicide, are epidemic. 'Stop the world! I want to get off!'

47 Read Hebrews 11:25

might have just been the words of a song of yesteryear. Or were they? Where is the fully human, fully alive vision? Where is the utopia each presidential candidate promises with his 'new deal?'

"The path before us may encircle the globe. Yet, it is a straight path, for we are to take it one step at a time. His Lamp is not a beam that throws light a mile down the rail, but it is a 'Lamp to our feet and a Light to our path.'[48] 'The steps of a righteous man are ordered of the Lord.'"[49]

Again, Ben Wagner paused. His deep breath, his firm grip on the podium, his intense expression—his whole demeanor let the audience know that he was coming to another summary point: "To the degree that we can resolve and lay to rest the anxieties of the future and commit each tomorrow to His keeping, to the degree that we can hold the hand of the One who holds the future, leaning not on our own understanding, but acknowledging Him in all our ways, that He may direct our path—[50] to that degree we are free of ourselves so that we can choose to serve others: To 'take up our cross daily, and follow Him to Calvary.'[51] To 'walk through the valley of the shadow of death.'[52] To 'walk in the light of His countenance.'[53] To 'walk through the open door of ministry that He has set before us.'"[54]

Ben Wagner again stood for a long, silent moment. He looked exhausted. It was as if he had given birth to a thousand thoughts. But he found strength to continue. "My dear friends, this is my heart; my passion. Let me summarize:

"There are basically three questions to life:
- Where did I come from?
- Why am I here?
- Where am I going?

48 Read Psalm 119:105   49 Read Psalm 37:23   50 Read Proverbs 3:5-6
51 Read Matthew 16:24   52 Read Psalm 23:4   53 Read Psalm 89:15
54 Read I Corinthians 16:8-9

"To the degree that we are able to resolve and lay to rest the laments of our past, the frustrations of our present, and the anxieties of our future, to that degree are we able to see clearly every situation from God's perspective as a leader and minister unto people from His perspective as a servant.

"May God add His blessing to the sharing of His Word. Amen."

The audience sat in silence. Pastor Snowdown stood beside Ben Wagner. The hush was in holy awe of what had just been shared. Simplistic? No. Simple? Yes. So simple that a child might understand it. But, then, that is the way of Jesus.

The meeting had ended, or so it seemed, but no one left. The silence was broken by many coming, without invitation, to the altar for prayer. The others seemed to want to stay just a little longer. There was only quiet talking.

Kevin broke the silence around him. Yet, he too, spoke in hushed tones. "Wow! Did you get all that? You could tell from his sincerity that he has learned that by experience. But for me to assimilate it all in one sitting is impossible. I'm sure going to order the tape."

Jason turned toward the exit. "Look over there! Melanie is leaving with Kyle. I wonder what that means?"

"It means that they really like each other," Helen said. "And they are struggling through a very tough issue. Next to salvation, it is probably the most basic." After listening to all that was said that night, Helen really wanted to help Jason. He just didn't seem to get it. *How could his first comment be about Kyle and Melanie,* she thought.

Slowly, in groups of twos and threes, the crowd began to leave, quietly, though, because many still remained at the altar. The three missionaries-in-training and their budding support teams congregated in the foyer.

"Pastor Dan, thank you for inviting all of us to this meeting," came a chorus of appreciation from Helen, Kevin, and Jason, as they and their friends crowded around Pastor Dan.

"He sure knows the Word," Helen said, as others agreed.

"I'm sure experience has taught him a great deal," Pastor Dan said. "And his ministry is a testimony to God's faithfulness in his life. But (and I'm sure he would admit this) like Paul the Apostle, our words—a true reflection of our belief—oftentimes go beyond our life experiences. What am I trying to say? Only this: We are all 'flesh and blood.' We need to be careful not to pedestal any man. You certainly don't like it when people 'fawn' over you about how great you are, planning to go to the mission field. Right?"

"You're right," one of Kevin's friends said. "Hey, this getting together is not only excellent training, but an encouragement."

"I'm glad you came," Pastor Dan said, smiling at the group. "Pastor Joe says he has another speaker scheduled for next month. We'll get an invitation out to you soon enough for you to invite your support teams again."

Kevin turned to Helen. "Helen, I can see how the 'comfort of the pew' could overwhelm people coming to your church for the first time. Not only a beautiful sanctuary and fabulous organ, but a full schedule of programs. I've been looking through your church bulletin."

"Kevin, being impressed would last only for a few

weeks, at the most. There's such an involvement here that very few can just settle into that comfort. Those who try usually move on to another church where they can just take in and not contribute anything." Helen was glad she could speak positively about her church.

"Later!" Jason threw over his shoulder, as he left with his three friends.

"Later!" Kevin laughed his word back at him. *Oh, to be a high school graduate again,* he thought.

"Good night, Jason," Helen said with as much kindness as she could muster.

A long evening was over. Intense! But the training yet awaiting these four would lead them deeper into their commitment.

PERSONAL NOTES:

7

THE HEART OF ONE WHO GOES

It was one month later when Kevin pulled his beat-up Toyota into a church parking lot. This time it was not his own church. It was Helen's church. The contrast between his church and hers was as obvious as night and day, and he felt a twinge of embarrassment driving his old, rust-spotted car before such majestic buildings. Even the parking lot of Helen's church was impressive: smooth and black, with clean, crisp white lines designating hundreds of even spaces. Quite different from his, where one pulled onto the grassy, gravel-studded meadow adjacent to the simple wooden structure and decided this would be a good place to start a line of cars.

Manicured lawns and planters spilling over with brightly colored seasonal flowers, invited people to the broad steps leading up to the several large buildings, each as beautiful and well-positioned as Jason had remarked.

When Kevin had come to Helen's church last month, he had sensed the Spirit of God there. It was no less present in his own church. He knew they worshipped the same God. But he had to admit to himself that the koinania he felt at his own church was more comfortable.

As he walked up the stairs to the four sets of double, glass doors, his thoughts soared miles away to his chosen field of service. *What would their worship feel like? Would he be able to join in? Would they accept his "American" ways? Or would he be able to adapt to theirs?*

Beautiful organ music welcomed him into the sanctuary. And there was Jason, standing in the aisle near the back, looking the same as he did when last Kevin saw him, big hair and all.

"Hi, Jason," Kevin said as he came along side of him. He put his hand on Jason's shoulder.

Jason had been standing at the doors of the sanctuary, mesmerized by what he saw.

"Hi, Kevin," he said dreamily, without taking his eyes from the room. "Do you see who's playing the organ? That's Helen. Man, that is sweet."

"Helen? Or the music?" Kevin said wryly.

"Both. And you know it," Jason said, the dreamy tone replaced with sudden defensiveness. He shook his head and cracked a smile when he saw Kevin's gentle grin. He was only teasing. *There I go again, putting my big mouth before my brain. Was that trigger response to assumed attacks ever going to go away?* lamented Jason.

"Don't get bent out of shape," Kevin said. "I was only teasing." His voice was now sincere and congenial. "Hey, do you think you can take a bit of counsel from one only four years older than you?"

"Try me," Jason said. In truth, he welcomed it.

"I don't know quite how to say it, Jason, but it seems that words come out of your mouth before you give much thought to them."

"I know. I was just thinking that! And lamenting the fact, too." Jason looked him square in the eyes. "But that still cuts me to the quick, hearing it from you."

"I'm sorry. I didn't mean to hurt your feelings. I'm just trying to help."

"That's okay. That's exactly the issue I'm trying to deal with. Can you help?"

"Scripture, dude. Scripture is the only thing that provides an answer for a problem like that. James gives us a real tongue-lashing about how wicked our tongue really can be. 'Like a spark of fire burning down a whole forest,' he says."

"Yeah, I'm only too familiar with those words. Our pastor encouraged us to do a personal Book study. Because I knew that James talked about the tongue, I started there. 'Even fresh and salt water don't come out of the same spring. Yet, good and evil comes out of the same mouth. This should not be,'[1] But he doesn't really tell us how to control our tongue."

"I discovered the same thing when I decided that I needed a better control of my words. David often prayed, 'Lord, guard my lips. Lord, put a bridle on my tongue.'[2] Can you picture it? A little leather harness around my tongue with the Lord holding the reigns." Kevin tried to say that with his tongue sticking out.

They both had a good laugh as they pictured it in their minds. Their laughter attracted Helen's attention, and she turned on the organ bench and frowned. They gestured that they were sorry and quieted down, as Helen went back to her music.

"Well," Kevin said, that might make an amusing picture, but it still didn't give me the 'It is written' that I needed to use when satan would tempt me to use bad

1 Read James 3:1-12   2 Read Psalm 39:1; 141:3

or hurtful words. But one day, in the normal course of my Bible reading, I came to Ephesians, Ephesians 4:29, to be exact. The words of that verse just stood out on the page. I knew that the Holy Spirit had chosen those words for me to use to control my tongue. Listen: 'Let there be no more foul language, but good words instead; words suitable for the occasion, that God can use to help other people.' Jason, I memorized that verse. I meditated—and continue to meditate—on that verse. I'll be the first to admit, my tongue still isn't perfect. But I can assure you that it's under better control now than before that day I decided to cry out to God and allow Christ to have victory in that part of my life."[3]

"The way you said 'that day' makes me think something pretty radical must have happened for you to cry out to God," Jason said.

Just as Kevin was about to tell his crisis story, Kyle and Melanie joined them. "Hi Kyle. Melanie," Jason said, flashing a white-toothed smile. "Good to see the two of you together. It just looks right. You both look—" Jason paused. Kevin glared. This time he choose his words carefully, "—happy! Yes, happy!"

Kyle beamed "We are, Jason. We've met a couple of times with Pastor Carl. Melanie, tell them the good news."

Melanie blushed at his gaze. "I'm glad you see it as good news, Kyle. I know it isn't exactly what you had hoped for, but we'll leave that to God."

"Tell us! What's the good news?" Kevin said, anxious to hear the resolve.

Melanie's face grew serious. In soft tones, she whispered behind a cupped hand, "You haven't heard about salvation through Jesus Christ?"

They all laughed. Kevin persisted, "Come on! You

3 The concept of having a "stockpile" of "It is written's" as Jesus had, recorded in Luke 4, is fully discussed in the book, *Prepare For Battle*, Neal Pirolo, ERI, 1997.

know that isn't what I meant."

"I know, I know. Well, we've come to this compromise. I really believe Kyle and I are meant to be together. I realized that on that one stupid date I had with Kyle's best friend. Not that his friend was stupid. I was. I probably made him miserable—just being with me. What's with that grin on your face, Kyle?"

"Oh, nothing. Okay, okay," Kyle chuckled. "Brandon gave me his rendition of the date. As much as he would have enjoyed developing a relationship with you, he too got the message: Back off, she still belongs to Kyle."

"Did you and Brandon set that up?" Melanie said, her eyes narrowed at Kyle.

Kyle smiled. "No, but I think maybe the Lord did."

"Well, Melanie, what's the compromise?" Kevin asked again.

"As I said, we believe we're still meant to be together. But at this time, I just can't see myself as a missionary. So we're putting our relationship on hold for these two years. I'm not going to bug Kyle about coming home to me. And he's not going to try to persuade me— I can hardly think of the thought—to be a missionary. We're going to keep our relationship in prayer and see how the Lord moves in our hearts." She turned to Kyle. "Is that a fair summary of our agreement?"

"Fair enough. I'm just glad you're here with us tonight." Kyle was still beaming.

"Flattery will get you everywhere," Jason said.

Kevin poked Jason sharply in the back, a friendly reminder of what they had been talking about before Kyle and Melanie showed up. Jason said no more. But he wondered, *Will Scripture really help me control my tongue?*

"Jason, flattery is *not* what is on my mind," Kyle re-

sponded. "No, I'm just glad to be with her." Kyle's statement of assurance was more for Melanie than for Jason. Kyle was sincerely glad, still knowing that it would
have to be God, not him, who brought change, if any,
into Melanie's heart.

The organ music stopped, and they watched Helen
step down to join them. "Helen, that was beautiful. I
didn't know you were so talented on the organ," Kevin
said.

"There's probably a lot you don't know about me."
Just as she had been with Jason last month, Helen
found herself short with Kevin, now. Why was she doing that? She was sure it was just a sincere compliment. She should have just said, 'Thanks.'

"Is that an invitation to get to know you better?" Kevin said, groaning in his mind as soon as he said it.

At the same time he was saying, "I'm sorry," Helen
cut him off with a sharp, "No!"

Jason joined in the fray: "Man! Did she tell you!"

"No, Jason. I didn't mean to sound harsh. I just
think those of us who have made a determination to go
on this two-year commitment can't let ourselves become sidetracked. I just want to stay focused. Don't you
think I'm having my own struggles? Besides wor-
shipping God—as I always do when I get to play the organ—I keep thinking, on the field where I'm going, there
will be no pipe organ—no organ at all! They have to sing
in whispers, if at all. It'll be a real challenge to me to
join them in making 'a joyful noise unto the Lord!'"

Jason, trying to choose his words more carefully,
said, "You always seem so cool—so together. I didn't
think anything could bother you. I'm sorry for making it
harder for you with my crazy words."

Helen smiled, saying nothing, but thinking, just

possibly under that huge head of hair there might be a real sensitive guy.

Kevin slapped his forehead with a "whap!" He hadn't even heard Jason's thoughtful words. He was thinking of his own situation. "Wow! You know how I love soccer. And I'm going to get to do soccer clinics and set up tournaments, and—"

"And probably a lot of other things that won't be just 'fun and games,'" Pastor Jim added, joining the group.

"Yes, I'm ready for that, too. At least I think I am," Kevin added.

"Hey guys, look who's coming," Jason said. "Hi, Andy. Meet some of my friends. These are the other three who are going on a short two-year ministry outreach. Kyle, and his girl friend Melanie, who's staying at home; Helen, and Kevin. And this is Kevin's pastor, Jim. Sorry, I don't know your last name, Pastor."

"Whitney. My name's Jim Whitney. Glad to meet you, Andy," he said, extending his hand.

"Aw, come on," Jason said, giving Andy a playful fist in the arm. "Andy's a hugger."

Andy and Jason embraced.

"Helen," Jason said, "I want you in particular to know that with your prodding, I not only listened to the tapes and read the book, but the Lord also directed me to ask Andy to be my liaison—my team leader. We went through the material together, he prayed about it, and then said, 'Yes.' His major task is keeping the team focused on their commitments while I'm gone. You know, none of this 'out of sight, out of mind' excuse when I come home. By the way, did you know there's another book specifically about coming home? In fact, two books. The one for us is called *Reentry*, and the one for our support team is titled, *The Reentry Team.*"4

"Well, Jason, I'm happy for you," Helen said. "By the way, are you and your church leadership any closer in deciding when and where you're going to go?"

"Oh yeah, man, that's exciting news too! That happened this month. We got that literature about the OM ship. Filled out and sent in the application. The references have even been sent in already. Now we wait for the okay. A new crew musters on twice a year. So after approval, I'd have to wait until the next muster. Could be a few months."

"Have you ever been on a ship?" Kevin asked.

Jason shook his head no. *What's coming next,* he wondered. He braced himself for—he didn't know what!

"Have you heard about seasickness?" Kevin said, wryly.

"Kevin! What are you trying to do?" a voice behind them spoke. They turned. It was Pastor Steve.

"Oh, hi, Pastor Steve," Kevin said. "Just a little teasing. Jason's never been on a ship."

"There will be a lot more than seasickness on his mind," Pastor Steve assured them all. "That ship ministry is demanding. Two years in the boiler room of an ocean liner will make a man out of him."

The excitement in Jason's voice was suddenly washed away in the undertow of reality. His smile flattened. It was good that he and Pastor Steve had attended those classes and had sorted out his motivation. 'Are we having fun, yet' sure doesn't apply to what he had to anticipate in a hot, greasy, smelly boiler room. "But, hey, somebody's got to do it," Jason thought out loud.

"Pastor Steve, do you know what the speaker is talking about tonight?" Kyle asked.

4 *Reentry,* Peter Jordan, YWAM Publishing, 1992. *The Reentry Team,* Neal Pirolo, ERI, 2000.

"I heard he has a lesson from Paul's farewell address to the elders of Ephesus. I don't know any more about it than that."

"Well, we'll find out soon enough. There he is with Pastor Joe, going up to the platform now," Helen said. She encouraged them all to sit down.

"Good evening. It's good to see you all here," Pastor Joe said aloud. "There's quite an exciting move going on among four of our churches in Middletown. Close to the same time four of our young people each went to one of their pastors and said the awesome words, *'I think God wants me to be a missionary.'* Through these last months they have been dealing with a number of issues that are good to get serious about before they head to the field. They've also gotten involved in some of the ministries to internationals who live among us right here in Middletown.

"I think all four of them have also been diligent in building their support teams. You know, one of the myths in the church at large is: 'All a missionary wants is my money!' On the contrary, a missionary needs care in at least six areas, that even Paul, the Apostle asked for. In a minute we'll be calling on my good friend, Pastor Hank Willis. But first I would like the four missionaries-in-training to stand with their pastors and their developing support teams."

There was a smattering of applause, not something that happened often in this church. Then it broke into a reechoing of sound. Those standing were embarrassed at the attention. But it did bring back to mind what they had learned about church people putting missionaries on the pedestal.

They were about to sit down when Pastor Joe said, "No, no! Stay standing. I think it's important to see that mission endeavor is a team effort. Notice that I didn't draw attention to the four who are going. Though they may be like the pitcher on a baseball team or the quarterback on a football team, it takes all of the other players doing their part to win the game. And we have more than just a game to win. Souls for the Kingdom is our objective. Now you may be seated." He directed those words to the mission teams and their pastors.

"Before I call our speaker to the podium, there's another bit of excitement to share. Carl Peters is the missions pastor at a sister church here in Middletown. Won't you come and introduce Adam and tell us what happened to him?"

As Pastor Carl stood, he quietly said, "Praise the Lord." *This pastor just called us a 'sister' church. Unity is what you want, dear Lord.* Thoughts like that register and resonate in the mind and heart of a true pastor. He literally ran to the platform, anxious to fully express his feelings about what happened. This disturbed the decorum of a few of the older members of this church.

"Adam, won't you come and join me on the platform?" Pastor Carl asked.

Adam ambled to the front and up the three steps, guitar strapped across his back. He bent over, full posterior to the audience, and picked up the amplifier cord for his guitar. The people couldn't help themselves. They broke into laughter. Adam was young, energetic and zealous for the Lord, but lacked some of the finesse of stage manners. *No matter,* Pastor Carl thought as he looked at him. *He loves the Lord. And look what He has done for and through him.*

Turning to the audience, Pastor Carl began. "A lot of excitement is being generated in our church as we prepare to send Kyle out on his first missionary venture.

Adam came to me one day a couple of weeks ago, looking pretty glum. 'What's wrong, Adam,' I asked. This was so unlike the young man I knew.

"Adam knew his problem. He stated it easily. 'There's a lot of excitement over Kyle and the development of his support team. I thought, what can I do? All I do is play my guitar at a home fellowship. That doesn't seem to be much in comparison to what Kyle is going to do.'

"'Oh, Adam,' I said. 'We are all a part of the Body of Christ. We are each important to what God has called us to do.' I knew that he sometimes wrote his own songs, so I challenged him. 'Listen,' I said, 'Psalm 67, verses one and two, has a powerful missions theme. Why don't you write a chorus, using those words?'

"Well, the very next day, Adam was back, beaming from ear to ear—like he is doing right now. I think I have embarrassed him. But listen to the powerful song that God gave to him for us."

Adam began strumming his guitar. As he sensed the Spirit of God, he began singing:

> "I hear the cry of kids that sounds through the
> streets;
> I hear the cry of mothers and fathers who are
> hurting;
> I hear the sorrow of girls and boys—young
> ones—who are going there;
> Everyone knows where, but they are silent.
> That's why I shout:
>
> Lord, be merciful to us and bless us;
> Lord, shine Your face upon us;
> May every nation see that You are Lord;
> That they might know Your way on earth
> and Your salvation among all nations.

I see nations lost without You;
I see countries bloodied by wars;
I see devils' curses upon those who are
   going there;
Everyone knows where, but they are silent.
That's why I shout:

Lord, be merciful to us and bless us;
Lord, shine Your face upon us;
May every nation see that You are Lord;
That they might know Your way on earth
   and Your salvation among all nations."[5]

Adam unplugged his guitar before the sound man had turned his amplifier off. Apart from the loud screech, the room was silent. Powerful words sung so sincerely spoke volumes. Adam joined the audience, placing his guitar under the pew in front of him. He looked up, still beaming.

"Powerful! That is powerful," Pastor Joe said as he motioned for the speaker to join him at the pulpit. "Well, Hank, I don't want to take any more time away from you, but I'm excited to see what God is doing through His people in Middletown. Church, please give a warm welcome to Pastor Hank Willis, Pastor emeritus, conference speaker, world traveler—what else? Friend!"

Willis took the stage. He was a humble, shy looking man with small round glasses and soft, thinning brown hair. But when he spoke, he was anything but soft. "Thank you for those kind words, Pastor Joe. I embrace your excitement. Though in some churches, missions is taking a back seat (Actually, some churches have completely removed that back pew!), many churches are coming alive to a new, yet 2000 year old, commission: *Go! Preach! Go! Teach!* Really, in Greek 'go' is under

5 This challenge given to Adam was literally given to Laci Adamovich, a Slovak man, when he expressed Adam's thoughts. It was translated into English by Ivetka Higgins.

stood in the more active sense of 'as you are going.' This takes it out of that 'special calling' that some people consider is necessary before they become 'witnesses unto Him' cross-culturally. But that's another subject for another time.

"What I want to share with you this evening would be titled, 'The Heart of One Who Goes.' I cannot agree more heartily with Pastor Joe that it takes a team. In fact, to change the metaphor, it takes a whole army! For missions is war; a war that is more critical than the sum total of all secular wars. It's a battle for the eternal souls of all mankind. But now let's look at a missionary from the First Century: Paul, the Apostle. In all of his letters you can see him challenging and/or commending the people for their partnership in the Gospel.

Hank Willis took off his glasses and leaned forward on the podium. "In Acts 20—and it might be good for you to open your Bibles and follow along—in Acts 20, Paul was on his way to Jerusalem. He had stopped at many cities, encouraging the churches and collecting an offering for the poor Christians in Jerusalem. He wanted to get there by Pentecost. He was returning from his third and most extensive trip. He had such a deep relationship with the elders of the churches he had planted in the region of Ephesus that he knew if he went there, they would delay his progress to Jerusalem in time for Pentecost. So he stayed in a seaport city of Miletus, calling the elders to come to him there. On their arrival, Paul, the Apostle shared a farewell address expressing the heart of one who goes."

Several on Kyle's team gave him an encouraging look. *How did they know I was thinking of my farewell 'address' to Melanie,* he thought. He glanced at Melanie. *Could she see her part in my team, as Adam had just shown?* he wondered. Probably not. Though she had come to an agreeable resolve, she was still shy of anything that would look like missions involvement.

The speaker slipped his glasses back on and looked down at his notes, and then back at his audience. "I'm going to expand the words of his farewell address with supportive Scripture from his other writings and from Luke's record of the Acts of the Apostles. Though I'm not going to be able to give you every reference, you'll soon hear almost all Scripture, though some of it might not sound familiar, coming from various translations. I'll try to keep my own words to a minimum. Paul begins in verse eighteen of Chapter 20:

*"I have lived among you.'*6
"Paul, the Apostle, was a man of no small heritage, both as a Jew and now as an apostle to the Gentiles. In his own words, not the Lord's, to the Christians at Corinth, he did a little foolish boasting: 'I am a Hebrew. I am an Israelite. I am a descendent of Abraham. I am a minister of Christ. I have worked harder than any of them.' (Those with whom he is foolishly comparing himself.) 'I have served more prison sentences. I have been beaten times without number. I have faced death time and again. I have been beaten the regulation thirty-nine stripes by the Jews five times. I have been stoned once. I have been beaten with rods three times. I have been shipwrecked three times.' Another was yet to come on his way to Rome. 'I have been twenty-four hours in the open sea.'"

I wonder if those OM ships ever crash, Jason thought. *Twenty-four hours in the open sea; man, that would be wild! There's more?* Jason questioned, as the speaker continued.

6 For you, the reader, the phrases in *italics* are from Acts 20. Because so many Scriptures are used in this chapter, we did not attempt to footnote them all. Sometimes there is just a phrase from a verse; sometimes many phrases from different passages are put together. We did attempt to bracket them all with 'single' quotes.

"'In my travels I have been in constant danger from rivers and floods, from bandits, from my own countrymen, and from pagans. I have faced danger in city streets, danger in the desert, danger on the high seas and danger among false Christians. I have known exhaustion, pain, long vigils, hunger and thirst, doing without meals; I have been cold and have lacked clothing.

"'Apart from all these external trials, I have the daily burden of responsibility for all the churches. Do you think anyone is weak without my feeling his weakness? Does anyone have his faith upset without my longing to restore him?

"'In Damascus, I escaped by being let down the wall in a basket. No, I don't think it's really a good thing for me to boast at all, but I will just mention visions and revelations from the Lord Himself.'[7]

"'I have lived among you,' he said. 'I have not demanded five-star hotels or first class, wide-bodied jets. I have not insisted upon the sumptuous cuisine of princes,' he would probably say today."

The audience sensed that Hank Willis was insinuating that this practice is not uncommon among missionaries today. Once again he removed his glasses and leaned forward for emphasis, speaking directly into the microphone. "I have lived among you. The heart of one who goes to preach Christ and Him crucified; the heart of one who goes to teach people how to live by the commandments of Christ will insist on living among the people. It was said of Christ, 'The Word was made flesh, and dwelt among us.'[8] Yet taxi drivers in major cities of the world 'automatically' take the missionaries to the elite sections of town. Nationals, who have related with missionaries over the years, will not 'respect' a new

7 Read II Corinthians 11:22-12:1   8 Read John 1:14

missionary unless he lives in the 'American' sector. 'No, I have lived among you ever since I first came to Asia,' answered a missionary statesman."

Jason's mind was going a "thousand miles a second" as he considered the tight bunk quarters and the narrow passageways he would be sharing with workers from 60 different cultures.

"'I have served the lord....'
"Though thousands in the first century and millions through the centuries of time have been benefactors of Paul's ministry, he served the Lord. 'Whatever you do, do it heartily as unto the Lord.' 'Keeping our eyes fixed on Jesus, the source and goal of our faith,' 'we endure hardness as a good soldier of Jesus Christ. We do not get entangled in the affairs of this world so that we may please the One who has called us to be a soldier.'

"To change the analogy, the house we build by our own instruction is a house of cards (wood, hay, and stubble) destined for sure to collapse in the storms of life. The house we build on the Rock (using gold, silver and precious stones) will withstand every tempest. In building his house (his life), Paul the Apostle affirmed, 'I have served the Lord.'

"'...with all humility of mind.'
"The heart of one who goes does not come with the excellency of human speech or of man's wisdom. But, in fertile new fields (as Corinth was at the time) 'I am determined to know nothing before you except Christ and Him crucified.

"'As a matter of fact, I was with you in weakness, and in fear, and in much trembling. And my speech and my preaching were not with enticing words of man's wisdom. But in demonstration of the Spirit and of power: Plainly that your faith should not stand in the wisdom of men, but in the power of God.'

"'We preach not ourselves, but Christ Jesus the Lord; we are your servants for Jesus' sake. This treasure is held in clay pots, to show that the splendid power of it belongs to God and not to us." To emphasize his next Scripture, Hank held up his hand, raising his fingers, point by point. "Let your light so shine before men... that they may see your good works... and glorify your Father in Heaven. The first two phrases of that Biblical injunction are not at all difficult to do. But to accomplish the third—that God would receive all the glory, Paul knew, requires that we serve the Lord with all humility of mind.'"

There is that 'pride' issue again, several of the students thought, remembering Jason's experience with his church family.

"*...and in tears.*'
"Solomon said that there is 'a time to laugh and a time to weep.' Jesus' heart was 'moved with compassion as He saw the multitudes that were sheep without a shepherd.' Paul's yearnings for the flocks of God under his care caused him, 'out of much affliction and anguish of heart, to write to them with many tears.'

"There is an intensity to the battle; It is hand-to-hand combat with the enemy of our souls. There is a great prize of victory; from every tongue and tribe, every nation and people, will come a Bride for Christ. And there is a privilege in our participation: 'All power in Heaven and earth has been given to Me, therefore (you) go.' A good starting place for our involvement might be in our closet of prayer crying out for the mercy of God on this sin-sick world. When was the last time we wept for the lost of the world? Paul the Apostle did—often."

Andy, Jason's team captain, noted this point. He knew it would be his responsibility to keep the team focused on the thousands of non-Christians who visit the ships each year. And on Jason's lifestyle, which will be 'read' by all those people. *Am I up to this responsibility?* Andy was wisely making a serious reality check on what he sensed the Lord wanted him to do.

"'...in trials and tribulations.'

"At least by the time Paul was in Ephesus, he had come to appreciate the fact that, with every open door of opportunity, there would be adversaries."

He paused to let a heavy silence weigh on the audience, for he knew what he was going to say next. "The enemy is satan. The people who will allow him to use them as pawns may be from any strata of life relationships. In one situation, because the Sadducees were against him, the Pharisees took a strong stand for him. Other times religious parties joined forces to attack him. Prominent citizens joined hands with 'certain lewd fellows of the baser sort' and 'set the city in an uproar.'

"'I've gotten to the place where I expect anything. All I know is that the Holy Spirit has warned me that imprisonment and persecution await me in every city that I visit.'

"Too often today, when one who is preparing for field work faces his first 'adversary', he shudders in his boots and says, 'I think God is closing that door on me.' Nonsense! That's just the beginning of the trials and temptations that await you as the 'big toe' of satan's adversaries are sticking out behind every door of opportunity, trying to trip you up. We must remember that open doors set before us by God, no one can shut!"

The four missionaries-in-training tried to catch the eyes of their pastors. They had all heard this before, and they knew clearly what Pastor Willis was talking about. They were experiencing it right now in these months of pre-field preparation.

Willis continued. "Rather, our attitude should be as James talked about: 'When all kinds of trials and temptations crowd into your life, don't resent them as intruders but welcome them as friends.'" Hank looked up. "—not as a masochist who enjoys pain, I would add— 'but realize that they come to test your faith and produce in you the quality of endurance.' And, if there is a quality that missionaries need in order to *thrive* on the mission field, it is endurance. 'It is through much tribulation that we enter the Kingdom of God,' said a missionary of centuries past.

"Notice that I also emphasized the word 'thrive'. Too often missionaries go to the field hoping that they will be able to 'survive the rigors' as they 'miss the comforts of home.'" Pastor Willis said those two phrases with a mock tremor in his voice to emphasize his disagreement with such an attitude. "Nonsense!" he shouted. "Missionaries face challenges to their new culture, for sure. But, *true* missionaries find ways to thrive in those new discoveries. But let's get back to Paul.

"'I have never shrunk from telling you anything that was for your good.'
"The heart and mind of Paul was free of the debilitating preoccupation with self. As with Jesus, he knew where he had come from: 'I am the chiefest of sinners.' He knew why he was here: 'You are chosen to be My ser-

vant.' And he knew where he was going: 'I have finished my course—a crown of righteousness awaits me.'

"As he instructed the Ephesians, so he practiced: 'Let there be no more foul language, but good words instead; words suitable for the occasion, that God can use to help other people.'"

Kevin mouthed the words with the pastor, and then said a silent, "Thank you Lord!"

As the passage was spoken, Jason also recognized its association with his own life. Lessons of truth were coming together as people from different backgrounds were saying the same thing.

I can have better control of my tongue, Jason assured himself. (Or was it Someone else assuring him?)

"The heart of one who goes is yearning to tell the nationals all that is for their good. 'Avoid fables and ill-informed controversies, which lead inevitably, as you know, to strife. Filter out all cultural gospel; treat as chaff the winds of doctrine;' defer the desire to share 'my soapbox', my doctrinal excess. Know nothing before them but the Gospel and teachings of Christ."

This teacher sure knows the Word, Helen thought. She knew that her depth of understanding of the Scriptures had been put there by her Christian-based home-school curriculum.

"So strongly bound to this commitment was Paul, that he said, 'Yes, if I, or an angel from heaven preach any other gospel, may I be anathema! Accursed! Cut off!' These are the powerful words of this pioneer missionary.

"'I have taught you both in public and in your homes.'
"While Paul was waiting in Athens for Silas and Timothy to join him, 'his soul was exasperated beyond en-

durance at the sight of a city so completely idolatrous.
He felt compelled to discuss the matter with the Jews in
the synagogue, as well as the God-fearing Gentiles, and
he even argued daily in the open marketplaces with the
passersby. He spoke to the council of the Epicurean
and Stoic philosophers at the Areopagus.'

"He wanted to enter the arena at Ephesus. He was
given permission to speak on the steps of the barracks.
He spoke in dungeons; he spoke by the riverside. He
spoke in third-floor, smoke-filled rooms—all night long!
He spoke on ships; he spoke on the seashore. He spoke
in the palace of kings; he spoke before the Sanhedrin;
he spoke in the court of Caesar Nero. He spoke in the
home of Simon, the tanner, as they labored in making
tents.

"As did Jesus, he was willing to speak to thousands,
or to take the time with a single soul seeking the Savior. The heart of one who goes has a compassion for the
lost that will have them instant in season and out. Willing to talk with many, or few. Present a scholarly discourse, or answer the simplest of questions: 'Sirs, what
must I do to be saved?'"

Helen realized that her testimony in a Muslim-
dominated country would come mainly from her lifestyle, not her words. She prayed that her work among
the children would bear good fruit.

*"I have most emphatically declared to both Jews and
Greeks...."*
"Peter had his 'sheet of unclean animals' experience to
convince him that the Good News is for the Jew and
Greek. What revelation of God was given to Paul is not
clear. But the testimony of his life and ministry declared: 'Whosoever will may come.'

"The heart of one who goes must become culturally adaptive, whatever the group: 'For though I am no man's slave, yet I have made myself everyone's slave: To the Jew, a Jew; to those under the Law, I put myself under the Law; to those who had no Law, I myself became like a man without the Law, but still bound to the law of Christ; to the weak, weak. In short, I have been made all things to all men so that by all means I might win some to Christ.'

Kevin thought of his 'all means' of sports clinics. He had read many testimonies of how sports had provided an entrance for the Gospel. He so wanted that to be true of his life.

"Zeal without knowledge is dangerous. But knowledge without zeal is a real drag! Paul's life demonstrated a zeal for God, which when tempered with the knowledge of the Holy One, motivated him to 'not consider his own life valuable so long as he could preach Christ and Him crucified.' Words spoken with conviction by Paul, the Apostle."

Hearing of Christ's crucifixion, stirred thoughts in Jason's mind. He had had time since that meeting months ago to come to grips with those two kinds of deaths. He was embarrassed to remember his outburst. But he was coming to a more mature perspective on even his easy-going, honest lifestyle.

Mr. Willis looked in his Bible to reference the next phrase. To his audience he said, "I trust you are following me. We continue at the second half of verse 21.

"'...repentance toward God and faith in our Lord Jesus.'
"Paul understood the simplicity of the Gospel message. In his letter to the Christians at Corinth, he said: 'Christ died for our sins according to the Scriptures,

was buried, and rose on the third day according to the Scriptures.' 'To write the same things to you--to me is not grievous, but for you it is safe.'

"The message, burned deep in the heart of one who goes, will have a ring of clarity and sincerity every time it goes forth. 'For I take no special pride in the fact that I preach the Gospel. I should feel utterly miserable if I failed to preach it,' testified one Paul of Tarsus."

Again Helen was brought face-to-face with the fact that it would be her lifestyle that would be doing most of the 'preaching' for her.

"'I am compelled in the Spirit...'
"Paul had moved through the districts, developing a church-planting strategy with some orderly pro- gression. The next district was Asia. 'But the Holy Spirit prevented them.' Okay, we'll go north to Bithynia. 'But when they got to Mysia, the Spirit of Jesus would not let them go!' On to Troas. The Macedonia vision: 'As soon as Paul had seen this vision, we made every effort to get on to Macedonia, convinced that God had called us to give them the Good News.'

"Let me insert a thought here: It is considered by many that it was at this point that Doctor Luke joined the team. Before that sentence, all of the pronouns were of others; now he is writing in the first person, saying 'we' and 'us.'"

Kyle knew this from his study of Biblical Greek. *But it was an interesting aside for the speaker to add,* he thought.

Now, as at several previous times, a certain look of compassion filled the speaker's face, letting the people know he had a serious summary statement to make. "The heart of one who goes has a deep, satisfying re-

lationship with the Father: I am loved. He has a re-
markable union with Christ that gives him a sense of
worthiness: I am complete in Him. And he has an intimate, secret dwelling place with the Holy Spirit that
gives him a sense of competence: I have been born of
the Spirit. It is in this third relationship—with the Holy
Spirit—that too often we fall short."

An uneasy quiet settled over this congregation of
mixed theology. What was Hank Willis going to say?
Doesn't he know that this issue is the subject of so
much controversy in the church? Surely, he does!

Pastor Willis smiled. "Yes, I hear the silence. Let me
continue. We have all had a father—good or bad—but
that somewhat helps us to relate to God, as a Father.
The Son. Yes, our elder Brother. He lived on earth. We
can understand. But, Holy Spirit—a Holy Ghost? The
Spirit has been that elusive Person of the Godhead
throughout the centuries.

"In His Mount of Ascension discourse, Jesus emphatically declared, 'Wait in Jerusalem for the Father's
Promise.' Personally, I don't care what you call 'it'; I
don't care when you get 'it'; just *don't leave home without it!*"

The tension in the audience was eased with the welcome pun, and even brought a few verbal "Amens!"

"'It' is referring, of course, to a personal, intimate,
knowledgeable, dynamic, ongoing, powerful, life-
directing and comforting relationship with the Third
Person of the Trinity, God, the Holy Spirit.

"While Apollos was in Corinth, Paul found twelve
disciples in the upper coasts of Ephesus. 'Have you received the Holy Spirit since you believed?' he asked.
They had not heard of Him; they had only heard of the
baptism of John. After some instruction, they were bap-

tized in the Name of Jesus. This is the testimony of a first century missionary.

"False spirits Paul was able to cast out. 'I command you in the Name of Jesus to come out of her,' he spoke to the demon possessing the damsel at Philippi. John said we are to 'test every spirit, to see whether it is of God or not.' The heart of one who goes becomes sensitive to the direction of the Holy Spirit of God. So lived one missionary, Paul the Apostle.

"Paul continues in his farewell address.

"'I do not know what may happen to me.'
"At best, I can only identify with one of Paul's traveling companions. And, at that, the continual state of uncertainty boggles my mind. Paul is preaching away. His co-workers are praying. There's euphoria of revival in Salamis and Antioch in Pisidia and Iconium. They are being acclaimed as Jupiter and Mercury, with an oxen ready to be sacrificed to him. And now, in Lystria—a healing! Then some Jews arrive and stone him. Drag him outside the city, thinking him dead. 'But when the disciples gathered around him, Paul got up and walked back into the city!'"

"That takes guts," Jason said. But this time in only a whisper. *Maybe God is already helping me to control my tongue,* he thought.

"Certainly Paul must have had Proverbs 27:1 memorized: 'Boast not thyself of tomorrow; for thou knowest not what a day may bring forth.' Could any two days in the life of Paul ever have been the same?

"The heart of one who goes must be prepared for the uncertainties of the culture, religion, politics, and economics of his host county. Anything less will shatter the 'comfort zones' of the uninitiated, often with devastating results. 'I have been made all things to all men,' said a culturally-adaptive missionary of long ago.

"Frankly I do not consider my own life valuable to me.'
"'It all accords with my own earnest wishes and hopes, which are that I should never be in any way ashamed, but that now, as always, I should honor Christ with the utmost boldness by the way I live, whether that means I am to face death or to go on living. For living to me means simply "Christ", and if I die I should merely gain more of Him. I realize, of course, that the work that I have started may make it necessary for me to go on living in this world. I should find it very hard to make a choice. I'm torn in two directions—on the one hand I long to leave this world and live with Christ, and that is obviously the best thing for me. Yet, on the other hand, it is probably more necessary for you that I stay here on earth. That is why I'm pretty well convinced that I shall not leave this world yet.'

Jason was not yet fully convinced that he was ready 'to leave this world.' He realized he had some 'closet work' yet to do on this one.

"The heart of one who goes must face the reality of 21st Century martyrdom. It does happen. But far more significant is the 'living sacrifice' of Romans 12:1-3: 'With your eyes wide open to the mercies of God. I beg you, my brothers, as an act of intelligent worship, to give Him your entire being, a living sacrifice...not letting the world squeeze you into its mold, but letting God renew your minds from within. Not cherishing exaggerated ideas of yourself or of your own importance, but having a sane estimate of your capabilities by the standard of the faith that He has given you,' instructed the Apostle to the Gentiles."

"As the overcomers of Revelation, Paul did not cherish his life even in the face of death. He had a correct attitude toward life and death."

After that Biblical study with Pastor Jim, Kevin certainly had a clearer understanding of Christ's call on his life. "It is Christ who is alive in me," he mouthed silently.

"'I just want to finish my course and complete the ministry which the Lord Jesus has given to me.'
"The Lord dealt gently with Ananias as he questioned the wisdom of 'handing himself over' to this Saul who had letters for his arrest in Damascus. 'Go on your way,' the Lord said, 'for this man is My chosen instrument to bear My name before the Gentiles and their kings, as well as the sons of Israel. He will suffer....'

"Years later, Paul had not diminished the Damascus Road experience. As he stood before King Agrippa, Bernice and Festus, he reiterated his call. And concluded, 'I could not disobey that heavenly vision.'

"Throughout His life, Jesus was able to testify to the fact that He neither said nor did anything but that which the Father told Him to say and do. The heart of one who goes is beating with the heartbeat of God— 'not willing that any perish, but that all come to repentance.' And he is able to focus on fulfilling those 'good deeds that He beforehand planned for him to walk in, for we are His most finely crafted work of art, created in Christ Jesus.'"

That Scripture has come up so often, recalled Helen in her own thoughts. *It is clear that He has a plan for my life.* She took comfort in those Words of Truth. *It's not all about me, but about Him and my part in His plan.* She cemented those words in her mind by clasping her hands firmly together. *I really want to see my life from God's perspective,* she affirmed in her mind.

"'I know that you are not going to see me again.'
"A lot of life is not super-spiritual, but rather mundane. Paul was a traveling man. Logistics played a big part in his life. It's amazing to 'pull out' of Scripture all of the passages that deal with just the ordinary. Yet, these are vital to the spiritual, for we are a whole person.

"For fun, read the 16th chapter of Romans. In this great theological treatise on Grace..., And it is that," Hank emphasized, "...notice that Paul devotes a full chapter—one-sixteenth of the Book—to the everyday business of saying, 'Hi!' Forty-two specific names are given in these exchanges of greetings. In fact, in verse 22, Tertius, who wrote this Epistle, must have leaned over to Paul, and in the excitement of all of these salutations, asked Paul if he, too, could greet the people. For, it says, 'I, Tertius, who wrote this Epistle, salute you in the Lord.'

"The heart of one who goes will soon learn the loneliness of separation, will feel the pain of friends who forget, will experience the frustration of unanswered letters."

This really perked up Karen's ears. She had been quietly following all Mr. Willis was saying, but now... She had agreed to be Helen's communication coordinator. They would have to exercise extreme care, considering the limited access country to which Helen was going. But Karen just now made a strong determination that the people back home would not lose contact with Helen.

Another dart of loneliness hit Kyle's being as he thought about life without Melanie being with him. He shot a sideways glance at her, wondering what thoughts she was having. *I must keep focused,* he determined.

"Though tempted to lament, 'May we not travel with a Christian wife as the other messengers do?' the heart of one who goes must take comfort in Christ's words: 'I promise you, nobody leaves home or brothers or sisters or mothers or fathers or children or property for My sake and the Gospel's without getting back a hundred times now in this present life—and in the world to come, eternal life.'"

Kyle felt Melanie squeeze his hand. It assured him of her sincere commitment to their agreement. "Thank You, Lord," he silently mouthed. He looked at her and smiled his appreciation.

"'I tell you solemnly today that my conscience is clear.'
"'The Way (by some called, heresy) is in fact the fulfillment of the Law and the Prophets. My hope is in the resurrection. With this hope before me, I do my utmost to live my whole life with a clear conscience, void of offence, before God and men.'

"Heavy on Paul's mind might have been the words of Ezekiel 3 and 33. God had set Ezekiel as a watchman to the House of Israel. Clear, unequivocal instruction had been given him as to whom to warn of judgment and what would be the consequences of his obedience or lack thereof: 'Because thou hast not given him warning, he shall die in his sins; but his blood will I require at your hands.'

"Paul bore the responsibility of his calling: Sent by God to the Gentiles to 'open their eyes, turn them from darkness to light and to turn them from the power of satan to God so that (and here begins the work of the

Godhead) they may know forgiveness of sins, be sanctified by the faith that is in Me, and receive an inheritance among the saints.'

"The heart of one who goes also bears the responsibility to 'go out to battle for right, armed with faith and a clear conscience.' He will pursue 'the ultimate aim of the Christian ministry, which after all, is to produce the love which springs from a pure heart, a good conscience and a genuine faith.'

"The heart of one who goes knows that a clear conscience protects him 'from men who would slanderously speak against him—who would try to libel his name.'"

The four missionaries-in-training simultaneously realized that nothing had yet been said about this subject. *A clear conscience,* Kevin thought, making a mental note to ask Pastor Jim about it.

Hank Willis continued, seeming to gain energy from the Lord. The power behind his words made an indelible impression on his hearers.

"'I have never shrunk from declaring to you the whole counsel of God.'
"Paul was a student of the Word. It was his final authority. 'All Scripture is inspired of God and is profitable for doctrine, for reproof, for correction, and for instruction in righteousness.'

"When he did not have Scripture to support his position, he admitted it: 'Now concerning young women, I have no commandment from the Lord.' Yet, at other times, he would say, 'I believe I have the mind of the Lord in this matter.'

"The Word, the Whole Counsel of God, 'is quick and powerful, and sharper than any two-edged sword.' It is the Spirit's Sword, entrusted to our hand. Yet, He re-

tains the responsibility of being the ammunition choos-
er ('My Word, He said, will not return void.') and the
guidance system. (It is the Word of God that 'divides between the thoughts of the mind and the motivations of
the heart.'

"The heart of one who goes, fearlessly thrusts the
Sword (at the Spirit's command) to cut that de-
generative spiral that begins with temptation and ends
in spiritual death talked about in James, Chapter One.
That chain of events is best cut with a sharp, 'It is written...' from the Word of God that Jesus used. With that
same Sword, the one who goes is able to 'prick sinners
in their heart' so that they cry out, 'What must I do to
be saved?' And, again, with that Whole counsel of God,
he can begin with Moses, go through the Psalms and
the Prophets, so the Christian says, 'Didn't our hearts
burn within us as He talked with us along the road?'

"Oh, how 'severe' are the words, 'Work out your own
salvation with fear and trembling....' But, the Whole
Counsel of God does not end there. It goes on: '...for it
is God Who is at work in you, both to will and to do of
His good pleasure.' Verse twelve of Philippians Two is
not a complete thought without verse thirteen.

Pastor Steve noted with what force Hank Willis emphasized that passage. *I wonder if there is some serious
background to that. Maybe he was only taught the first
half of that thought in his youth,* he mused.

"The heart of one who goes will declare the unique-
ness of a loving, infinite, personal, all-wise, all-powerful
God. He will also make known: 'It is a fearful thing to
fall into the hands of the living God.'

"The Sword slashes from both edges. 'I have not
shrunk from declaring to you the Whole Counsel of
God,' declared this first century missionary.

"Now be on guard for yourselves.'
"'I run the race with determination. I am no shadow boxer, just beating the air. I really fight. I am my body's sternest master, keeping it under subjection, lest that by any means, when I have preached to others, I myself should be a castaway.'

"'Some, alas, have laid these simple weapons, faith and a clear conscience, contemptuously aside and, as far as their faith is concerned, have run their ships on the rocks.'

He's talking now about a clear conscience being a weapon, Kevin mused. I have to talk with Pastor Jim about this. Is a clear conscience a weapon or part of our armor? Or may it be both?

It is interesting how the same words can speak differently to different people. Jason was muttering under his breath, "There he goes talking about shipwrecks again. Man, is this a forewarning or something?"

"The heart of one who goes 'will stir up the gift of God, which is in him by the putting on the hands of ordination.' 'For God has not given us a spirit of fear, but of power and of love and of a sound mind,' admonished Paul, the Apostle to the Gentiles.

"'I tell you to keep on the alert.'
"'Be alert, not only for yourselves, but for every flock of which the Holy Spirit has made you guardians; you are to be shepherds of the Church of God, which He won at the cost of His own blood,' Peter told his fellow elders. Jude began his brief letter with the words, 'I exhort you to earnestly contend, in hand-to-hand combat for the faith, for evil men have entered the church....' Paul continues, 'I know that after my departure savage wolves will come in among you without mercy for the flock.

Yes, and even some men from among you, will arise speaking perversions of the truth, trying to draw away the disciples and make them followers of themselves.' It is a warning as vital today as it was when Paul spoke it.

"'Now I commend you to the Lord.'
"Paul and Barnabas were excited. Commissioned by the Holy Spirit and their church, they were off on their first journey. New believers—and adversaries—in every city. They reached Derbe, and realized that they had not established any type of leadership structure in the churches. 'And when they had preached the Gospel in that city and made many disciples, they turned back to Lystra, Iconium, and Antioch. They put fresh heart into the disciples, urging them to stand firm in the faith. They appointed elders for them in each church, and with prayer and fasting, commended these men to the Lord in whom they had believed.'

"On later journeys, Paul had other members of his team for that work. Titus and Timothy each got personal letters instructing them.

"The heart of one who goes, sensitive to the Holy Spirit, 'will find faithful men (national, for sure) and entrust to them all he has heard (of the Gospel and teachings of Christ). And he will do it in such a way that they will be able to go out and teach others.'

"Look at what Jesus did with the two disciples on the road to Emmaus: He came along side and walked with them; He 'hid' His own identity; He listened to them; He revealed Himself through the Word; He stayed with them until their hearts were rekindled with the fire of God. Then, when they were able to carry the Message of His resurrection back to Jerusalem on their own, shouting, 'He's risen! He's risen!,' Jesus disappeared.

His physical presence wasn't needed there anymore.

"The heart of one who goes, therefore,

- Will come alongside the nationals and will work with them;
- Will minimize as best as possible his identity as a foreigner;
- Will listen to their hearts and felt needs;
- Will reveal Christ by the Word;
- Will stay with them until the fire of the Spirit is kindled (or rekindled) in their hearts;
- Will get out of their way when they can minister on their own.[9]

"As Watchman Nee once said, 'A missionary at best should regard himself as scaffolding. When the church is built, you take it down and move it on to the next location'

"The heart of one who goes 'commends the brethren to the Lord and the message of His grace which can build you up and give you a place among all those who are consecrated to God.'

"'And with these words—and others—he knelt down with them all and prayed.'"

And that is exactly what the congregation in that Middletown church did. Without a dramatic appeal, a wave of the Spirit of God rolled across the auditorium. One by one, row by row, the people went to the altar, kneeled at their place or just bowed their head in prayer as the Holy Spirit moved in each of their hearts.

Sometime later, as people began moving about, the four pastors, the missionaries-in-training and their fledgling support teams came together for a final huddle. Each was sober in thought, yet excited with anticipation. Certainly the Lord had good plans for each one of them.

9 This six-point summary of Luke 24:13-35, is the foundation of ERI's teachings, and our strongest encouragement to those who would minister cross-culturally.

PERSONAL NOTES:

EPILOGUE

A new family of believers left the building that evening. Many took a fresh look at their own lifestyle, asking the question, "What does God want of me?" Priorities were set in order by others. The camaraderie among the Christians in Middletown was beginning to be felt everywhere: In the marketplace; in the workplace; in the home. God was awakening this city to His plan and His purposes: That the whole earth would be filled with His glory![1]

And what happened in each of the missionary's lives?

They continued for a while in their own churches, developing a ministry among the internationals living in Middletown.

Kyle set up a class in a local empty storefront to help those who wanted to practice their conversational English. He was able to enlist the help of members from his church as the program grew. Melanie even came to help on several occasions. More and more people were wanting this kind of help. Eventually he had to find someone else to head up the class. That was not an easy task. For a while Kyle even thought that God might want him to stay and continue to run it himself. This would have pleased Melanie.

1 Read Numbers 14:21

Jason went to the illegals living in the canyons surrounding the city. Their life was not an easy one. Desperate for work, they cautiously came out of their run-down, dilapidated shacks they had to call "home"; always fearing that the INS would send them back to their home country. Jason started by just bringing food and blankets. But his acts of kindness won the hearts of some who began listening to him share the love that Christ has for them.

Helen offered her gracious services to the Chamber of Commerce. When visitors—business people and others—came to the city, she gave them tours, took them to the zoo and other points of interest—anything that would make them more comfortable in a foreign land. Yes! America is a 'foreign' land to those who come here. No 'gospel message' was ever preached. But Helen was a 'living epistle read among men' as she befriended these internationals.

Kevin volunteered at the local continuation school, working in the child care center. Nine out of ten of the children could not speak English. As their parents studied in the formal classes upstairs, Kevin gave his own lessons to the children.[2]

As the four of them became active in these ministries, they still kept their goal in mind: distant cross-cultural ministry. So they met with and continued to solidify the responsibilities of their support teams. As Jason had done, the other three were also able to identify and turn the leadership of the team over to a liaison, the person who would act as the contact between the missionary and the rest of the team. Financial and prayer support commitment was firmed up. At each meeting they spent some time in prayer, not only for their missionary but also for the people among whom

---

2 A series of 12 essays under the title, *Internationals Who Live Among Us*, introduces nine distinct types of internationals in America and ways to minister among them. The series is available through ERI's website: www.eri.org.

they were going to minister. And each team member recognized that to the degree of his active involvement to his commitment, he, too, would face the spiritual warfare. For the enemy of our souls will attack at any level of our involvement.

Logistical details were formalized. Jason protested his need for a will. "A 'final testament?'" he wailed. After all, he owned nothing but a beat-up ten-speed and a room full of motocross pictures.

A communications coordinator learned, and then taught the teams, in the do's and don'ts of e-mail and Instant Messenger. This was especially important for Helen's team, as she was going to a restricted-access country where very special care had to be taken in what to say and what not to say. In fact, it was finally decided that all communication would pass through her communications coordinator's computer and censorship. Helen would delete her existing e-mail address and use only the one agreed upon between her and the coordinator. Some may think this is too restrictive, but it has been proven to be necessary in some situations.

In two of the churches, the teams were already studying the book, *The Reentry Team*,[3] knowing that, although their missionary was planning on a two-year commitment, an emergency might bring them home early.

And then their big day came. Each in their turn had their commissioning service, bon voyage potluck good-bye outing, and they were off.

Helen went to a country where Christ is proclaimed in secret meetings. But she wasn't even allowed to attend those meetings. Rather, she worked in an orphanage for physically and mentally handicapped children. At first, through tears of sorrow for them (and some-

3 *The Reentry Team: Caring For Your Returning Missionaries*, Neal Pirolo, ERI, 2000.

times tears for herself) she only held and massaged their almost lifeless limbs. But one day, to her amazement, she realized that they were responding to her music. She had been softly humming her favorite choruses as she worked. At first, they just listened. Then she saw 'life' in their eyes. She began singing the words. Little by little, she saw them beginning to mimic the words. Soon, they were able to memorize simple words, then phrases, and then whole sentences as she put them to catchy melodies on the piano. They were learning their own language as fast as Helen could learn it! Tender, young hearts were open to the beauty of Christ seen in her.

Much to the surprise of everyone, Jason shaved off all his hair. Man, did he look different! There was no way for him to maintain his thick Afro in the boiler room of a ship. Things were going well for him. He had found that his roommate had an equal zest for motocross. The ceiling and the little space on the walls between the bunks was soon plastered with pictures they were collecting at each port. When the ship called at a port, Jason joined the drama team that worked with the local churches.

But Jason came home early. As his ship was fighting against the heavy winds and strong current in the treacherous waters of the Beagle Channel, having just left a great port stay at Ushuaia, Argentina, she struck the edge of the submerged rock shelf of Solitario Island. "Man," Jason recalled later, "what a grinding sound reverberated through the engine room that night!" Jason was knocked to the floor. But he had learned his lessons well. A ship has very rigid emergency rules, and they practice them weekly. At the captain's order to abandon ship, all 139 of the ship's company safely (but not without much difficulty) launched the lifeboats and were rescued. In the early morning light, Jason could see a rainbow. Its arc spread across the sky and curved downward to come to an end across the bow of the ship. But the ship remained stuck, where it remains to this day.[4]

How did Jason take it? When asked in public, he replied, "If I'm going to keep up with Paul, I have only three more shipwrecks to go!" But in private, he admitted that it is hard. He still has those nights of flashback. But a select reentry team is there for him—to listen to him and pray with him as he processes the events of those dramatic hours. And he is awaiting the next mustering of the ministry's other ship.

Kevin joined a collegiate sports ministry. He is now traveling the world, playing—not soccer—but basketball! He is quite good under the hoops. He can often share his testimony on court and off. He participates in clinics for the young people who are only too eager to emulate the stars. Kevin has learned that the life of a traveling man is not all 'fun and games' as his pastor had warned; there's a different bed almost every night, hours of travel by every means—from jumbo jets to camels. Yes, that's right. Camels! Once in northwest Uganda, a village out in the middle of nowhere wanted to see this team from America play basketball. He almost died of heat stroke. But he is praying about asking to extend his two-year commitment another two years.

Kyle was able to find someone to take over that fabulous local cross-cultural ministry the Lord had allowed him to start. He was able to use his writing skills and what he learned while working on the college newspaper, as he joined an organization in Eastern Europe

---

4 Though Jason is a story character, the events recounted here actually happened to the OM ship, Logos. You can read about this ship's ministry in the book, *The Logos Story*, Elaine Rhoton, OM Literature, 1988.

that trains local ministries how to write Christian magazines and journals. Their success was heard of in Asia. What a trip that was as they did a week-long training there. Some people with whom he worked in Europe have even taken positions with local newspapers and secular magazines. He has decided to continue his education at a European university.

What about Melanie? She did have the courage to visit Kyle in Austria once. But alas, she is at home—single. And lonely.

Kyle still prays for her, but his life is becoming fuller and fuller at God's direction. And it doesn't seem so necessary for Melanie to be a part of that life anymore.

THE END!
...OR, THE BEGINNING!

ERI RESOURCES

PUBLICATIONS

• *SERVING AS SENDERS: How to Care For Your Missionaries—While They are Preparing to Go, While They are on the Field, and When They Return Home.* (Available in English, British English, German, Dutch, Swedish, French, Russian, Czech, Romanian, Spanish, Portuguese, Korean, Chinese, Japanese and Indonesian.)

• *THE REENTRY TEAM: Caring For Your Returning Missionaries.* (Available in English and Dutch.)
Reentry is the least understood aspect of missionary care. Following chapters on A Shared Responsibility, A Biblical Foundation and The Human Dilemma are seventy stories written by returned missionaries. Commentary follows each story to help the reader first identify with the situation, then, second, translate the situations into help for his own returning missionary friend.

• *PREPARE FOR BATTLE: Basic Training in Spiritual Warfare.* (Available in English and Russian.)
Making reference to over 700 Scriptures that point to victory in battle, Neal covers the basics: Spiritual Armor, Spiritual Weapons, Our Attitude Toward War, Tactics of satan, Spiritual Authority, Principles of War, and Strategies for Battlefield Living. Each chapter is followed by *Practical Insights* written by Yvonne Pirolo from her life experiences.

- *I THINK GOD WANTS ME TO BE A MISSIONARY*
In a sometimes humorous, sometimes serious—always dramatic dialogue, four young people discuss with their pastors and friends scores of issues to consider long before they (you) say, "Good-bye."

- *Critical Issues in Cross-Cultural Ministry* are 4-6 page essays on vital missions topics. Available back issue reprints include:
    Series I: *Mobilizing Your Church*—15 essays
    Series II: *For Those Who Go*—15 essays
    Series III: *Serving As Senders*—12 essays
    Series IV: *Internationals Who Live Among Us*—12 essays

SEMINARS

- *Nothing GOOD Just Happens!* —This is an intense, 21-hour seminar to train church missions leadership in how to mobilize their fellowship in cross-cultural outreach ministry.

- *For Those Who Go*—The sessions of this 6-hour seminar help the potential cross-cultural worker look beyond the "romanticism" of missions and deal with some very practical issues of going.

- *Serving As Senders*—The lessons of the book, *Serving As Senders*, are presented in a 6-hour interactive format.

- *Building Your Support Team*—This 4-hour seminar speaks to the missionary in the same six areas of care as *Serving As Senders*, but is teaching them how to develop such a team.

- *What's the BIG DEAL? They're JUST Coming Home!*—"Too little; too late!" comes the heart cry from many returning missionaries. After establishing the simply stated, five-step process of reentry from the Book of Acts, this seminar deals with the many human dilemma factors which make this process so difficult to follow.

Then, using actual reentry stories written by returning missionaries, participants explore the issues that confront them. And search out the solutions for their own friends.

• *Steps to the Field*—For missionaries to arrive safely at the "regions beyond," requires many careful steps. Unfortunately, unlike Neal's adventure in Paris where he could not avoid any of the 762 steps to reach the observation deck of the Eiffel Tower, one preparing to go to the field can skip many of the steps—to their own (and their church's and agency's) peril! An outline of five major "flights of stairs" gives some direction to this round table discussion: Motivation, Confirmation, Destination, Preparation, and Ordination.

• *Eight Possible "Next Steps"*—Having been challenged to consider personal involvement in cross-cultural ministry through the Perspectives Class, a good missions book, a missions conference, a visiting missionary, or a "new" reading of the Bible, one may still wonder, "What next?" There are (at least) eight avenues—paths—roads on which one may embark to find fulfillment in cross-cultural ministry; some involve going, some sending and some mobilizing.

ACTS VIDEO/AUDIO TRAINING TAPES

• *Prepare for Battle: Lessons in Spiritual Warfare*—This 9-hour video or audio training tape series comes with 19 pages of Student Notes and Assignments, and a Study Guide for Groups or Individuals. It follows the chapters of the book, *Prepare For Battle.*

• *Building Your Support Team*—This 2-hour, 20-minute audio training tape series is the counterpart of the book, *Serving As Senders,* instructing the missionary in how to develop relationships with the caregivers in the six areas of support.

- *Solutions to Culture Stress*—This 4-hour video training tape series helps prepare a short-term missionary for the culture stress of going overseas and returning home.

- *ACTS Audio Library*—Various one-hour audio lessons on cassette or CD are available. Specific titles are on the website: www.eri.org.

ACTS TRAINING COURSES

- *ACTS Team Orientation*—2-10 hours of cultural, interpersonal relationship and spiritual warfare training for short-term teams. Offered by request.

- *ACTS Boot Camp*—One week of cultural, interpersonal relationship and spiritual warfare training for those serving up to six months. Offered by request.

- *ACTS 29 Training Courses*—An intensive 4- or 10-week immersion in a second culture to learn how to live and minister in another culture. The courses include: Cultural adaptation, language acquisition, interpersonal relationships, spiritual warfare, unculturating the Gospel and Teachings of Christ, primary health care and contingency training. This field training incorporates classroom study with community experience while living in the home of a Mexican family. Offered by request of eight or more participants.

ACTS MINISTRY TRIPS

ERI leads three- or four-week trips as schedule permits throughout the year. Pre-field training, a demanding "hands-on" experience, a good reentry and "next step" follow through helps the church leadership develop a consistent involvement in missions. We look for participants who are interested in a deeper involvement in missions: As a goer, sender or mobilizer. You definitely experience what life on the mission field is really like!

SPEAKERS BUREAU

Neal and Yvonne Pirolo, and Associates of ERI are available as speakers on a variety of subjects, all challenging to a personal involvement in cross-cultural outreach ministry.

ERI Advocates, located around the world, are available to assist you in the development of missionary support teams. Their names and contact information are available on ERI's website: www.eri.org.

Additional copies of this book and more information on these and developing resources to equip you and your church for cross-cultural ministry, are available through:

EMMAUS ROAD INTERNATIONAL
7150 Tanner Court, San Diego, CA 92111
Phone/Fax: 858 292-7020
E-mail: Emmaus_Road@eri.org
Website: www.eri.org